TORQUEMADA
& THE INQUISITORS

TORQUEMADA
& THE INQUISITORS

JOHN EDWARDS

TEMPUS

First published 2005

Tempus Publishing Limited
The Mill, Brimscombe Port,
Stroud, Gloucestershire, GL5 2QG
www.tempus-publishing.com

© John Edwards 2005

British Library Cataloguing in Publication Data.
A catalogue record for this book is available from the British Library.

ISBN 0 7524 3532 9
Typesetting and origination by Tempus Publishing Limited
Printed in Great Britain

Contents

Introduction

In 1968, the historian and sociologist Julio Caro Baroja published a collection of studies entitled *El señor Inquisidor y otras vidas por oficio* ('The Lord Inquisitor and other lives according to occupation'). In the initial chapter, which surveys those who held the office of inquisitor in Spain between 1478 and 1834, he begins by discussing the question of biography in general, suggesting that: 'Biography is a literary genre which from time to time is said to have just been discovered'.[1] The present book takes up anew the challenge of attempting not just to describe but also to penetrate the characters and personalities of some of the leading men (they were of course all men) who exercised the office of inquisitor in Spain. It does so on the grounds that there must, at least in principle, be something interesting about those who presumed to enquire, with the authority of both Church and State behind them, into the inward as well as the outward religious life of Spaniards. Yet it may well emerge that real inquisitors were not, on the whole, the wild-eyed and fanatical figures of later legend and artistic depiction, but are better characterised as soulless bureaucrats, who succeeded in detaching themselves from the human cost of the work they did.

In my earlier study, *The Spanish Inquisition*, since republished under the title *Inquisition*, the emphasis was on the ideological basis of such institutions and on the organisation of such heresy-hunting in Spain between 1478 and the early nineteenth century.[2] That book explains how the notion of excluding, and otherwise punishing, believers who fell short in terms of orthodoxy of belief or social behaviour, was built into the life of the Christian Church in its earliest years, as described in various books of the New Testament. It outlines the course of the introduction of specialised tribunals to identify and repress heresy, which began on papal initiative in the early thirteenth century in Italy, France and Catalonia. The present work, on the other hand, is not intended as an institutional survey of the post-1478 Inquisition in Spain, though the tales it tells will inevitably reveal much of the interior life of the so-called 'Holy Office'. Instead, it will look at the lives of some of those who took charge of the Inquisition, and hence helped to give it its evolving character. Most of the men studied in this book, but not all, held the office of Inquisitor General, which was inaugurated by Tomás de Torquemada. Some others, who worked for subordinate tribunals, are included because they came to prominence in relation to a particular issue in their own time. One of the major subjects of Chapter 6, Melchor de Macanaz, was not an inquisitor at all, and was a layman rather than a cleric. In the first half of the eighteenth century, though, his approach to the Inquisition, which was both supportive of religious ortho-doxy and deeply critical of the ways of the Holy Office, achieved a higher political profile than any inquisitor of the period could manage.

As the successive chapters concentrate mainly on the great issues in the history of Spain with which the inquisitors had to grapple, brief biographies of the main protagonists are added at the end of the book, along with a chronological table, to help orientate the reader. Inevitably, though, the result of studying prominent inquisitors over such a wide sweep of Spanish history helps to illuminate not only the evolution of the notorious institution over which they pre-sided, but also the varying contexts in which it operated. The book is offered to those who wish to see the 'human side' not just of those thousands who suffered at the hands of the Spanish Inquisition, but also of some, at least, of the men who inflicted that travail upon them. Finally, it is proper to acknowledge, freely and with gratitude, the labours of so many students of the institution who have helped to provide a basis and a context for what follows here.

Oxford, February 2005

I

Tomás de Torquemada: The Model Inquisitor

Tomás de Torquemada was born in 1420, the son of Pedro Fernández de Torquemada and Mencía Ortega, in the town of the same name in the Castilian diocese of Palencia in northern Spain. As was customary in the period, in his early teens he entered the Dominican order of friars, at the priory of San Pablo ('St Paul'), Valladolid, having completed his theological studies at least to the level of Bachelor of Theology. He became an enthusiast of the 'Observant' reform of his order, which was officially known as the 'Order of Preachers'. The 'Observance' was part of a general movement in religious orders in the fifteenth century, which tended to stress the spiritual life

rather than the intellectual aspects of religion which had
been so important throughout Dominican history. In 1455,
he was elected prior of the Dominican house of Santa Cruz
('Holy Cross') in Segovia, retaining that post until his death
in 1498. He became confessor to Cardinal Pedro González
de Mendoza, Archbishop of Seville and then Toledo, and
afterwards chaplain and confessor to Isabella and Ferdinand.[1]
Tomás had been introduced to the Order of Preachers
(Dominicans) by his uncle, Cardinal Juan de Torquemada,
Master of the Sacred (papal) Palace and a noted theologian,
who had been elected as cardinal of St Sixtus in 1439.[2]

Ever since their own day, there has been controversy over
whether uncle and nephew had Jewish origins, credible evidence that they did apparently being provided by Hernando
del Pulgar, chronicler to Ferdinand and Isabella, himself of
convert blood. In his pen-portrait of Juan, first published
in 1486, Pulgar makes a firm assertion to this effect, which
seems not to have been contradicted by Tomás: '[Juan's]
grandparents were of the lineage of Jews converted to our
holy Catholic Faith'.[3] If it were true that the first Spanish
Inquisitor General was partly Jewish, this would give a
poignant gloss to his activities, but it is impossible to be
certain, because his precise religious ancestry is not known.
An argument against his being Jewish, though certainly not
an incontrovertible one, is his stipulation, when founding
a new Dominican priory in Ávila in 1482, that none of its
members should have any degree of Jewish origin. Such
'purity of blood' (*limpieza de sangre*) statutes were then a
fairly new concept, but would survive throughout the entire
existence of the 'Spanish Inquisition'.[4] Despite his immense
influence on Spanish life long after his own death, and his
notoriety in recent times, Torquemada was typical of leading figures of his day in leaving behind no personal or
biographical material. Thus his character has to be deduced,

somewhat inadequately, from his own actions, official documents, and the work of contemporary commentators. The
friar was not directly involved in the new foundation of
the Inquisition from the very start, but royally-appointed
inquisitors had been operating in Seville for less than two
years when, on 11 February 1482, Pope Sixtus IV named
eight other Dominicans to assist them, and to extend their
work into the rest of the Crown of Castile. Among this
group was the prior of Santa Cruz de Segovia, Fray Tomás
de Torquemada, whose rise was soon to become meteoric,
no doubt assisted by his role as one of the royal confessors, in
which he had counselled Isabella before she became queen.[5]
On 17 October 1483, Sixtus appointed him, at the sovereigns'
request and at the age of sixty-three, to be the first Inquisitor
General for Ferdinand's territories, Aragon, Catalonia and
Valencia, on the implicit and correct understanding that he
already fulfilled a similar role in Castile.[6] Sixtus' legate in
Spain, Rodrigo de Borja (Borgia), the future Pope Alexander
VI, reported that Torquemada was fulfilling his duties vigor-
ously, and at an unknown date in 1484 the Pope sent him
a letter (papal brief), urging his 'beloved son' to 'persevere
with untiring strength, and to assist and promote the cause
of the faith'.[7] This he duly did, and on 3 February 1486
the new Pope, Innocent VIII, sent him a bull confirming
him as Inquisitor General of Spain and empowering him
to appoint new inquisitors, who might continue to receive
income, as absentees, from their benefices, while they were
engaged in the work of the Holy Office.[8] By the time this
papal document was issued, the outlines of Torquemada's
fifteen-year career as Inquisitor General had largely been
laid down. In Joseph Perez' words, Fray Tomás was 'a curious
mixture of austerity and magnificence'.[9] He seems to have
been abstemious in his habits and not personally ambitious,
refusing the rich archbishopric of Seville. He always dressed

in the simple habit of a Dominican friar and ate no meat, yet by the very nature of his inquisitorial work he found himself in rich surroundings, with numerous servants and a large personal bodyguard. According to the early-nine-teenth-century historian and critic Juan Antonio Llorente, by the end of his career this retinue consisted of fifty 'famil-iars' (lay servants of the Inquisition) on horseback and 200 foot soldiers. Llorente also claimed that Torquemada always had by him, when eating, the horn of a unicorn, which was meant to neutralise poisons.[10] He acquired a considerable financial fortune, but spent it on extending his priory of Santa Cruz in Segovia and founding and building the priory and college of Santo Tomás in Ávila. Nevertheless, the name 'Torquemada' has since become a symbol for fanatical and cruel violence, both personal and institutional. In the words of García Cárcel and Moreno Martínez:

> Fray Tomás de Torquemada... is, thanks to the literature, the model inquisitor *par excellence*. His zeal in inquisitive and inquisitorial tasks has become proverbial; a zeal in large part attributed to his *converso* roots. The dark shades in which he has been described have totally obscured his features.[11]

A good example of such an approach is to be found in a fairly scholarly work by the noted Italian novelist Rafael Sabatini:

> If ever a name held the omen of a man's life, that name is Torquemada. To such an extraordinary degree is it instinct with the suggestion of the machinery of fire and torture over which he was destined to preside, that it almost seems a fictitious name, a *nom de guerre*, a grim invention, com-pounded of the Latin *torque* ['twist'] and the Spanish *quemada* ['burnt'], to fit the man who was to hold the office of Grand Inquisitor.[12]

In fact the name derived from the town's Roman name 'Torre Cremata' ('Burnt Tower'), but this detail does not prevent the point about the verbal association with cruelty from being made. Indeed, it is supported, despite the attempted defence of García Cárcel and Moreno Martínez, by Meseguer Fernández, who writes:

> Torquemada has hunted with the *sambenito* [the robe worn at *autos de fe* by those convicted of heresy or apostasy] of all the institutional cruelty of which the Holy Office is accused, and [also] what came to him through his personal character and activity.[13]

By the time of his death on 16 September 1498, a network of inquisitorial tribunals had been established throughout Isabella's Crown of Castile and Ferdinand's Crown of Aragon. In addition, a central governing body, the 'Supreme Council of the General Inquisition', commonly known as 'La Suprema', had been established to co-ordinate the inquisitors' work. According to its main recent scholar, Rodríguez Besné, this increasingly influential committee most probably resulted from a meeting held in Seville in November 1484, at which rules were made for the procedures of the Castilian inquisitors. The suggestion is that the existence of the new organ of control was excluded from the documentary record in order not to further provoke the papacy, which was increasingly concerned at the extent of the powers which it had delegated in 1478 to Isabella and Ferdinand, and the use they were making of them.[14]

Although Torquemada was not directly involved in the sharp controversy which surrounded the introduction of the new Inquisition to Seville in 1480, he was inevitably at the centre of the political row which erupted as a result of his appointment as Inquisitor General in Aragon, Catalonia and Valencia. This nomination resulted from heavy pressure put on the Pope by Ferdinand, who had for several years been lobbying in Rome for greater power over the existing, papally-appointed inquisitors in Zaragoza, Barcelona and Valencia.[15] It is clear that the king wanted Torquemada to set up a new organisation on the Castilian model in his hereditary lands, but two problems loomed. Firstly, if the new Castilian Inquisition was to spread across the border, something would have to be done about the inquisitors already in post, and secondly, the fact that Torquemada was a Castilian, and hence a non-native, went completely against the deeply-cherished charters (*fueros*) of Aragon, Catalonia and Valencia. Although it was his subordinates, rather than himself, who suffered insult and rebuff as a result, leading in one case to death, it is clear that Torquemada himself was responsible, along with the king, for setting the new system in motion. Ferdinand called a combined session of the three kingdoms' parliaments (*Cortes*) in the Aragonese town of Tarazona in April 1484, and on 14 April Torquemada presided over a meeting (*junta*) there at which he announced the appointment of new inquisitors for Zaragoza, Huesca and Teruel in Aragon, Lleida and Barcelona in Catalonia, and for Valencia. In each case, while the Inquisitor General himself remained at one remove, trouble quickly broke out for his, or technically the Pope's, nominees. There was sullen constitutional resistance, but no notable violence, in Huesca, Barcelona or Valencia, but in Teruel military force was needed to impose Fray Juan de Solivera, after a stand-off which lasted from 23 May 1484 until 25 March of the following year. The town council's lawyers held, correctly, that Solivera, being a Basque subject of the Castilian Crown, could not legally hold office in Aragon, and that, as he was under forty years old (in fact just twenty-four), his appointment was illegal under canon law. Despite all this, Ferdinand's personal intervention and the use of force by his 'captain' in Teruel, Juan Garcés de

Marcilla, ensured that his subjects' resistance was futile. Worse still in terms of violence, in Zaragoza, on the night of 15-16 September 1485, one of the two new inquisitors there, Fray Pedro Arbués de Epila, already accustomed to wearing body-armour and a helmet under his clerical attire because of his unpopularity, was nonetheless murdered, while at his devotions (thus dressed) in the cathedral, by a group of *conversos*.[16] So Torquemada was not to be the first martyr of the 'new' Spanish Inquisition, and indeed he would die in his bed, but how, in religious terms, did he approach the task on which he and his colleagues embarked in the 1480s? In this connection it is intriguing to consider further the case of his uncle, who had first introduced him to the Dominican order.

Juan de Torquemada was born at Valladolid in 1388, into a *converso* family which, like many, had achieved integration by marriage into the Castilian nobility. As a boy, he entered the Dominican priory of San Pablo in his native city, and by 1403 he seems to have been a university student at his order's college of San Esteban, in Salamanca University. The elder Torquemada emerged onto the international scene in 1416, when the prior of San Pablo in Valladolid, Fray Luis de Valladolid, chose him to accompany the Castilian delegation to the Council of Constance, which ended the 'Great Schism' (1378–1417) of the Catholic Church. Between 1418 and 1426, Juan studied in Paris, becoming a Master of Theology, then returning to succeed Fray Luis as prior of San Pablo in his native city. Three years later, he moved to a similar post in San Pedro Mártir in Toledo, a house dedicated to the first Inquisition martyr, Peter of Verona, who had been killed by Cathar heretics in Lombardy in 1252. In 1485, it was to become for a time the headquarters of one of his nephew's tribunals. By now, Juan was well known at the Castilian court, and as a result was sent as a member of both the royal and Dominican delegations to the Church Council of Basle in 1432. After that, he spent the rest of his career in Italy, in the service of successive Popes, beginning with Eugenius IV, proving to be a loyal servant of the papacy and a distinguished theologian. His publications, offering a theological justification of papal supremacy, were to remain current for many decades. In addition, though, the anti-*converso* measures taken by rebels in Toledo in 1449 (see Introduction) provoked the cardinal, as he had become in 1439, to write a Latin tract, 'Against the Midianites and Ishmaelites' (*Tractatus contra Madianitas et Ismaelitas*), in defence of Christian converts from Judaism.

In this work, Juan states that the rebels were simply jealous of the *conversos*, and hence made false and malicious charges against them, but, given the nature of his nephew's subsequent career, the main interest lies in the theological arguments that he uses to justify a positive view of Jewish Christians. Following Paul's Epistle to the Romans (Ch. 11), he asserts that the continuing existence of unconverted Jews is necessary for the salvation of Gentiles (non-Jewish Christians), but he does not stop there. He adds that to attack the Jews, on the grounds that they are irremediably damned, is to blaspheme against Christ himself, who took flesh as a Jew. From this he goes on to argue that the very existence and nature of the Mass support his view. In a manner which must have seemed startling to conventional Catholics of his own day, who were brought up on a liturgy which generically condemned the 'perfidious Jews', especially on Good Friday, he points out that the flesh and blood that the priest consumed in every Mass, and the flesh that the people consumed during their Easter communion, were in fact wholly Jewish:

> Without slander against [the Mass] it is not possible to say that the race
> [*genus*] of the Jews has been damned in its faith, and is unbelieving,

when from that race was taken up the true flesh of Christ and His
most precious blood, which is placed before us in this sacrament for
the living sustenance of our souls [T4,3:158].

For the first Inquisitor General's uncle, Jews in fifteenth-
century Spain were just as beloved of God as their ancestors
in New Testament times, and only needed baptism in order
to achieve full redemption. Thus the Christ of the Mass was
Jewish, and so were many of the saints in heaven for whose
intercession Gentile Christians asked, including the Virgin
Mary herself, John the Baptist and the Apostles. For Juan,
Jews were not intrinsically bad, and their conversion was
essential for the salvation of non-Jewish Christians, 'Old
Christians' in the Spanish terminology of the day.[17] But did
Tomás heed his uncle's advice when he, in turn, was called
to pronounce on the proper relationship between Jews and
Christians, Judaism and Christianity?

In 1478, while concern was mounting, particularly in
Seville, about the supposed treachery and infidelity of
conversos, Tomás de Torquemada sat down in his priory at
Segovia to write a memorandum to Isabella and Ferdinand
on 'The things the kings (*reyes*) must remedy'. In it, he
took a very different tone from his uncle's, attacking both
Jews and Judaism in general as a harmful and contagious
influence on Christians and mainstream society. He proposed that old ecclesiastical and secular legislation should be
revived to counteract this perceived social menace, including the physical separation (*apartamiento*) of the Jewish and
Christian communities in Spain's towns and cities, and
the wearing by Jews of identification badges (in Spain,
traditionally red or yellow discs), in accordance with the
relevant decree of the Fourth Lateran Council of the Church
(1215). Interestingly, Torquemada makes no mention in this
document of the introduction of an Inquisition, but this

may have been in deference to the royally-sponsored campaign of mission and catechising among the *conversos* of the
dioceses of Seville and Cádiz, which was taking place at
the time under the authority of the archbishop of Seville,
Cardinal Pedro González de Mendoza, and which was led
by another of the queen's confessors, the Jeronymite Fray
Hernando de Talavera. Under their leadership, parish priests
in Seville archdiocese were attempting to instil orthodox
Catholic Christianity into their *converso* congregants, using
a pamphlet written by Talavera, 'in order that Christian
religion and life may grow and be practised in that most
noble city and in its monarchs'. The Cardinal had ordered
that placards should be placed on all the church doors in
the diocese, displaying Talavera's rules for Christian conduct
('the form which the Christian must keep from the day he
is born'), and also edicts which threatened dire penalties for
the disobedient.[18]

Despite all this, it is clear that Torquemada was fully aware
of the direction in which the political and religious wind
was blowing, and that he had effectively brought himself
to the monarchs' attention in case more drastic measures
should be introduced. Also, it appears that at this stage he
discounted positive arguments, such as those of his uncle,
concerning the role of Judaism in Catholic Christianity, and
accepted the view then prevailing in royal circles that many
outward Christians, in the archdiocese and elsewhere, were
in fact secret Jews, who were plotting with their former co-
religionaries to subvert majority society. Once he had been
summoned to join the new inquisitorial team, Torquemada
quickly became the leading brain behind the organisation
of the expanding network of heresy-hunting tribunals, first
in Castile and soon also in Aragon. The theoretical basis of
the organisation over which Torquemada presided is best
represented by the 'Instructions' for his inquisitors, which

were first issued on 29 October 1484 and supplemented, under his supervision, on 9 January 1485 and 27 October 1488. Finally, on 25 May 1498, in the year of his death, Torquemada issued a further set of instructions at a special assembly held in Ávila. Given the lengthy past history of inquisitorial tribunals in Spain and elsewhere, it is not surprising that the 1484 Instructions owed a great deal to earlier precedent, a major source being the fourteenth-century *Directory for Inquisitors* of the Catalan Dominican, Nicolau Eymerich.[19] Also, like most official documents of that period, the Instructions were drawn up by more than one author, in this case two legal assessors appointed by Torquemada, Juan Gutiérrez de Chaves and Tristán de Medina. The result was examined, in Seville, by a committee consisting of the inquisitors from the four tribunals then operating in Castile – Seville, Córdoba, Jaén and Ciudad Real – as well as Chaves and Medina and, as members of the newly-constituted Suprema, Alonso Carrillo, bishop-elect of Mazzara (Sicily), and two doctors of law, Sancho Velázquez de Cuéllar and Poncio de Valencia.

The twenty-eight articles began with an order that the setting-up of a tribunal should be announced throughout the district concerned, and went on to specify the issue of the 'edict of faith' (later 'grace'), which had first to be read publicly wherever heresy was suspected. Under its terms, all heretics and apostates, the latter being those who had returned to former errors which had previously been confessed and punished, were to come forward and confess their new sins within thirty days of its reading. As in the case of earlier tribunals elsewhere in Europe, those who confessed were to have their testimonies recorded by Inquisition notaries, who were sworn to secrecy, and be prepared to answer inquisitors' questions concerning their statements. They were also to report any heresy they knew of in others, and would, in any case in which their own admitted offence was not entirely secret and unfit for general knowledge, be absolved in public. Such notoriety was an intrinsic part of the Inquisition's supposedly 'secret' work. Those 'reconciled' (*reconciliados*) to the Church, after absolution, were certainly not exempt from penalties, and these were more drastic than those normally required of penitents at sacramental confession. Absolution by Torquemada's Inquisition involved exclusion in the future from jobs which carried public honour or recognition, and such people, supposedly 'reconciled', were forbidden to wear any kind of rich clothes or precious metals, as a sign of their former, and in effect continuing, degradation. In the words of the 1484 text:

> Item: [Torquemada's committee] decided that in as much as the heretics and apostates, however they might return to the Catholic Faith, and be reconciled in any way, are infamous in [Canon] Law, and because they must fulfil and comply with their penances with humility, grieving for the error into which they [once] fell, the aforesaid inquisitors must order that they should not hold, and may not hold, any public offices or benefices, nor should they be legal representatives (*procuradores*), or tax-farmers, or pharmacists, or spice-merchants, or physicians, or surgeons, or leeches [extractors of blood for medical purposes], or brokers. And they should not wear, and may not wear, gold, or silver, or corals, or pearls, or other [such] things, or precious stones, nor wear any silk, or ermine, nor wear [the latter] on their clothes or accessories, and that they should not ride on horseback, nor carry weapons, for the rest of their lives.

Nevertheless, people in the category of the 'reconciled' might pay for 'rehabilitation' (*habilitación*) from the Pope or, after a concession from Alexander VI dated 17 September 1498 and requested by the Crown, from the inquisitors themselves. 'Spontaneous' donations to the Church's work were also required of the 'reconciled', both kinds of payment being much to the liking of Ferdinand in particular, who wished the new Inquisition in Castile and Aragon to be a source of revenue rather than a drain on public funds.

All these provisions applied to those who came forward within thirty days of the reading of the Edict of Grace, but people who volunteered a confession after that time, without intervention from the inquisitors or any other official, would still have all their goods confiscated immediately, having morally forfeited them at the very moment of their first offence of heresy or apostasy. Those under the age of twenty, if they confessed voluntarily after the 'period of grace', were assumed to have been led astray by their elders. Nevertheless, for one or two years at least they still had to wear in public the *sambenito*, a robe of infamy, mainly yellow in colour, which graphically depicted their offence. They had to wear it when attending Mass on Sundays and festivals, as well as in religious processions, which for such ex-offenders were compulsory. In general, when a person was convicted, the inquisitors would try to establish the exact date of the beginning of the offence, in order to determine the proportion of his or her goods which should be confiscated. An established part of Inquisition practice, which was duly reiterated in Torquemada's first Instructions, concerned those who already found themselves in prison and at that stage decided to confess an offence. At least in theory, life imprisonment would be their lot, though theologians held that they would have at least a chance of reaching heaven, after time in purgatory, rather than the certainty of hell. If, however, the inquisitors suspected (and who could prove otherwise in these circumstances?) that a confession made thus was false, the 'false penitent' would be condemned to 'relaxation' (*relajación*), which meant being handed over to the secular authorities with a cynical verbal request for mercy but, in practice, with the inevitable result of being burned. The same fate awaited those who had confessed 'spontaneously' but were discovered to have held something back. The provision which applied in a normal oral confession, whereby forgotten sins are commonly offered, as it were, *en bloc* to God and absolved with the rest, did not apply within the precincts of the Inquisition. In general, it was very hard for anyone who had once entered the clutches of Torquemada's tribunals to escape from them. Those whom the inquisitors could not convict were simply described as 'impenitent' and remained subject to social disabilities as though they had indeed been found guilty, and at this early stage in the Spanish Inquisition's 350-year history torture was already authorised in cases where suspects remained recalcitrant. Another notorious provision, to be found in the 1484 Instructions, is the denial to the penitent, or his legal counsel appointed by the Inquisition, of a full copy of the evidence against him. Responding to a concern that witnesses might be intimidated, all particulars which might identify those who gave testimony were removed before trial documents were handed over. Both in the initial collection of evidence and during the torture of prisoners, the 1484 rules required that inquisitors should, if at all possible, be present in person, at least two in the case of torture sessions, though in practice their lay representatives or commissioners often had to collect testimony in outlying districts.

From the start, the Inquisition had to contend with suspects who fled rather than face trial. Such people might be processed in their absence, and if found guilty of relapsing into heresy be burnt in effigy. The 1484 Instructions not only permitted such trials, but also authorised the exhumation of deceased persons who had been accused of heresy. In the cases of the escaped and the dead, just as in those of the living, property would be confiscated and relatives lose their inheritance. A further instruction stipulated, no doubt as a result of early experience in Seville, that inquisitors should have full power to act in seignorial lands, and royal officials should assist them, thus strengthening the power of the Crown over areas which had previously been granted with jurisdiction to nobles. Returning to the fate of the 'heretics' themselves, the 1484 code stipulated that if someone who had been burned as a 'relaxed' heretic left children behind, the Crown would make a gift to them, in alms, of some of their parent's goods, while the inquisitors would be responsible for finding suitable persons to act as their guardians and bring them up in the Catholic faith. This instruction seems to have been honoured more in the breach than the observance. Torquemada's advisers also turned their attention to details of the property which might be confiscated from the accused. Those whose confessions were accepted during the 'period of grace' did not lose their goods, but if they held property belonging to others who did not qualify for this 'indulgence', as was likely in the case of close-knit *converso* families, goods in this latter category were liable to confiscation. The Christian, but not the Muslim, slaves of a person who had been reconciled without losing his property would nonetheless be freed, thereby causing their owner further loss. The Instructions then turn to the character and conduct of the inquisitors themselves. Reflecting Torquemada's own values and attitudes, the document states that these officials were to be incorruptible, in their own terms, and if they or other Inquisition officials were found to have taken presents or bribes, they were to be subject to complete excommunication from the Church, lose their posts, have to pay back what they had received, and pay a fine worth twice its value. Somewhat idealistically, Torquemada instructed that inquisitors should not have rivalries among themselves, or lord it over each other – for example if one of them received the delegated inquisitorial powers of his local bishop, thus increasing his own status and influence. Finally, inquisitors were to supervise their subordinates with zeal and, ominously, be given discretion to decide any matter not specifically covered in these twenty-eight instructions.[20] This was a recipe for totalitarianism.

In Seville, on 9 January 1485, a further eleven articles were agreed by the Suprema, tightening up the organisation of local tribunals and attempting to eliminate corruption among their officials. In future, a lawyer (*letrado*) was to be retained in Rome who would smooth the Spanish Inquisition's path there and be paid out of the goods which it had confiscated. It was agreed that all property contracts entered into before 1479 by those convicted as heretics should be counted as valid, but if any were proved to be false, the prisoner concerned should be given 100 lashes and branded with a hot iron. The offensive against 'lords of vassals' continued, with a demand that they hand over any goods that they held in confidence for fugitives from the Inquisition. One instruction which would inadvertently help later historians was that Inquisition notaries should keep registers of confiscated goods, while specialised receivers (*receptores*) should handle the disposal of the goods concerned. There should be an 'internal market' between the receivers of the different tribunals to ensure that each should receive his own dues and, to avoid corruption, each receiver should be accompanied while on duty by a constable, and should deposit goods confiscated with a third party. Evidently, accusations of financial abuse committed by the Inquisition were hitting home, and at Valladolid on 27 October 1488 the Suprema returned to these matters, demanding procedural uniformity among inquisitors and, alarmingly, urging that cases should not be held up by a desire for complete proof since, given the nature of heresy, this was impossible. It was in these instructions that the notion of regional tribunals reporting trials to the Suprema was first established, on the grounds that adequate advice was not always available locally. From now on, official advisers (*consultores del Santo Oficio*) would be retained by the Suprema, to review the sentences handed down by local tribunals. There had evidently been problems in keeping the 'secrecy' of Inquisition prisons, as the 1488 Instructions banned all contact between outsiders and prisoners, except for priests who might be permitted to hear their confessions. The inquisitors themselves should tour the Inquisition's gaols at least once a fortnight and no one inessential to the conduct of the tribunal's business should be present when evidence was being taken. The concern with record-keeping evidently continued, and local tribunals were ordered to keep proper archives, under lock and key. This was to facilitate the exchange of records when more than one tribunal was involved in a case. By 1488, there was an acute shortage of accommodation for those condemned to life imprisonment (*cárcel perpetua*) and the concept of house arrest was introduced. The treatment of child offenders and of the heirs of convicted heretics was tightened up, apparently to ensure their maximum degradation, and the Suprema announced in these Instructions that a specialised prison, complete with cells and a chapel, should be built in the headquarters town of each tribunal, so that the release of prisoners to house arrest could be avoided. Torquemada's Inquisition was evidently settling down for the long haul.[21]

Such organisational details do not, of course, indicate the religious content of the inquisitors' work under Torquemada's authority. In recent decades, a series of well-documented studies has greatly increased knowledge of the day-to-day workings of local tribunals in the early

days, for example in Trujillo (Extremadura), Ciudad Real
(the tribunal which in 1485 moved to Toledo), Jaén and
Seville.[22] Whatever the problems of assessing the quality
of the primarily *converso* religion that was examined by
Torquemada's first inquisitors, surviving trial records indicate clearly enough what the investigators were looking for.
Each tribunal had a prosecutor (*procurador fiscal*), who was
responsible for assembling cases against those who had been
or might be arrested on suspicion of heresy and/or apostasy.
If the inquisitors and their theological advisers (*calificadores*)
decided that there was a case to answer, the prosecutor
would draw up a standard questionnaire, to be put to the
accused and to witnesses. A case in point is that of Fernán
Rodríguez del Barco, a royal chaplain who brought all of the
Inquisition's cases in Ciudad Real, between 1483 and 1485.
First, he would charge the accused with having betrayed
the confidence placed by God and His Church in every
baptised Christian, and declare that his or her 'Christianity'
was a sham. He would then go on to specify a series of false
beliefs and practices associated with Judaism of which he
claimed the accused to be guilty. The tone of what followed,
in this and all other trials of 'Judaisers', could not have differed more from the respectful approach earlier adopted
by Torquemada's uncle in his 'Treatise'. Del Barco would
begin by detailing a set of prescriptions from the Mosaic
law concerning, for example, Sabbath observance, dietary
regulations and social and religious links with the local
Jewish community. He would then go on to specify the
failings of the accused as a Christian, the important point to
notice being that it did not help the defendant if he or she
had previously confessed any of the sins mentioned by the
prosecutor, as these were reserved to the Inquisition alone
and no other confessor could give absolution for them.[23]
It is evident that throughout his fifteen years as Inquisitor

General Torquemada fully supported the prevailing assump-
tion that thousands of Catholic Christians were in fact secret
Jews. For the entire period, these 'false' *conversos* were the
primary target of his tribunals, while other aspects of devia-
tion from official orthodoxy, whether by former Muslims or
'Old' Christians, were given little or no attention.

Perhaps the clearest manifestations of Torquemada's personal attitudes and aims came in the years after 1490, when
two episodes occurred which were to mark Spanish history
for centuries to come. The first was the case of the so-called
'Holy Child of La Guardia', while the second was the issue
in March–April 1492 of edicts expelling from Castile and
Aragon all Jews who refused to be baptised as Christians.
One night in June 1490, a *converso* called Benito García
was staying at an inn at Astorga, in north-western Spain
near the Galician border. Some kind of dispute broke out,
as a result of which other guests claimed to have found a
stolen Host, the consecrated unleavened bread of the Mass,
in García's luggage. In this period, those who removed
such wafers from churches were believed to be inspired
by the Devil, as Jews in general were thought to be. The
case was taken immediately to the vicar-general, deputy to
the bishop of Astorga, who passed it on to the Inquisition
at Valladolid, but Torquemada's personal interest quickly
became evident when the matter was transferred to his
current base at Ávila. During the succeeding months, the
inquisitors there attempted to unravel what they believed
to be a conspiracy involving up to ten *conversos* and unbaptised Jews, supposedly acting in concert. The story which
developed was that not only had a consecrated Host been
stolen for nefarious purposes, but a young boy from La
Guardia (Toledo) had been kidnapped from his parents
in Toledo, taken to a cave near his home town and made
to endure the same sufferings, including scourging and

crucifixion, as had been inflicted upon Jesus during His Passion. The case is technically interesting, in that the anxiety to secure convictions, very probably as a result of pressure from Torquemada himself, led the Ávila inquisitors to break various of the procedural rules in the Inquisitor General's own instructions. Instead of being kept isolated and interrogated individually and secretly, the accused were made to meet, in a desperate attempt to force their conflicting testimony into a coherent story. In addition, no dead and tortured child was ever found, and no parents apparently reported a missing son. Yet by November 1491 the inquisitors had evidently satisfied themselves and their master, Tomás de Torquemada, that young 'Cristóbal' (Christopher, the 'Christ-bearer') had indeed been spirited away from an Assumption-tide fair in Toledo and subjected to Christ-like torments. It was the result that counted, so the 'conspirators' were inevitably convicted, sentenced and subsequently paraded at an *auto de fe* in Ávila on 16 November 1491. The next day, a notary in Ávila, Antón González, reported to the municipal council in La Guardia that Benito García died as a 'Catholic Christian', in other words repentant, and that two other 'conspirators', Juan de Ocaña and Juan Franco, also showed remorse and were therefore strangled before their bodies were burned. The rest of the group were burned on a slow fire. What followed this tragedy was revealing, both of Torquemada's strategy and the intentions of his royal master and mistress. González told the La Guardia councillors that the Inquisition would send a delegate to tell them where the child had been crucified, though a divine revelation would be needed to reveal where his remains could be found. In the event, it would be several decades before they were 'discovered' and the full development of the cult of the 'Holy Child' could begin. In the meantime, though, Torquemada was determined to exploit the case, ordering that the trial proceedings should be translated into Catalan, for distribution in that Principality. A painting was produced at this time showing ugly, stereotypical Jewish men, all named, surrounding a crucifed blond boy (Illustration 8). It seems clear both that Torquemada was personally involved in the case, and that he and his colleagues were determined to exploit it in order to demonstrate the dangers implicit in allowing unbaptised Jews to continue to reside in Ferdinand and Isabella's kingdoms.[24]

The Ávila *auto* coincided with the climax of the ten-year war to end Muslim rule in the kingdom of Granada, but Torquemada and the Suprema continued with their campagn to gain control, by means of baptism and conversion, over the entire population of Spain. For this purpose, it was essential that the Castilian and Aragonese Jewish communities, possibly totalling up to 100,000 people, should be forced to convert or leave. If they chose to stay in Spain as Christians, the argument went, they would no longer be able to lead converts back to the old faith, but would instead be themselves subject to inquisitorial discipline. There seems to be little doubt that Torquemada and his colleagues not only urged the Catholic Monarchs to adopt this policy, but also largely drafted the resulting edicts for Castile and Aragon, which were eventually to be issued in April 1492, and give Jews only four months to decide whether to be baptised and stay, or else leave the country just with what they could carry. Torquemada's determination to achieve the implementation of this policy has often been dramatised, though on no serious documentary basis, especially in a scene during which he supposedly rebuked Queen Isabella for listening to petitions from the leaders of Castile's Jews, Abraham Seneor and Isaac Abravanel, for the edicts to be withdrawn. For Torquemada, according to this version, the queen's acceptance of the financial offers made by the Jews would, scandalously, be equivalent to the Jewish priests paying thirty pieces of silver to Judas for betraying Jesus [Matthew 26: 14-16, 27: 3-10]. Whatever 'victory' the first Inquisitor General may have achieved by obtaining the conversion and expulsion edicts, with all the suffering they caused for the exiles and for the reluctant converts who were baptised immediately or else returned within a few years as Christians, his own career was by now approaching its end. He was over sixty when he took up his post, and in his seventies began to show his age. Eventually, on 23 June 1494, Pope Alexander VI issued a bull appointing Martín Ponce de León, Bishop of Messina in Italy, Iñigo Manrique de Lara, Bishop of Córdoba, Francisco Sánchez de la Fuente, Bishop of Ávila, and Alfonso Suárez de Fuentesalce, Bishop of Mondoñedo, to 'assist' him in his inquisitorial work because of his advanced age and infirmities. Four years later, the fearsome Torquemada was dead, and the committee continued in his place until Diego de Deza succeeded him as sole Inquisitor General, under the terms of a bull dated 1 December 1498. One of Torquemada's last achievements was to obtain permission from Alexander VI, in a brief dated 12 November 1496, to exclude all *conversos* from the Dominican priory in Ávila, on the grounds that their hatred of the Inquisition would undermine the community there. There could be no clearer admission of the nature and consequences of Torquemada's work.[25]

Also during the reign of the first Inquisitor General of Castile and Aragon, a precedent was set for the persecution of Spanish bishops who appeared to most of their contemporaries to be model Christian leaders. The case involved the bishop of Segovia, Juan Arias Dávila, who eventually died in Rome on 28 October 1497, while

pleading his case there, at the age of eighty-seven. The Arias
Dávila family, which was of Jewish origin, had served the
Trastamaran monarchy, especially in the Segovia area, since
well before Isabella's accession in Castile. In 1486, though,
the inquisitors of Segovia, followed by those of Ávila, began
to interrogate witnesses concerning supposed 'Judaising'
by the bishop and his relatives. A full trial began in the
summer of 1490, at the same time as the supposed exposure
of the murder of the 'Holy Child' of La Guardia, and it
became a part of the pressure on *conversos*, masterminded
by Torquemada and his sovereigns, which would dominate
the succeeding decade, and outlast the Dominican's power
to influence events personally. Among those accused with
the bishop were his mother, Elvira González, and his late
father, the royal treasury accountant (*contador*) Diego Arias.
The case was first discouraged by the Suprema, but political
pressure and Torquemada's zeal soon overcame such objections, thus combining anti-Jewish prejudice with political
jealousy. A second, and significant, precedent was set when
the case was transferred to Rome, where the death of the
accused bishop overtook it. In contrast, however, with the
later and notorious case of Archbishop Bartolomé Carranza
(see Chapter 4), Juan Arias' cause was taken voluntarily to
the papal curia by the accused, and not transferred unwill-
ingly by the Spanish Inquisition itself. Unlike Carranza,
the bishop of Segovia was not under arrest in 1490, but
achieved what so many other *converso* prisoners could only
dream of when he was able to present his own case before
the Pope. Like the tale of the 'Holy Child', the expulsion
of unconverted Jews and the 'purity of blood' statute in
the Dominican priory in Ávila, the Arias Dávila case was
a marker for the conduct of Torquemada's successors over
many decades.[26] In this sense, the Castilian friar's subsequent
reputation as a zealot is not unjustified.

2

Conflict in the Church

After Torquemada's death, his office was exercised by Bishops Martín Ponce and Alfonso Suárez, who had been 'assisting' him previously. After a few months, though, they were succeeded as sole Inquisitor General of Spain by another Dominican, Fray Diego de Deza, who had already achieved prominence as tutor, chaplain and confessor to Ferdinand and Isabella's only son, Prince John (1478–97). Diego was born in Toro in 1442, the son of Antonio de Deza and Doña Inés de Tavera. He was probably not of Jewish convert (*converso*) origin, as some have suggested, but he certainly was the uncle of Cardinal Tavera who, as well as being archbishop of Toledo, was chancellor to the Emperor Charles V. The family appears to have originated beside the river Deza in Galicia, and Diego's paternal grandfather was

chief accountant (*contador mayor*) to John I of Castile. In
Toro, in his early years, Diego's main protector was Diego de
Merlo, a noted servant of the Castilian Crown, who secured
his appointment in 1461 as a royal page (*doncel*) to Henry
IV. In 1470, at the unusually advanced age of twenty-seven,
Diego entered the Dominican order, taking the habit at the
convent of San Ildefonso in his native Toro. Three years later,
he matriculated as a student in the University of Salamanca,
at the Dominican college of San Esteban, and his ability,
combined with his relative maturity, seems to have led him
to progress rapidly in his academic career. In the 1476–77
session, while still possessing only a bachelor's degree, he was
an official deputy for the distinguished and controversial
theological professor of the time, Pedro Martínez de Osma.
On 15 December 1476 he also competed unsuccessfully for
the chair of natural philosophy at Salamanca, and in 1479, by
this time having gained his licentiate, he acted as deputy in
the Vespers chair of theology, competing for the permanent
appointment on 5 July of that year. On 20 March 1480,
having by now obtained a doctorate, he finally took over the
lecturing associated with Pedro de Osma's Prime chair of
theology, and by this time he was also prior of San Esteban,
the Dominican college in Salamanca, becoming Provincial
of the order. Deza's was not just a regular, if distinguished,
academic career, though, and his succession to Osma's chair
was far from routine. In fact, he was instrumental in the
downfall of his predecessor, serving on the inquisitorial
tribunal, of the old-fashioned diocesan kind, which had
been assembled in Alcalá de Henares in 1479 by Archbishop
Alonso Carrillo of Toledo, to examine Osma's supposedly
heretical theological views. Although not sentenced to death
by the inquisitors, Osma died of natural causes on 14 April
1480, and in the following month Deza stepped into the
dead man's shoes at Salamanca. Thus began his career as an

inquisitor, though this was not to develop for a number of years thereafter. In the meantime, he was to make his name as a servant of the royal court, becoming tutor and chaplain to Prince John, probably in or around September 1485. The accounts of the royal treasurer, Gonzalo de Baeza, record a payment to him on 20 December 1485 of a third of a year's salary, being 33,333 *maravedíes* out of an annual salary set by the queen at 100,000 *maravedíes*. According to these records, Deza received a final salary payment as the prince's tutor on 5 April 1496, and in the meantime he was also given various bonus payments (*ayudas de costa*). In 1494, he was named by the Crown as bishop of Zamora, the appointment being confirmed by Alexander VI in April of that year, but, in the manner so fiercely criticised by both Catholic and Protestant reformers in the next century, he never resided in his diocese, instead administering it through a vicar general. Soon afterwards, in June 1494, he became bishop of Salamanca, a see which had, somewhat amazingly in view of Ferdinand and Isabella's much-lauded zeal for Church reform, been vacant since the death of Gonzalo de Vivero in 1480. The Pope, in turn, confirmed this appointment two years later. Following his pattern of calculated absenteeism, Deza waited until 23 May 1497 to take possession of the see, on his way back from Prince John's wedding in Burgos. Had it not been for the young man's premature death, it appears that Deza would have continued as his tutor, and possibly acted as mentor for his career as a student at Salamanca.[1]

Despite his frequent absences, Deza did take a lead in introducing reforming practices to his diocese, notably in the synod of 1497 and the diocesan constitutions drawn up in 1501. He also initiated a project to build a new cathedral in Salamanca alongside the old one, a scheme that came to fruition under his successor as bishop there, Alonso Manrique, who was also eventually to become Inquisitor

General of Spain (see Chapter 3). At this time, the king and queen made Deza their senior chaplain (*capellán mayor*), entrusting him with the task of visiting and reforming a wide range of religious houses in Castile. With the aim of carrying out similar reform among the clergy of his own diocese, the monarchs also negotiated with Alexander VI the grant to Deza of the power to present candidates to Salamancan benefices for six months of each year as a delegate of the Pope, who continued to appoint to those which became vacant in the other half of the year.[2]

Having had his beloved prince die in his arms at Salamanca, Fray Diego seems to have wished to leave the town for ever, and Ferdinand and Isabella obligingly arranged his transfer to the Andalusian see of Jaén in February 1498. His reign there was to be of the briefest, though, as on 1 December of that year he became Inquisitor General, as Torquemada's chosen permanent successor.[3] Thereafter, he moved fairly rapidly from one bishopric to another, first to Córdoba on 1 September 1499, then transferring to Palencia, in Old Castile, on 7 February 1500, holding a diocesan synod there and publishing its constitutions. He appears to have launched a powerful attack on the remaining Muslims (*mudéjares*) in his diocese. His harshness in this respect augured badly for his tenure as Inquisitor General of Castile and Aragon, but fitted in well with royal policy, largely based on experience in Granada, which would lead in 1502 to the forced conversion or expulsion of Castile's remaining Muslims. Deza had been able to witness the development of this policy at close quarters from his position as Chancellor of Castile, the chief legal officer of the kingdom.[4]

It was in 1501 that Fray Diego finally began work as Inquisitor General, setting up new tribunals in the university city and governmental capital of Valladolid, in Jaén (this later moving to Granada), in Llerena in Extremadura and in Durango (Vizcaya). In the mid-fifteenth century, this Basque town had been the centre of a supposedly heretical movement among Christians, but the inquisitors soon transferred themselves to Calahorra, finally settling in the Riojan town of Logroño. On 17 June 1500, in Seville, Deza issued seven chapters of new instructions to inquisitors, following them soon afterwards with six more, which were published at Medina del Campo. At this time, the friar was also urging Ferdinand to introduce an Inquisition on the Spanish model in Sicily, and the king duly did so, extending it later to the kingdom of Naples in order to stem the flow of Sicilians fleeing there to escape the new tribunal on the island.[5] Apart from his work in the Inquisition, Deza continued to carry out other ecclesiastical tasks for the Crown, as in 1502 when Isabella asked him to undertake the reform of the monastery of San Gregorio in Valladolid, which belonged to his own Dominican order. Alexander VI named Deza as judge of ecclesiastical appeals on his behalf, and he also became a member of Ferdinand's royal council.[6] Finally, in August 1504, the monarchs presented him to the wealthy and prestigious see of Seville, of which he took possession in October of that year, the relevant papal bulls being dated 21 December 1504. Although he took up this post at the time of Queen Isabella's last illness and death, she had recently shown her high regard for Deza by making him one of the executors of her will, alongside her own husband and Cardinal Cisneros.[7] Diego de Deza was to remain as archbishop of Seville until his death, which occurred on 9 June 1523, combining the supervision of the second most valuable and extensive Spanish bishopric with the general administration of the Inquisition. He began work with vigour in both cathedral and archdiocese, quickly holding three meetings with the cathedral chapter and, once again, drawing up new statutes.

Intellectually, as befitted a Dominican friar, Deza espoused a vigorous form of Thomism, the theology of the great theologian of the same order, St Thomas Aquinas (*c.*1225–74). While at Salamanca University, he had been an opponent of the two main rival theological schools of the period, Franciscan Nominalism and anti-papal Conciliarism, the latter having its main source in the University of Paris. In taking this view, he followed in the footsteps of the Dominican cardinal Juan de Torquemada, uncle of Inquisitor Tomás. Between 1515 and 1517, four volumes of Deza's works, including his defence of Aquinas' theological system, were printed and published by the distinguished German printer known in Spain as Juan Cromberger, who was based in Seville. This defence of Aquinas had previously been published in Seville in 1491 by Meinardo Ungut and Estanislao Polono, and although its title was printed in Latin, the text was in Castilian. Also in the collection were Deza's commentaries on one of the greatest authorities in medieval scholastic theology, Peter Lombard. Significantly, in view of his inquisitorial work, he also published a polemical attack on the theological views of two fourteenth-century converts from Judaism to Christianity, Nicholas of Lyra and Pablo de Burgos (or de Santa María). Deza also appears to have been the author of a twenty-five-page treatise on the Lord's Prayer, which was published in Seville in 1524, just after his death. It was dedicated, though, to Queen Isabella, and its climax is a *Very devout prayer at the elevation of the Body of Christ, put into verse by a very devout person.* In the preface to this work, which is addressed to the queen, Deza bemoans the lack of respect shown towards the Lord's Prayer by many Spanish Christians of his own day. His work in the Inquisition was, however, to excite wild controversy.[8]

Deza's initial appointment as Inquisitor General, on 1 December 1498, was renewed on 1 September of the following year and, in a brief dated 26 August 1500, Alexander VI confirmed that he should have exactly the same powers as his predecessor. A bull to the same effect was issued on 25 November 1501, with a further bull, at the petition of Isabella and Ferdinand, on 15 May 1502.[9] Yet while the papacy in the first years of the sixteenth century continued to affirm his position and powers, Deza was about to be threatened by one of his own colleagues, whose reputation for violence and cruelty was soon to become much greater than that of Torquemada. Fray Diego's own dignity would not survive the resulting political buffeting, and the 'Lucero affair' would for a time put the whole future government of Castile in question.

The second tribunal of the new Castilian Inquisition had begun work in Córdoba in 1482, and although most of its early documentation is lost, it appears to have undertaken the task of investigating 'Judaisers' without exciting great controversy, even though, up to 1498, it is known that at least forty-nine people, including some prominent inhabitants of Córdoba and the surrounding district, were burned after *autos de fe* in the city, forty of them in person and nine in effigy. These included several of the cathedral clergy, among them the treasurer, Pedro Fernández de Alcaudete, who was burned by the 'secular arm' in February 1484. Some of those burned in effigy had been tried posthumously, under the terms of Torquemada's Instructions. During this period, it appears that the inquisitors' work was supported by the city's ecclesiastical and secular leaders. Between 1482 and 1492, Córdoba acted as the rear base for the war against Muslim Granada, and on a number of occasions the inquisitors had to share the royal castle, which was their headquarters, with Queen Isabella and her court, as well as the royally-appointed head of the local government, the *corregidor*. During this time, there seems to have been a fairly general consensus that the

internal 'Judaising' enemy should be dealt with alongside
the external Muslim foe. Things were to change, though,
after Deza's appointment as Inquisitor General in December
1498, and the arrival in Córdoba in the following year, as
inquisitor, of a canon of Seville Cathedral, Diego Rodríguez
Lucero. It should be remembered that Deza was briefly
bishop of Córdoba, between September 1499 and February
1500, when he was transferred to the see of Palencia. As far as
Lucero was concerned, if Torquemada had been meticulous
and unfeeling, the new Cordoban incumbent would bring
true fanaticism to the task of the inquisitor.

In order to place his action in context, it is necessary
to stress the fact that he took up his appointment at a
time when Western Andalusia in general, and Córdoba
in particular, were being swept by a climate of religious
prophecy, with both Christian and Jewish dimensions. Thus
Lucero found on his desk, when he entered his office in
the royal castle at Córdoba, reports provided by the Toledo
Inquisition concerning prophetic and visionary activity in
the north of the historic 'kingdom' of Córdoba, around
Chillón and Herrera del Duque. On 24 April 1486, two
inhabitants of Chillón, Diego López and Master Antón
Rodríguez, had been burned as 'Judaisers' after an *auto de
fe* in Córdoba, but the special characteristics of religious
fervour in that area (which was under the lordship of
one of the leading regional magnates, Diego Fernández de
Córdoba, known by his office of 'Alcaide de los Donceles'
['Governor of the Royal Pages']) became clearer as the
semi-millennial year 1500 approached. In 1499, the year of
Lucero's appointment as inquisitor of Córdoba, a 'prophet-
ess' by the name of Inés, daughter of Juan Esteban, a citizen
of Herrera, came to the attention of the Inquisition in
Toledo. During her trial, and those of thirty of her followers, it emerged that she claimed to have been fetched

up to heaven by her deceased mother, and by a boy she knew who had also recently died. In her subsequent preaching, which merged Jewish and Christian ideas, she claimed to have passed through the Christian purgatory and then to have arrived in heaven itself, escorted by an angel. There, she claimed to have seen people sitting on golden thrones who, according to her guide, were *conversos* who had been burned by the Inquisition as Judaisers. She announced that her visions were authenticated by material 'signs' from above, these being a letter, an olive, and a large ear of corn. Thus far, the imagery in her tale seems to derive from the last book of the New Testament, the Revelation or Apocalypse of St John the Divine, but at this point directly Jewish references came into the story. Inés of Herrera apparently prophesied that Elijah would return in March 1500, and announce from a cloud the arrival of the Messiah, who would then lead the *conversos* from Spain to Israel, the Promised Land. This was evidently a reflection of the material Jewish, rather than the more spiritual Christian, notion of the Messiah. Before these mighty events took place, the *conversos* were to abandon Catholic Christianity and observe the Jewish Torah (Law), and witnesses stated to the Toledo inquisitors that many did so, including young children as well as adults. The movement quickly spread from Herrera to neighbouring Chillón and Almodóvar del Campo, and a summary of a lost document, formerly in the cathedral archive, indicates that news of the activities further north had reached Córdoba by May 1500. In August of that year, apparently fearing a major Jewish Messianic movement among the city's *conversos*, Lucero and his colleagues decided to act, and thus began an outburst of violent persecution that would lead, eight years later, to his enforced retirement. The Córdoba Inquisition published an edict of grace, urging all those involved with the prophecies to confess. Eventually, an *auto de fe* was held on 13 February 1501, after which eighty-one people were burned.

By taking this decisive action, Lucero evidently attracted the attention of the king, who wrote to him on 11 December 1500, urging the inquisitor to ever greater zeal against the 'heretics', and especially against those who had previously been punished but had then lapsed. Ferdinand would support Lucero's repressive campaign for several more years. In February 1501, for example, he asked his son-in-law, King Manuel of Portugal, to return to Lucero's charge a group of Cordobans who had fled across the border to escape trial. In the following month, Ferdinand authorised the receiver (*receptor*) of confiscated goods for the Inquisition in Córdoba, Andrés de Medina, to engage two assistants to help him deal with his increased work-load. Lucero was evidently responding to his sovereign's urgings, but by November 1501 he was also beginning to face opposition from the formerly supportive authorities and the 'Old Christian' citizenry of Córdoba. As a result of complaints received, the Suprema sent Dr Rodrigo Sánchez del Mercado down from Castile to investigate the 'prophecy' trials and report back to the king and queen and to Deza. This development had probably been precipitated by an incident which apparently took place during the previous summer. According to a royal letter dated 6 September 1506, the chief constable (*alguacil mayor*) of Córdoba, Gonzalo de Mayorga, had been expelled from the area, and the chief magistrate (*alcalde mayor*) Diego Ruiz de Zarate, who was the other assistant to the city's chief royal official (*corregidor*), Diego López Dávalos, had been suspended for six months, both of them being charged with attempting to interfere with an auction of confiscated property which had been organised by the Inquisition.

Crucially, Sánchez del Mercado declared as a result of his investigation that 'the business of Elijah [in other words the prophecies] was true', and recommended to the Suprema and his royal masters that Lucero's work should continue, even though the inquisitor was by now on a collision course with the Cordoban authorities. No doubt buoyed up by this official approbation, Lucero organised a further *auto*, on 1 May 1502, after which another twenty-seven people were burned. Despite its growing doubts, on 27 April the city council had ordered a platform to be built, from which it could watch the main proceedings of the *auto*. But Lucero's greatest and most controversial case was about to begin.

In July 1502, the Inquisition began an investigation into the activities of Bachelor Alonso de Membreque, who was accused of preaching 'Judaising' heresy to the *conversos* of Córdoba and others, as part of the prophetic movement. The resulting trial lasted until 1504, and was probably one of several such investigations, for the rest of which documentation has not subsequently appeared. By the end of the process, in an echo of the case of the 'Holy Child' of La Guardia, Membreque and other followers of the prophetesses were being accused of the 'ritual murder' of Christian children. Lucero appears to have come to the sincere belief that Córdoba contained a network of secret synagogues where Jewish worship took place, and Catholic Christianity was thus being systematically subverted. In September 1502, Dr Sánchez returned to the city, this time accompanied by a colleague from the Suprema, Licentiate Gumiel. According to the account later produced for the Crown and the Suprema by the royal chronicler Lorenzo Galíndez de Carvajal, both men rejected the accusations of child crucifixion and murder, but they differed on the subject of the 'secret synagogues' and Membreque's preaching.

The local political temperature had evidently risen over the summer, and by 1503 Córdoba city council was beginning to put economic pressure on Lucero and his colleagues. The councillors (*veinticuatros*) began to demand tax arrears from the Inquisition, and defiantly granted exemption from direct taxation (*pechos*) to all those who had had their goods confiscated by the local tribunal. Inquisitor General Deza, who seems to have regarded Lucero as his protégé, now felt constrained to act. In November and December 1503, a team of High Court judges (*oidores*) was in Córdoba, on the orders of the monarchs and Deza, to review Lucero's actions once again, but they also took at face value the confessions concerning secret Jewish preaching and the prophetesses, and permitted the current trials and investigations to continue. Things were now reaching a climax, and on 14 June 1504, while Deza was still bishop of Palencia, the trial began of another *converso*, Juan de Córdoba Membreque, who was accused of offering his house as a venue for his brother Bachelor Membreque's preaching. Lucero's investigations in this case resulted in a further *auto de fe* on 22 December 1504, in the presence of the city council, after which over 100 people were burned. Finally, Lucero, who seems by now to have believed that he was omnipotent in Córdoba, was beginning to head for a fall. By this time also, Deza had become archbishop of Seville, the neighbouring diocese to Córdoba.

On 26 November 1504, Queen Isabella had died at Medina del Campo, in Old Castile. Now her daughter Joanna, soon to become known as 'the Mad', reigned in her mother's kingdom with her husband, the Habsburg Philip I, as her consort, and Ferdinand, who had been Lucero's stoutest supporter, had no further official role in that kingdom. At first, the Cordoban inquisitor continued on his grisly path. In May 1505, a further *auto* was held, after which twenty-seven men and women were burned, and the trial was undertaken of Martín Alonso Membreque, a spice-dealer who was supposedly linked with the secret Jewish preaching. By now, though, Diego de Deza had begun to intervene directly, and did so in support of Lucero. He ordered the arrest of various suspects who had escaped to other parts of Castile, but at this point King Philip entered the picture, and not in favour of the Inquisition's activities in Córdoba. During Isabella's last years, a growing number of Castilians had made the journey to the Netherlands, hoping to ingratiate themselves with the new regime. Philip had been brought up in an entirely non-Spanish environment, and seems to have felt no affinity at all for the special way in which Spain attempted to resolve its religious problems. Thus there were high hopes that the new king, who heard about Lucero's activities while he was still in Brussels, would abolish the Inquisition. Indeed, on 30 September 1505, before leaving for Spain, he ordered the suspension of its activities until he was able to investigate in person, thus halting Deza's inquisitorial work. But the friar simply delegated his work to his nephew Juan Pardo de Tavera, who was administrator (*provisor*) in the archdiocese of Seville and would later be Inquisitor General (see Chapter 4). Thus Philip's measure was ineffective, but the new Habsburg king did obtain action from Rome. At his request, in April 1506 Julius II went further, and removed Deza from his post as Inquisitor General, replacing him with Diego Ramírez de Guzmán, Bishop of Catania, who, according to Cordoban sources, sent a representative, Licentiate Osorio, to the city with a message of encouragement that the change of regime at the top would curtail Lucero's rampagings. Philip's sudden death, though, in September 1506, introduced new uncertainty. Deza was restored to his post, and Lucero carried on his ghoulish

work, in the midst of what had developed into a full-blown
social and economic, as well as political and religious, crisis,
including famine and epidemic, in the Córdoba region. In
these circumstances, though, Ferdinand, who had regained
control in Castile after Philip's death, found it increasingly
difficult to go on supporting Deza and Lucero. At this
point, he seems to have recognised that Castile and his
own Crown of Aragon would have to go their separate
ways in inquisitorial as in other matters. Thus, for the first
time since Torquemada's double appointment in the 1480s,
the Castilian and Aragonese Inquisitions were separated,
with Cardinal Cisneros in charge of the former and Juan
de Enguera of the latter. Eventually, between 1 June and
1 August 1508, an *ad hoc* ecclesiastical 'Congregation', which
included Crown servants and in which Ferdinand took a
personal interest, met at Burgos in order to examine the
Lucero case, and, as a result, more of the events that had
taken place in Córdoba came to light.

According to the minutes of the Burgos Congregation,
Lucero did not speak in his own defence, though the rest of
his team was interrogated. These were Sancho de Castilla,
deputy (*provisor*) for the bishop of Córdoba, Licentiate
Alonso Rodríguez Castrillo, precentor (*chantre*) of Ávila,
and Licentiate Francisco de Yepes. In contrast to the impression of their great cruelty and violence in this case which
has been given up to now, it is interesting to see how the
inquisitors defended themselves. Their case was forcefully
presented in the opening statement by the Córdoba tribunal's prosecutor, Antón Francés, on 1 June 1508. He asserted
that the procedures used by Lucero and his colleagues
to investigate the prophetesses and the secret preaching
were entirely in accord with Torquemada's Instructions of
1484–98. The Inquisition possessed over 400 confessions
from prisoners stating that there was indeed a Judaising

conspiracy, not just in Córdoba but elsewhere in the kingdom. In addition, after the *auto* held on 22 December 1504,
four or five other Cordobans who had not previously confessed had come forward to do so. Witnesses had given
evidence, 'fathers against sons, and sons against fathers, and
against brothers and relations', for which reason, Francés
argued, 'it should not be believed or presumed that they
said it out of malice and accursed thought of their souls and
conscience, when it was not true'. Many of these confessions, he stated, had been obtained without torture, but all
agreed on the reality of the conspiracy. Those who gave
evidence were either *conversos* who had been reconciled
to the Church after previous offences, or else the sons
or grandsons of heretics. He argued that witnesses who
gave evidence in these cases, after previously being reconciled for earlier offences, were unlikely to make false
confessions or accusations in such serious matters, as 'they
were bound to be relaxed and burned, as indeed they were,
and their lives could not be spared'. For this reason they
had no incentive to do so. Francés pointed out to the
Congregation that many of these confessions and trials had
already been reviewed and accepted by the royal judges and
representatives of the Suprema who had come to Córdoba,
and observed that, where torture had been used, this had
been done entirely in accordance with proper procedure.
None of the 100 or more prisoners who had been burned
in December 1504, 'when they came out of the gaols, or in
the streets, or onto the catafalque, complained and shouted
and cried to heaven'. It might therefore be assumed that
they were guilty. The 'Jewish' preacher himself, Bachelor
Alonso de Córdoba Membreque, did not protest either,
but Antón Francés revealingly admitted that the Inquisition
notary who had been present at the time could not be
certain of this, since 'because of the gag he had had on, the

Bachelor had a very swollen tongue and could not speak clearly'. As far as the Inquisition was concerned, this was an exemplary investigation, carried out entirely according to form. What, though, had been Diego de Deza's attitude towards these proceedings?

The then Inquisitor General inevitably came under the spotlight during the Burgos Congregation of 1508, and it is worth going back, with this aspect in mind, over the events which had led up to the Burgos Congregation. According to the chronicler Lorenzo Galíndez de Carvajal, Deza did not react to the events in Córdoba until the middle of 1505, by which time several hundred people had been burned there. The archbishop apparently became totally convinced that a nationwide Judaising movement, spread by prophetesses who were trained by the cathedral authorities, was radiating from Córdoba. He responded by having numerous suspects arrested in Valladolid and other places in Old Castile, and transported to his home town of Toro, where they were interrogated by members of the Royal Council and the Suprema. Witnesses were brought from prison in Córdoba to testify against them, in some cases after torture. Deza's account of events in 1506, following Philip I's suspension of the Inquisition's work, is to be found in an important document addressed to the councillors of the Andalusian town of Jerez de la Frontera, and dated at Seville on 19 December 1506. Deza's account covers the months after Philip banned a further *auto*, which Lucero had proposed to hold in Córdoba in June of that year, and obtained the appointment of an outsider, the bishop of Catania, to investigate the Cordoban inquisitor's activities. The suspended Inquisitor General's letter to Jerez was intended to counteract the anti-inquisitorial propaganda which was being distributed in the region by Córdoba city council. In it, he claimed that during the period of the bishop of Catania's activity, which had ended with Philip's death in September, he had, on his own initiative, released several people who had previously been reconciled, on the grounds that they claimed to have given evidence 'for fear of the tortures which the inquisitor Lucero gave them and threatened them with'. Deza claimed to have known about such accusations since the previous year, and to have told Lucero and his colleagues not to arrest any more 'Old' Christians or 'officials' until he had sent judges to Córdoba to investigate. The Cordobans had rejected his offer of judges and appointed their own investigators, but Deza had gone ahead nevertheless, and named Licentiate Torquemada, Archdeacon of Aza, as well as the archdeacon of Córdoba, to look into the matter. In response, the city authorities requested a joint commission, including their own representatives and Deza's, but the archbishop refused this on the grounds that both the local council and the cathedral chapter were interested parties. Deza claimed to be afraid that, in this overheated climate, councillors or their agents might do harm to *conversos* who had testified against leading citizens, 'which would be on my conscience'. At this time, the leaders of the two main noble factions in Córdoba, the Marquis of Priego and the Count of Cabra, who were exploiting the prevailing instability in the kingdom to restore their former influence, went to see Deza to intercede for the city, but they received a dusty reply. The archbishop rebuked them for not doing more, 'as leading men there', to prevent violence in Córdoba. Then, on 8 November 1506, the Inquisition prosecutor, Arriola, was arrested by the local authorities, 'with a great disturbance of armed men, and many insults and blasphemies against the ministers of the Inquisition'. After this undoubted provocation, a Cordoban delegation went to meet Deza in Seville and ask that Lucero should be arrested, this

meeting taking place in the presence of the Duke of
Medina Sidonia and members of Seville Cathedral chapter.
The encounter was stormy, with the Cordobans refusing to
offer evidence of their complaints to Deza, and the latter
refusing to act without it. He did, however, appoint the
archdeacon of Almazán, 'who is a native of Córdoba', to
head a new investigative commission. The Cordoban delegation left in anger, though, and Deza's three new judges
were roughly treated when they arrived in the city. The
Inquisitor General not unnaturally felt that the Cordoban
authorities had obstructed all his attempts to discover the
truth, and resorted to litigation against the city council and
the cathedral as 'abettors' (*fautores*) of heresy, for obstructing
the work of the Inquisition. He sent yet another judge, the
archbishop-designate of the Indies, Pedro Deza, to pursue
the case.

It is clear that by this time the councillors and canons were
in alliance against both Lucero and Deza, and were determined to turn the behaviour of their local Inquisition into
a national issue. On 15 October 1506, the council appointed
four representatives to meet the cathedral chapter, to discuss
'the infamy which is being uttered against the knights [*cabal-
leros*] and clerics of Córdoba concerning the things of the
Inquisition'. On 9 November, the day after the arrest by the
secular authorities of the Inquisition's prosecutor, Arriola, a
civic member of the joint Cordoban commission, Diego de
Aguayo, issued a formal legal demand (*requerimiento*) to the
corregidor to quell disorder, and within a few weeks things
had deteriorated so much that the council ordered a general
levy of all fit men between the ages of seventeen and sixty.
Although no military action followed, Córdoba adopted
an increasingly rebellious posture during the rest of 1506
and in 1507. As well as sending appeals for support to other
Andalusian towns such as Jerez, as already noted, the city

despatched a delegation northwards to present its case to Ferdinand's government in Burgos. The civic and cathedral authorities in Córdoba responded to Deza's litigation by naming their own judge, the head of the Mercedarian friars in the city, to investigate the local Inquisition's activities. Lucero, rightly sensing a crisis, escaped from Córdoba in disguise, but his next move would have the effect of precipitating his permanent removal from office there. He now accused the venerable Jeronymite friar, Hernando de Talavera, Archbishop of Granada and former confessor to Isabella, of being an instigator of the supposed secret synagogues in Andalusia, even having one within his own household. In return, the Cordoban authorities claimed that Deza, too, was publicising the claim that there were 30,000 'heretics' in Andalusia, their city being the centre of a Judaising network. During 1507, events approached a climax. The bishop and city council of Córdoba appealed to Rome for Lucero to be removed and investigated, not by Deza, but either by the bishop of Catania or by Cardinal Cisneros. Meanwhile, at court, moves were made to prevent the trial of Hernando de Talavera, while between March and June 1507 royal investigators began to interrogate witnesses who had testified against the 'prophetesses'. Relatives and servants of the saintly archbishop were, however, arrested by the Inquisition. Lucero's fate was sealed when, at the beginning of June 1507, Pope Julius II accepted Deza's resignation as Inquisitor General, replacing him, as noted above, with Cardinal Cisneros, Archbishop of Toledo, in Castile and by Juan de Enguera, Bishop of Vich, in the Crown of Aragon.

Now Ferdinand was forced to listen to the complaints about the excesses of the inquisitors. On 15 September 1507, just after his return from Naples to take up the reins of government in Castile, a powerful delegation from Córdoba, Toledo and Granada met him at Santa María del Campo, between Burgos and Palencia. The spokesman for the city was the royal chronicler, Gonzalo de Ayora, a native and absentee councillor of Córdoba, who rehearsed the now familiar charges against Lucero, which involved abuse of process, injustice and cruelty, adding the accusation that the inquisitor had, on more than one occasion, arrested Cordobans, including Old Christians, on spurious charges of heresy in order to procure sexual favours from their wives. In one case, the chronicler claimed, Lucero desired the wife of Julián Trigueras, and took her away. Her husband, who was apparently an Old Christian, protested to Ferdinand, but he simply delegated the case to Deza, who returned it to Lucero. As a result, Trigueras was processed with unconscionable speed and burned after an *auto* held just three days later, while his wife became the inquisitor's mistress. In a second case, Ayora claimed that Lucero took a fancy to the daughter of Diego Celemín, 'who was very beautiful', and, as her parents and husband refused to hand her over to him, he had all three of them burned as heretics, and kept the girl for his delectation in the royal castle of Córdoba. Gonzalo de Ayora's statements, which cannot now be independently documented, were supported by the Toledan and Granadan delegates, whose cities had been implicated by Lucero in the supposed Jewish conspiracy. The Cordoban inquisitor was also accused of using false prisoners to teach Jewish prayers to the innocent, inside the Inquisition cells. With Cisneros now in post as Inquisitor General, though, Ferdinand asked him to act, and in November 1507 the cardinal began assembling the relevant documentation.

The resulting 'Catholic Congregation', which met at Burgos in June of the following year, was an irregular and unusual assembly, which mixed ecclesiastical and secular delegates but was not a Church council, a committee of the Inquisition, or a secular court of law. It included four bishops, the Inquisitor General of the now separate tribunal of Aragon, Fray Juan de Enguera and various other inquisitors and members of the Suprema. The 'Congregation' may best be described as an administrative tribunal, which perhaps helps to explain why Lucero was not allowed to speak in his own defence. Yet the surviving minutes of the assembly make it clear that, while individuals were to be condemned, the corporate standing and reputation of the Inquisition as a whole were to remain untarnished. Thus it concluded that, in the words of the town chronicler of Salamanca, Pedro de Torres, 'the Jews and heretics who were burned were justly burned'. Although the charge of Judaising in the household of Archbishop Talavera was rejected, the Burgos meeting appeared to accept that there had been prophetesses and secret synagogues in Córdoba and its region, and no general rehabilitation of Lucero's prisoners was ever issued, much to the annoyance of the inhabitants of that city and of many other Andalusians. As Inquisitor General, Cisneros received a difficult inheritance from the partially discredited Deza who retired to his post of archbishop in Seville, as did Canon Diego Rodríguez Lucero, whom he may well have brought to Córdoba in the first place. The memories of these traumatic years would last long, both in Andalusia and further afield.

In fact, Lucero had been unpopular in the cathedral in Córdoba since before his appointment as inquisitor in the city, because he had effectively looted the canonry in Seville, to which he returned after his removal, from one of the Cordoban canons, the archdeacon of Castro. After Lucero's departure, the local tribunal in Córdoba seems to have become somewhat less draconian, so that when the pending trial of Martín Alonso Membreque was finally concluded in 1513, instead of being burned, as would most probably have happened in earlier years, he was given only minor penances, including the requirement to go on a pilgrimage. Thus the Inquisition saw its honour as being satisfied, while it avoided further raising the political temperature. Nevertheless, resentment at what had gone on before remained strong in the city. A year later, the city council was still so concerned about the subject that it deputed one of its number, the *veinticuatro* Francisco de Aguayo, to speak further to the local inquisitors about 'the story of the synagogues'. Anxious to remove eyesores and 'in order that such a memory may disappear', the councillors wanted to rebuild on the sites of houses in the town which had been demolished as supposed synagogues. They seem to have felt, not unreasonably, that they and their city were being victimised in that, while Archbishop Talavera had been 'rehabilitated' at Burgos in 1508, they had not. The matter still rankled in 1521, by which time Cardinal Adrian of Utrecht was Inquisitor General as well as regent for King Charles and his mother Queen Joanna. In response to protests from Cordoban citizens, Adrian attempted to restrain the local inquisitors from keeping the problem alive, by compiling genealogies of various families, with the more than suspected intention of identifying possible further 'Judaisers'. The relevant minute of the council meeting in 1514, at which Francisco de Aguayo was deputed to act on its behalf, provides a valuable insight into the social vocabulary of the time. In the city's statements to the Crown about the Lucero affair and its aftermath, the prevailing language is that of human honour and purity. By ordering the compilation of family genealogies, the bloodthirsty inquisitor's successors had touched a raw nerve in Córdoba and throughout Spain. Back in 1508, in the memorandum sent with their representatives to Burgos, the city council and the cathedral chapter used the words 'clean' (*limpio*) and 'cleanliness' (*limpieza*) five times within a few lines, to indicate Córdoba's true state, as opposed to Lucero's accusations. To suggest otherwise

was to impugn the city's 'honour', as expressed in particular
in its people's military and economic sacrifice during the
conquest of Muslim Granada. Behind these protestations,
of course, there was no consolation for those who saw a
place for Jewishness in Christian society, and it is clear from
other evidence that many Cordobans understood all too
clearly the message that any element of their ancestral faith
and culture was regarded as a dishonour by those who governed their native city. On this subject, the trial by Lucero's
Inquisition, in 1502–4, of Juan de Córdoba Membreque,
on the accusation of using his house as a secret synagogue,
played a major part both in fomenting hostility against the
tribunal among Cordobans and in justifying its actions in the
eyes of its defenders at the Burgos Congregation of 1508.
The surviving records make it possible to say that testimony
against Juan, which would lead to his death by burning,
was given initially by his family's Muslim slave-girl, Mina,
and then by his wife and two daughters. Between 17 July
and 6 September 1504, though, no fewer than ninety-three
witnesses gave evidence against Juan, and what emerges is a
picture of a neighbourhood community, much of it *converso*,
which lived around the axial trading street of Córdoba, the
Calle de la Feria (Fair Street).[10]

   Over twenty years later, a novel in dialogue form was
published, probably in Venice, probably in 1528, and probably written by a Cordoban priest called Francisco Delicado.
The heroine, who gave the book its title, *Lozana andaluza*
('The brave Andalusian beauty') came from a broken home,
had a disastrous early love life, and eventually arrived in
Rome in March 1513, at the time of the coronation of
Pope Leo X. She would stay in the 'Eternal City' until
1527, fleeing after the 'Sack of Rome' and retiring from
her occupations as a prostitute and procuress and apparently having a kind of religious conversion. While she was

still in Spain, her father died; she and her mother failed to
win the title to their Cordoban house at the High Court
in Granada, and she stayed for a while with an aunt in
Seville. Here she naturally spoke of her early upbringing,
and especially her cooking exploits:

> And couldn't I just do pickled meat? When that appeared, all the
> cloth-merchants in the Calle de la Feria wanted to try it, especially
> when it came from a good breast of lamb.[11]

Delicado's text is full of innuendo, most of it sexual, but
the author firmly places Aldonza, as she was known before
she acquired the nickname 'Lozana', both in the heart of
the *converso* community in Córdoba, which had suffered so
severely from Lucero's actions during virtually the whole
of her early life, and later in the refugee community in
Rome, some of whom (all female) explicitly affirmed to her
that they too came from Andalusia and had fled from the
Inquisition. The members of the large Spanish expatriate
community in Rome towards whom she gravitated when
she first arrived were either Jews or *conversos*, and she quickly
told them, too, that she had been born near the Calle de
la Feria, continuing to protest her pride in her Cordoban
origins. Given her primary occupations in Rome, it may
be supposed that she was a fictional, or possibly a true, representation, of the group upon whom Lucero preyed, and
a likely potential subject of Gonzalo de Ayora's more lurid
accusations against the inquisitor.[12]

It remained to be seen how the somewhat tawdry situation of the Inquisition, in Córdoba and elsewhere, would
be affected by the death of Ferdinand, its arch-protector,
and the succession of his grandson, Charles of Ghent, as
Charles I of Spain and, soon, Charles V of the Holy Roman
Empire. In the meantime, though, Diego de Deza remained a

confidant of Ferdinand, even being entrusted in November 1508, after the Congregation of Burgos, with the delicate task of restoring royal authority in the lands of the rebellious Duke of Medina Sidonia, whose Cordoban neighbour, the Marquis of Priego, had also rebelled during that year. Until his death in June 1523, Deza seems to have continued to act as a conscientious diocesan bishop, in accordance with then current notions of Catholic reform. He held a diocesan synod in Seville in January 1512, and in 1522 was even proposed by Charles V as archbishop of Toledo. The offer came too late, however, and the former inquisitor, so little loved in Córdoba, was laid to rest in his own cathedral in Seville. Lucero, or 'Tenebrero', the man of darkness (rather than light) to his enemies, lived on in his Seville canonry for a further decade, until 1534. In that year, on 10 December, he made his will, setting up a chantry chapel in the parish church of Moguer, his birthplace, in which twenty Masses a month were to be celebrated for the repose of his soul. In addition, 300 Masses were to be said for his soul in Seville Cathedral and in the monasteries and churches of the archdiocese. Unrepentant to the end for his hatred of Jews, he stipulated that the celebrants of all these Masses should be 'Old Christians, and of good life and fame'. To his nephew, Juan Rodríguez Lucero, he left 400 ducats in cash, a chestnut horse, and his books of civil and canon law. To his other nephew, Diego Lucero, who was a Dominican friar in the priory of San Pablo in Seville, from which Alonso de Hojeda had demanded an Inquisition of the queen in 1478, he bequeathed his theology books and his Mass vestments. Lucero's will also reveals that he was a slave-owner, having bought about a dozen Muslim captives as a result of the rebellions in Granada in 1499–1502, as well as possessing, according to the custom in Andalusia at the time, various 'white' North African and black West African slaves. Very belatedly, Lucero attended to their rights in his will, granting them freedom. Also, in the nepotistic tradition of the late medieval Church, he created an ecclesiastical dynasty by securing cathedral canonries in Seville for his nephews Juan Rodríguez Lucero and Diego Rodríguez Lucero. Many of the *conversos* whom he had pursued, in Córdoba and elsewhere, during his career as an inquisitor, had a less peaceful end than their tormentor.[13]

3

The Inquisition in Crisis: Cisneros, Adrian and Manrique

When Cardinal Francisco Ximénez de Cisneros, Archbishop of Toledo, replaced Archbishop Diego de Deza as Inquisitor General in 1507, he was already seventy-one years old, and had considerable experience both of high office and of resisting the Muslim opponents of the Christian faith. He was born in 1436, at Torrelaguna near Madrid, the son of Alonso Ximénez and María de la Torre, and was baptised Gonzalo. His early studies were in Roa and Cuéllar, after which he matriculated in the University of Salamanca, graduating as a bachelor

in canon law in 1456. Between 1460 and 1465 he was in
Rome, whence he returned with a papal letter entitling him
to the first Spanish benefice which might become vacant.
As a result, in 1473 he became archpriest of Uceda, thus
incurring the enmity of the diocesan, Archbishop Carrillo
of Toledo, who demanded that he leave this post. Cisneros
refused, and after being removed to Santorcaz by the archbishop's officers, was imprisoned there for six years. Once
released, he returned to Rome to fight his cause, and in 1480
was successful in obtaining other benefices, as chaplain in
Sigüenza Cathedral, and *provisor* and vicar-general (deputy)
for the bishop of that diocese, his long-standing patron
Pedro González de Mendoza. In 1484, at the unusually
advanced age of forty-eight, he made his profession, under
the 'religious' name of Francisco instead of his baptismal
Gonzalo, as a member of the Observant Franciscan order, in
the convent of San Juan de los Reyes in Toledo, which had
been built by Ferdinand and Isabella as a celebration and
thank-offering for their victory over the Portuguese at Toro
in 1476. He soon acquired his first significant experience
of government, when a Toledan magnate, Alonso de Silva,
Count of Cifuentes, entrusted to him the administration
of his estates when he left to take part in the Granada war.
Eventually, in 1492, Cisneros became a confessor to Queen
Isabella, and in the following year he was elected Provincial
of the Franciscans in Castile. From then on, he took a leading role in the spreading of Observant practices among the
unreformed 'Conventual' houses of the order. This aim was
strongly supported by the king and queen, who two years
later made him Chancellor of Castile, and thus the effective head of the royal administration. At the same time, in
February 1495, he was appointed archbishop of Toledo.

As an intimate counsellor of the rulers, as well as leader
of the Spanish Church, he was closely involved in the

formulation of policy in the former Muslim emirate of Granada, where his militant conversionist methods appeared to contradict not only the pact which had been made between the 'Catholic Monarchs' and the defeated Nasrids, but also the gentler approach of the first archbishop of Granada, the elderly Hernando de Talavera, a Jeronymite friar, long-standing spiritual adviser, and former confessor to the king and queen. Although Cisneros' policies of mass baptism and the burning of books in Arabic, including copies of the Koran, appeared to provoke the violent revolts which took place in Granada itself and in the barren and mountainous Alpujarras nearby, as well as the Sierra Bermeja, between 1499 and 1502, his agenda for the future, aiming at a militant and reformed Catholicism, was fundamentally accepted in both Church and State.[1] His appointment as Inquisitor General on 5 June 1507, once Ferdinand had regained his former influence in Castile, together with the grant by Julius II of a cardinal's hat on 17 May of that year, thus seemed to be a logical progression.[2]

When Cisneros took charge of the Inquisition in 1507, its initial period of formation and experiment was coming to an end. It thus fell to the new Cardinal to convoke the 'Catholic Congregation' at Burgos in 1508, which investigated the Lucero affair (see Chapter 2). The aftermath of the events in Córdoba continued, for the rest of Cisneros' period in office, to affect the Inquisition's work politically, morally and financially, this last as victims of the scandal, in Córdoba and elsewhere, tried sometimes successfully to regain their confiscated goods. Cisneros presided over a time of consolidation, in which the institution became a solid prop of the monarchy. No doubt because of the Franciscan's often violent zeal in Granada, Diego de Deza expressed to the king his fears for the effect of his likely successor on the Inquisition, but, from the point of view of the institution itself, his worries seem to have been largely unfounded. Deza thought that Cisneros would be too much the creature of Ferdinand, and suggested alternative candidates for the post, including Juan Ruiz de Medina, Bishop of Segovia, and Alfonso Carrillo de Albornoz, Bishop of Ávila, who were known to be loyal servants of the Crown and proponents of Catholic reform. Deza would, however, be proved wrong, as Cisneros soon showed that he was perfectly capable of combining strong support for the king with enthusiasm for the work of the Inquisition, even though his powers, unlike those of his predecessors Torquemada and Deza, were confined to the Crown of Castile. The surviving records indicate his concern for correctness and integrity in the Inquisition's procedures. He investigated the conditions, often poor, in which prisoners were held, and attempted to tackle corruption among the tribunals' officials with a zeal which matched that with which he had earlier pursued his unreformed Franciscan brothers. He was also worried about the quality of the evidence that the inquisitors used in order to achieve convictions, in one case of supposed 'Judaising' urging officials not to imprison men 'if they had no other suspicion or indication to go by than partial circumcision… for there were no definite rules in such cases, and it seems to me that one must proceed with discretion'. The main problem which faced Cisneros, as well as his Aragonese colleague Juan de Enguera, was however a powerful revival of resistance by *conversos* to the Inquisition and its work. In Aragon and the Catalan territories, this resistance mainly took the form of protest on constitutional grounds, as in the earlier opposition to Torquemada. In Castile, on the other hand, the *conversos*' main weapon was bribery.[3]

The Cortes of Monzón, held under Ferdinand's aegis between 1510 and 1512, launched a critical assault on the Inquisition of the Crown of Aragon. The inquisitors themselves were attacked for corruption and abuse of their powers, and for interfering in categories of cases which were traditionally reserved to the ordinary Church courts, such as bigamy, usury and blasphemy, which did not appear to represent systematic heresy. Cortes members urged that diocesan bishops should become more involved in such case, thus restricting the freedom of the Inquisitor General of Aragon, Juan de Enguera, and his colleagues. The parliamentarians were also concerned to protect, and if possible extend, the legal rights of the Inquisition's prisoners, including the power to denounce and have discounted by the tribunal false witnesses (a theoretical right that was often denied in practice) and to establish effective appeals procedures. Also raised was another long-standing grievance, which dated back to the days of Torquemada. This was the problem of the severe economic consequences which automatically affected the relatives of those arrested by the Inquisition. At Monzón, the representatives proposed that the innocent wife of an accused man should be able to retain her original dowry, and that economic transactions made by a prisoner before his arrest should remain valid. There is no doubt that these demands reflected widespread discontent, and not only in Aragon and Catalonia, at the personal distress and the general social and economic disruption which were caused by the inquisitors' activities. In 1512, Juan de Enguera swore to accept these demands, and Ferdinand also took an oath to ensure that they were put into practice. The king may have taken this uncharacteristic action because of his need of political and economic support for his planned campaign against the Muslims in North Africa, but in any case the new laws remained largely a dead letter. Ferdinand, having personally supported the full rigour of the Inquisition since its inception, was never likely to accept its weakening in this way, and in 1513 duly

obtained from Pope Leo X a dispensation from his oath to
the Cortes of Monzón. Nevertheless, the weakening of the
Inquisition in Aragon and Catalonia was continued by the
issue of further procedural instructions in 1514, by the next
Inquisitor General of the Crown of Aragon, the Cistercian
monk, Luis Mercader. In this brief document, he introduced
some reforms in the appointment of the lay assistants of the
Inquisition, the *familiares*, who were responsible for identifying and helping to arrest those accused of heresy. There was
thus some weakening in the position of the Aragonese and
Catalan tribunals in the latter years of Ferdinand's reign, up
to his death in January 1516, but the Castilian Inquisition,
for which Cisneros was personally responsible, continued to
consolidate its position as an intrinsic part of society in that
kingdom.[4] Nevertheless, the departure of Ferdinand, and his
replacement by Charles of Ghent as effective ruler of Castile
(as Charles I) on behalf of his mother Joanna, who was held
to be mentally incapable, led to another crisis similar to
that which had occurred after the death of Isabella in 1504.
Once again, leading *conversos* lobbied, this time at Charles'
court in Brussels, for a reduction of the Inquisition's powers.
As a bribe, they offered to fund the young king's war to
secure Navarre, which had been invaded by Ferdinand in
1512, as a permanent part of the Crown of Castile. Cisneros
persuaded Charles to reject the bribe, 'for he wished to
place devotion and observance of the Christian religion…
above whatever riches and gold there were in the world'.
The Franciscan cardinal also successfully begged Charles
'to keep before his eyes the singular and recent example
of his grandfather and not allow the court procedure of
the Inquisition to be changed'. In particular, the elderly
Inquisitor General was concerned that the anonymity of
witnesses should be retained. He told the king that their
lives would be in danger if their names were disclosed to

defendants and their counsel, deploying for the purpose the story of a *converso* who 'discovered who was the witness who had denounced him. He sought him out, confronted him in an alley, and ran him through with a lance'. On the basis of such cases, Cisneros urged that 'No-one will come forward to denounce a person at the risk of losing his life', and drew the logical conclusion: 'That [proposed change] spells ruin to the tribunal and leaves the Divine cause without defence'. The cardinal succeeded in persuading the king to leave things as they were, stating that he had corrected abuses in procedure. Thus not only was there no need for any further changes, but it would actually be 'sinful' to make any. It was in this condition that the Inquisition entered the Habsburg era.[5]

When Ferdinand died on 23 January 1516 at an inn in Madrigalejo, a village near the Marian shrine of Guadalupe in Extremadura, while on his way to Seville to take charge of a further expedition against the Muslims of North Africa, he had already made a will, in which he named his grandson Charles 'to govern and administer the realm on behalf of the Most Serene Queen, the Lady Joanna, his mother and my most dear and beloved daughter'. He also appointed Cardinal Cisneros to act as regent in Castile until Charles could arrive, 'so that the said Cardinal may do what we would do or have the authority or obligation to do, until Charles decides on a course of action… trusting in his conscience, religion, rectitude and good will'. When the terms of Ferdinand's will were communicated by the Castilian Royal Council to Charles' representative in Spain, Adrian of Utrecht, who would soon himself succeed Cisneros as Inquisitor General, the phrase 'until Prince Charles decides on a course of action' was omitted. Thus there seems to have been a determination on the part of the councillors that Cisneros should indeed take over as regent until the king came to Spain in person, as well as continuing in charge of the Castilian Inquisition. The cardinal would still experience problems with the institution's unpopularity, though, and, when Charles eventually arrived in Spain in 1518, the Castilian Cortes once more demanded changes.[6]

Nevertheless, during his tenure, and despite his public affirmation of the validity and the propriety of his Inquisition's work, Cisneros in fact presided over actions which served to undermine both its efficacy and its standing in the eyes of much of the Castilian public. Since the very beginning of Torquemada's reign as Inquisitor General, tribunals had been subject to two pressures. The first of these consisted of complaints to the papacy about supposed procedural abuses, and the second involved the desire, especially on the part of the wealthier *conversos*, to mitigate social and economic damage to themselves and their families by obtaining documents of 'rehabilitation' (*habilitación*), which would enable them and their relatives to resume, without stain (*tacha*), their former position in society. In 1503, while Deza was still Inquisitor General, Pedro de Villacís, a citizen of Valladolid in Old Castile, came to settle in Seville. Villacís was a sharp individual, who specialised in estimating the value of other people's property. In Toledo, his calculations had been so highly regarded by the authorities that the fines paid for rehabilitation by the city's *conversos* were simply based on his estimation. Such skilled financial advice had its price, of course, and his commission was one-eighth of the sums raised, but Seville would offer him much richer pickings, under authority granted by the Suprema on 18 January 1503. It had come to the attention of the councillors of the Inquisition that, since its inception in 1480, the Seville tribunal had failed to confiscate all the property owing to it from those whom it had tried as heretics. Now Villacís was to reclaim these goods, and hand them over to the local tribunal's new receiver (*receptor*), Pedro de Mata. The investigator worked under the protection of King Ferdinand himself, and thus survived the fall of both Lucero and Deza (see Chapter 2). On Ferdinand's initiative, and apparently without any reference to Cisneros, Villacís was instructed, in a royal letter dated 22 April 1510, to cross to Portugal and arrest three escaped 'Judaisers', Bachelor Alonso de la Pedrada from Jaén, Marica de Moza from Córdoba and Gómez Tello from Seville. They were all duly detained and brought back to Spain for punishment, with the active assistance of King Manuel of Portugal. Thus, while Lucero peacefully lived out his days in Seville, those whom he had pursued continued to suffer arrest and investigation for their religious beliefs.

In 1507, just as Cisneros was taking over from Deza as Inquisitor General, the receiver of goods for the Seville tribunal, Juan Gutiérrez Egas, died, probably of the plague. On 3 September 1507, Cisneros named Pedro de Villacís to succeed Egas, and a new and intriguing phase began, in which, as well as continuing to collect confiscated goods from prisoners and their families, he and the equivalent officials in other tribunals also calculated and collected payments from individuals who had received dispensations, commutations and lesser penances which did not involve an appearance at an *auto de fe*. The receiver of goods in the neighbouring diocese of Córdoba had already received authorisation from Ferdinand to act in this way, and Villacís did so under a royal order dated 11 August 1508, at the very culmination of the Lucero crisis. From then on, Villacís and his colleagues pursued a dual, and apparently contradictory, policy. On the one hand they used their financial and detective skills to locate goods to which the Inquisition was entitled, but which had not been seized 'through the fault and negligence of past receivers and through other frauds, collusions and concealments'. Not surprisingly, *conversos* complained violently about this action to the local secular authorities, but Ferdinand merely reiterated his full support for what Villacís and his colleagues were doing. Alongside this effort, though, the receivers also turned their attention to 'compositions' and other agreements with offenders. Such arrangements had been made with certain individuals ever since the 1480s, and the king's finances had greatly profited as a result. It remained to be seen whether Cisneros would be so tolerant, or even enthusiastic about them, given his stout public defence throughout his tenure of the Inquisition's primary functions of identifying, reconciling and punishing 'heretics'.

In the event, traffic in 'compositions' and other commutations continued unabated between 1507 and 1517. Juan Gil, in his monumental study of the Seville tribunal, plausibly suggests that such financial extorsion from *conversos* merely continued, after baptism, the regime of exactions under which Jews in Spain and elsewhere had lived during the late Middle Ages. On 16 April 1508, four men and a woman were burned as Judaisers, after an *auto de fe* in Seville. On 28 October of that year, though, Ferdinand entered the city, through the Macarena gate, with his second queen, Germaine of Foix, to be received by Archbishop Deza. An *auto de fe* was duly held on the following Sunday, 29 October, and the goods of notorious suspects were confiscated. One example was the *lombardero* (artilleryman) Maestre Alonso, who had served in vital campaigns during the Granada war, but was now pursued from his refuge as a lay member (*donado*) of the Dominican priory of San Pablo, and accused of Judaising. Alongside this, though, and with the explicit prior approval of Cisneros and the Suprema, Ferdinand used his time in Seville to make a financial composition, on 7 December 1508, with the city's *conversos*. With at least apparent reluctance, the royal and Inquisition treasuries (which in practice were hard to distinguish) agreed to abandon claims on the goods of those involved in the deal, 'because they were litigious and expensive, or because of the actions of people, or for [private] interests, or through negligence, or because they had not come to [the Inquisition's] notice, or through malice, or for whatever other causes'. The terms were wide-ranging. The accused *conversos* in the archdiocese of Seville and the diocese of Cádiz had to pay the considerable sum of 20,000 ducats to the Crown, in return for which they would regain possession of any property which had been confiscated from them between the introduction of the Inquisition to the area in 1480 and 30 November 1508. These terms applied even if the individuals concerned had been found guilty and reconciled to the Church under penance, and if the goods in question had belonged to their parents and grandparents. Curiously, the only exception, at the request of Queen Germaine, was that goods confiscated from those who had been processed in her presence at the *auto* of 29 October 1508 should remain in the Inquisition's hands. Anyone who refused to accept the agreement would be subject to the normal procedures and penalties. Nevertheless, the authorities, including Cisneros, were evidently keen to involve as many *conversos* as possible in the deal. In addition, individuals were in some cases allowed to arrange the size of their contributions among themselves. An earlier attempt in 1494 at such an agreement, during the last years of Torquemada's reign, had foundered because the Inquisition insisted on fixing all the contributions itself. Significantly, both for Cisneros' period of office and for those of his successors, the practice of negotiating 'compositions' continued to be a regular feature of the activity of the Holy Office. In 1509, a further agreement was made in Seville, involving the considerable sum of 40,000 ducats, and the surviving lists of participants, compiled in that and subsequent years, provide a valuable and detailed insight into the character of the major Spanish *converso* communities. The 1509 Seville composition, like other such documents, was not all-embracing, though, so *autos* and burnings continued, but in 1511 another composition was concluded, this time involving the sum of 80,000 ducats. Again, the king was present in Seville, hoping to arrange a further expedition against the Muslim powers in North Africa. In the following year, and at least in part with the same motive, compositions were made with *conversos* in Córdoba, Jaén and León. This ambiguity of practice, in relation to the Spanish Inquisition's original and still main 'client group', the Jewish *conversos*, would continue during the tenure of Cardinal Adrian and Alonso Manrique de Lara, but without the backing of Ferdinand's religiously bigoted yet financially mercenary zeal.[7]

The next Inquisitor General of Spain, Adrian Dedel, or Boeyens, was born in the Netherlands, in Utrecht, on 2 March 1459. He was educated by the Brethren of the Common Life, a group of Christian brothers who followed a simple but wholly orthodox version of Catholicism. He studied at the University of Louvain, becoming a doctor of theology there in 1492, then canon and later dean of Utrecht Cathedral, and in 1507 he was chosen as tutor to Charles of Ghent. In 1517 he accompanied his young charge to Spain, and soon became bishop of Tortosa in Catalonia. Indeed, after Ferdinand's death, and even more after that of Cisneros, which occurred at Roa near Burgos on 8 December 1517, he became a crucial figure in the establishment of Charles' regime in Spain. In the latter year he became Inquisitor General of Aragon, and also Navarre, taking up a similar role in Castile in 1518. He accompanied his master to the Cortes of La Coruña in 1518 and 1520 and Santiago, also in 1520, and was named regent when Charles departed for the Low Countries, leaving Castile in a state of imminent revolt (the rebellion of the '*Comunidades*', see below). After a stormy time as the head of the government of Castile and Aragon, to the surprise of many, but with Charles' vital support, he was elected Pope on 9 January 1522, unusually retaining his baptismal name as [H]adrian VI. He died, after a short and controversial reign, on 14 September 1523. Thus Adrian 'of Utrecht' spent little more than three years in the reconsolidated post of Inquisitor General of Spain, leaving it vacant after his own election as Pope until, on 10 September 1523, he authorised the appointment as his own successor to the Spanish post of Alonso Manrique de Lara. Nevertheless, during his brief period of office, Adrian had considerable influence over the king in inquisitorial as well as other matters, and it was during the years 1518–22 that the first impact of Martin Luther's ideas was felt in Spain. No major changes were made during this period in the organisation and functioning of the Inquisition in the country.[8]

Alonso Manrique, who took up his post on 19 September 1523, five days after his predecessor's death in Rome, was the first Inquisitor General of Spain to come from the Castilian upper nobility. He was born in Toledo, the son of Rodrigo Manrique, Count of Paredes and Master of the Military Order of Santiago. He was the nephew of Iñigo Manrique, who was both archbishop of Seville and president of Ferdinand and Isabella's Royal Council. The distinguished court poet Jorge Manrique was his brother, as was one of the finest soldiers in the Granada campaigns, Pedro Manrique. In 1488, Alonso matriculated at the University of Salamanca, where he made an unsuccessful attempt to join the friars of St Augustine. He nevertheless obtained a doctorate, became chancellor of the university, and held several prominent posts in Salamanca Cathedral, including those of canon and head of the cathedral school. He also became, as an absentee,

archdeacon of Toro in the neighbouring diocese of Zamora.
On 28 September 1499, he was appointed bishop of Badajoz
in Extremadura, where he took a more active role, holding a diocesan synod in 1501 and publishing the resulting
legislation. In 1515, he was translated to the see of Córdoba,
where he also held a synod and published the results, as
well as initiating a building programme which involved the
destruction and replacement of a large part of the famous
mosque, which had become the city's cathedral after the
Christian conquest in the thirteenth century. In 1516, he
presided over the ceremonies held in Brussels in memory
of Ferdinand 'the Catholic'. Shortly before his appointment
as Inquisitor General, he was translated from Córdoba to
the archdiocese of Seville, taking possession of the episcopal
see there on 13 May 1524. He had begun his work as Inquisitor
General, and also as the tribunal's Judge of Appeals on behalf
of the papacy, on 4 January of that year. The latter measure,
enacted by the Dutch Pope, effectively ended the possibility of
appeals against the Inquisition to Rome, which had irritated
Spanish monarchs and inquisitors since the 1480s. On 29
November 1529, Clement VII made Manrique a cardinal.
The latter eventually died in Seville on 28 September 1538,
being buried in the Franciscan convent of Santa Clara de
Calabazanas, in the diocese of Palencia, which had been
founded by the Manrique family. The main significance of
Manrique's period in office was that it fell to him to face
the first major impact on Spain of ideas from elsewhere in
Europe concerning the reform of the Catholic Church in
the west, which would eventually split it between 'Catholics'
and 'Protestants'.

In the earlier years of his reign, though, Manrique's
Inquisition remained mainly focused on the group which
it had been targeting since 1478 – the *judeoconversos*. Thus up
to 1530 the onslaught against actual or supposed 'Judaisers'

continued unabated. In Valencia, for instance, an average of forty-five *conversos* a year continued to be tried, and the local inquisitors had become even more ferocious when a secret synagogue for crypto-Jews was supposedly discovered in the city (possibly encouraging Inquisitor Lucero in his work in Córdoba). Perhaps the most notable among these *conversos* were the family of the distinguished humanist Juan Luis Vives, later adviser to Henry VIII's first wife, Catherine of Aragon, in England. His story was suppressed for centuries, but it is now clear that Vives' absence from Valencia was primarily due to his fear of the Inquisition. His mother was first arrested as a 'Judaiser' when she was just fourteen and, at an *auto de fe* in Valencia on 9 September 1524, just after Manrique had taken up the reins, the humanist's father, Luis Vives Valeriola, as well as his grandmother, Esperanza Valeriola, were burned for the same offence. Six other relatives and friends were also burned at this time, the whole episode providing a violent and ominous prologue to Manrique's operations against newer, Christian 'heresies'. Juan Luis Vives, who left Spain for good at the age of sixteen, never subsequently referred directly in his written works to the Inquisition which had burned his father and condemned his mother to be burned in effigy. Yet, in a manner conventional in the Renaissance period, he often talked of 'Fortuna' as the arbiter of events and, more particularly, he dedicated one of his works, *De pacificatione* ('On peacemaking'), to the noble Manrique himself, using these pointed words:

> To be an inquisitor of heresies is such a dangerous and exalted undertaking that, if you were ignorant of its true purpose and aim, you would sin gravely, particularly because in [the Inquisition] are put into question the lives, the properties, the reputations and the existence of many people. It is extraordinary that such wide-ranging authority

should be granted to the judge, who is not free from human passions, or to the accuser, who for many reasons may be a cynical slanderer, moved by hatred.

Inquisitor General Manrique was on notice.[9]

At the beginning of his period of office, Archbishop Alonso also addressed himself to the growing awareness among the 'Old Christian' majority in Spain that Muslim converts might be as 'suspicious' in the Christian faith as their Jewish contemporaries. Up until then, the Inquisition in Castile had treated relatively lightly those Muslims, in the kingdom of Granada and elsewhere, who had been baptised as Christians as a result of the royal edict of 1502. In the Crown of Aragon, meanwhile, there were few such converts, since Muslim subjects were still allowed to practise their faith freely. During Cisneros' period as Castilian Inquisitor General, and as early as 1509, there had, however, been some trials of 'Islamicisers', in the Valladolid area and in the southern part of the archdiocese of Toledo. Nevertheless, it appears that from 1510 or thereabouts Ferdinand and Cisneros agreed on a policy of moderation in the treatment of those who had recently converted from Islam. A bull was sought from Julius II, allowing those who relapsed an extended period of fifty days in which to be reconciled to the Church without the normal requirement to abjure their errors in public and, crucially, without their goods being confiscated. As a result of this measure, between 1512 and 1515 property was returned to former Muslims (*moriscos*) in Valladolid, the Campo de Calatrava and Hornachos (Badajoz). Nevertheless, some local inquisitors continued to strain at the leash, and at the very end of Cisneros' life, in 1517, some *moriscos* were investigated by the tribunal in Logroño. Under his successor Cardinal Adrian, between 1518 and 1521, there was a systematic investigation of *moriscos* in the diocese of Cuenca, under the terms of an edict of grace issued by the Inquisitor General himself. In parallel to this procedure, the inquisitors of Cartagena investigated the *moriscos* of the valley of Ricote, and Manrique inherited similar investigations in Segovia, Cuenca and Palma del Río (between Seville and Córdoba). He decided to take control of the situation and, on 28 April 1524, issued, with the Suprema, a set of instructions for how to deal with those accused of relapsing into Islam. In future, such investigations and trials were to take place only if there was solid evidence, and all doubtful cases were to be referred to the Suprema for decision. Much later, even the highly critical Juan Antonio Llorente (see Chapter 7) praised Manrique and Charles V for the statesmanlike nature of this measure.

Any optimism at the time concerning Manrique's attitude towards the Castilian converts from Islam (*moriscos*) was, however, soon to evaporate, as the main surviving Muslim communities which were unconverted, in Aragon and Valencia, came under ever-increasing pressure from 1525 onwards. Trouble for the Muslims of Valencia, who had been allowed to survive the conquest of the kingdom in the 1230s with their traditional faith and way of life largely intact, had already been attacked during the *Germanías* ('Brotherhoods'), a local Valencian rebellion against Charles V, in 1521–22. In the summer of 1521, numerous Valencian Muslims, who were still the backbone of the rural labour force in the centre of the kingdom and had normally been protected by their Christian lords, were forcibly baptised, while some of their mosques were consecrated as churches. When the rebellion was crushed, and many of the converts returned to Islam and seized back the new 'churches', the inquisitors in Valencia took action. While the *Germanías* themselves had defied royal authority, their victims were now in trouble with the Inquisition, and Charles and Manrique felt it

necessary to crack down on Spanish Islam, not least because
of the growing Turkish threat in the Mediterranean. In this
process, the Inquisition naturally played a crucial role, using
its network of tribunals to collect evidence of the circumstances in which baptisms of Muslims had taken place, to see
whether force used by the rebels should, under canon law,
free those involved from their baptismal vows. The Church's
policy in this matter was not helpful, since it had been established, ever since the period following the forced baptism of
French and German Jews during the First Crusade in 1096,
that unwilling converts might only be absolved from their
vows if they had physically resisted the administration of the
sacrament – something hard to achieve when they had been
told that refusal meant certain death. Thus it was no surprise when, in March 1525, a special inquisitorial meeting,
held in Madrid in the presence of the king, ruled that the
violence employed by the Valencian rebels was not 'specific
or absolute', so that the baptisms were indeed valid, and
the new converts (moriscos) 'should be compelled to keep
Christian faith and doctrine'. A campaign of instruction and
reconciliation of the penitent to the Church was begun
at once, using not the Valencian inquisitors themselves but
'guest' preachers, including the highly distinguished humanist friar, Antonio de Guevara. From the beginning of the
previous year, Charles and Manrique had been working
closely together with the aim of converting to Christianity
all the remaining Muslims in the Crown of Aragon. Vital
in this process was a bull issued by Pope Clement VII
on 15 May 1524 which, even before the forced baptisms
were declared valid, had laid out a plan for the gradual
conversion of the Muslim population which corresponded
closely to the wishes of both king and Inquisitor General.
Thus Charles was absolved from the oath which he had
taken, in the Aragonese, Catalan and Valencian Cortes at

the beginning of his reign, not to expel Muslims from these realms. He was to urge the inquisitors of the Crown of Aragon to preach the Christian faith to the Muslims (*mudéjares*), who, if they did not convert within the interval stipulated by the Inquisition, should be expelled from Spain. If they refused to go, they might be made slaves, a fate which had not befallen the country's Jews in or after 1492. The inquisitors were to be free to use all their existing powers in this case, including the right to enlist the 'secular arm' if necessary. In the words of Rafael Benítez Sánchez-Blanco, 'The bull grants the Inquisition such a major role that it is hard not to see in its content the inspiration of Alonso Manrique and Charles V'.

After at least the nominal conversion of those Valencian Muslims forcibly baptised by the rebels had been achieved, royal and inquisitorial attention turned to the remainder. In the latter part of 1525, the leading authorities in that kingdom, including the vicereine, who was none other than Ferdinand the Catholic's widow, Queen Germaine, continued to resist a wholesale 'conversion', but a Muslim delegation failed to persuade the emperor to change his mind. Eventually, an agreement was reached at Toledo on 6 January 1526, the feast of the Epiphany, or the 'showing of Christ to the Gentiles'. It has generally been supposed by historians that this excluded the Inquisition from acting against the *moriscos* in Valencia for a period of forty years, but this is not so. Certainly, the twelve Muslim religious leaders (*alfaquíes*) had sought to negotiate the preservation of their cultural traditions, including dress and language, for that period. They asked that during that time the Inquisition should not investigate them or confiscate their goods, and also that Muslim cemeteries should be left undisturbed in perpetuity. For themselves, they asked that, as Christians, they should still receive the rents from taxation that had previously been paid to them as Muslim religious leaders. At the community level, they asked that the existing community entities (*morerías*) in royal towns should continue to exist, though now integrated with the Christian majority. Nevertheless, they asked for the converts to be freed of the restrictions normally placed on Muslims, such as a ban on carrying weapons and on moving house, and of the demand for special taxes. All these requests were put to the king but on some of them, concerning religious matters, clothing, language and cemeteries, Manrique was consulted as well. As a result, the *moriscos* were at least temporarily given what they wanted in the matter of cemeteries, and it was conceded that their old *morerías* should remain under royal, rather than seignorial, jurisdiction. They would also be allowed to carry arms and be exempted from the discriminatory taxes formerly collected from them as Muslims, but the king reserved the power to modify these concessions if circumstances seemed to warrant it. Manrique also agreed that converts from Islam should be permitted to continue wearing their traditional form of dress and speaking Arabic, but only for the next ten years, and not the forty which were requested and which historians often state to have been granted. In answer to the most important request from the Muslim leaders, that the converts should be free of the attentions of the Inquisition for a period of forty years, Manrique stated that 'what is enforced and done with them should be the same as was done with the Moors of Granada, who were baptised and remained as Christians'.

It is sometimes suggested that this decision was intended to be kept secret, but in fact Manrique asked Queen Germaine to have his and the king's verdicts on the subject published in all the remaining Muslim communities (*aljamas*), avowedly to encourage the *mudéjares* to come forward for baptism. This duly occurred, and it was only two years later that problems began to arise concerning Manrique's ruling on the main question – the relationship between the Inquisition and the *moriscos*, including those newly baptised. On 4 April 1528, he and the Suprema urged the vicereine and the other authorities in Valencia to comply with the 1526 concordat, since the *moriscos* had complained that they were still suffering from the discrimination and restrictions which had faced them as Muslims. On 21 May, while in Valencia, Manrique confirmed the concordat, while, at Monzón on 17 July 1528, Charles in turn reiterated that its terms should also apply in Aragon and Catalonia. Trouble seems to have broken out because the Aragonese Muslim delegates to Monzón were under the impression that they would receive a forty-year dispensation to continue their traditional customs without molestation from the inquisitors. Realising the confusion and its likely consequences, Charles and Manrique decided to act. On 30 September, Charles wrote to the viceroys of Aragon and Valencia, instructing them to publicise the correct interpretation of the 1526 concordat. Manrique specifically reiterated that he had not granted a forty-year respite to Valencia's *moriscos*, but:

> ...that what would be done to them would be what was done with the new converts in the kingdom of Granada, that is to say, that for trivial things and weaknesses which they may commit through lack of care, not being ceremonies of the damned sect of Muhammad, except for things in which they might fall back into old customs and not in order to separate themselves from our holy Catholic faith... they should be kindly treated.

In reality, Manrique's policy in this matter coincided exactly with that of his predecessors, Cisneros and Adrian.

One consequence of the Inquisition's policy towards *moriscos* was a growing hostility towards it from the seignorial nobility of the Crown of Aragon. While Charles V officially supported the operations of the Holy Office, on a day-to-day basis the tribunals' officials suffered harrassment, obstruction and even violence. In Valencia, the lords claimed the right, on the basis of charters (*fueros*) dating back in many cases to the thirteenth century, to take back any goods which were confiscated by the Inquisition from their direct *morisco* vassals. They also demanded that converts from Islam should not be tried for heresy unless they had previously received Christian instruction, this being a problem because of the negligence and absenteeism of local clergy. This opposition was duly reflected in the Valencian Cortes, and in 1533 the Inquisition was largely defeated, being forced to accept an uncharacteristically gentle process, in which dissident converts would be allowed to confess Islamic belief and practice to their parish priests, rather than inquisitors, thus risking less severe penances. If this approach failed, they would have to confess to the Inquisition, but they would not have to abjure in public at an *auto de fe*, and their goods would not be confiscated. There were similar concessions in cases where goods had previously been confiscated from convicted 'Islamicisers'. Heirs who showed themselves to be faithful Christians would be allowed by the Inquisition to inherit half their relatives' property, but the king feared that mass emigration of thrifty *moriscos* to North Africa would nonetheless still occur and on 24 December 1533, after the Cortes had finished, he ordered that heirs to property in that category should be permitted to inherit all the goods concerned. Manrique's men in Valencia resisted this order, but were forced to capitulate three years later, when the relevant bull arrived from Rome. The Inquisition was not in a mood to surrender, however, and in March 1537 the Suprema instructed the Valencia tribunal to investigate *moriscos* who were fasting during Ramadan and carrying out other Islamic practices. They were not, however, to confiscate the goods of the accused, as was required in other such cases. At the Cortes of 1537, the inquisitors tried to win the propaganda battle against the recalcitrant lords by publicising the prayers for Muslim victory against Charles V's attack on Tunis, which had been organised, along with the Ramadan fast, by Valencian religious leaders (*alfaquíes*). The manoeuvre was not entirely successful, though, as the emperor's senior officials, his secretary Los Cobos and his chancellor Granvelle, while allowing the Muslim leaders to be flogged, would not permit the Inquisition to confiscate their goods. More than this, Charles took the opportunity to extend the existing privilege from the 'newly converted' to their descendants, though he did grant a subsidy to the Inquisition to compensate for its being deprived of the confiscated property. As Manrique was dying, in 1538, his determination to extirpate Islam from the kingdom of Valencia was still meeting stout resistance from the Christian leaders of local society, as well as the *moriscos* themselves. There is less information available about the kingdom of Aragon, where other Muslim or *morisco* communities still remained, but it appears that the issues, and the resulting disputes between the inquisitors and secular leaders, took a similar course to that in Valencia. The other main front in Manrique's campaign against Spanish Islam was, however, the kingdom of Granada.

In 1526, while at the Alhambra palace in Granada on his honeymoon, having recently married the beautiful Isabella of Portugal in Seville in March of that year, the emperor returned to the question of the *moriscos* in that kingdom. As soon as he arrived in the city, he was faced with complaints from *morisco* city councillors about the treatment that they were receiving from their 'Old Christian' colleagues. On the other side, members of Christian religious orders in Granada complained to him about continuing

Islamic practice, especially in the Albaicín quarter. A tour of the kingdom by royal inspectors revealed a depressing picture, from the government's and the inquisitors' point of view:

> They found that many injuries were being done to the *moriscos*, and that, along with this, the *moriscos* were very fine Moors. It was twenty-seven years since they had been baptised [during Cisneros' time in Granada], and they did not find twenty-seven of them who were good Christians – not even seven.

To tackle this matter, Charles V summoned to the Royal Chapel, alongside Granada Cathedral, where his grandparents Ferdinand and Isabella were buried, a special 'Congregation'. The Councils of Castile and of the Inquisition took part, along with the bishops of the Granadan dioceses, the royal secretary Francisco de los Cobos, Friar Antonio de Guevara, and the royal chronicler Lorenzo Galíndez de Carvajal. The decisions arrived at in this meeting, which followed on from a 'junta' held in Madrid in the previous year, constituted a fierce legislative attack on Islamic life and culture. The use of Arabic was to be banned, as were traditional clothing and ornaments. The authorities were to take firm control of bathhouses, to prevent their use as part of Islamic religious ritual, and of butchers' shops, to prevent the halal preparation of meat. *Moriscos* were to be restricted in their movements, and forbidden to possess weapons and slaves. Corresponding efforts were to be made to strengthen the position of Christianity. As the Church in the kingdom of Granada was directly under the control of the Crown, through the post-1492 concession by the Pope of the *Patronato real* (royal control of Church patronage), the Council of Castile would look after ecclesiastical rents and church-planting, as well as the prevention of the abuse of *moriscos* by feudal lords or royal officials. Meanwhile, the Granadan bishops would take charge of clerical discipline and the religious instruction and social control of the converts, in order to inculcate Christianity and root out Islam. However, it was stipulated that the prelates would have to share these tasks with a third group, Manrique's Inquisition. The influential Carvajal wanted the inquisitors to act with moderation in Granada, concentrating on teaching rather than punishment, 'because burning them and seizing their property would leave little else to be done'. The old question, which had been there since the start in 1480, of the inquisitors' being motivated by financial greed, rather than zeal for the faith, surfaced once again, though, in the Granadan context, and Carvajal urged that, as in Valencia, the goods of the *moriscos* should not be confiscated. On 7 December 1526, the emperor published the Congregation of Granada's decisions in the form of a pragmatic and, on the same day, Alonso Manrique signed an edict of grace in which, contrary to normal practice, he absolved the *moriscos* of religious sins previously committed, and exempted them from having to confess to inquisitors, rather than other clergy, enabling them to do so without suffering confiscation of property or any other penalty. A week later, Charles wrote to Rome asking Pope Clement VII to ratify the Granadan measures, but making the additional request that Manrique should be allowed to act in such matters without further reference to the Holy See. Thus the Inquisition's role in Granada closely paralleled that in Valencia and Aragon, but the rest of Manrique's period as Inquisitor General was to see constant difficulties in the implementation of this supposedly co-ordinated royal, episcopal and inquisitorial policy. As far as the Inquisition was concerned, not only was its activity obstructed by the resistance of the *moriscos* themselves, but it was also undermined by the religious and social concessions which Charles V felt the need to make to the former Muslim population, in return for financial contributions. Firstly, in 1527–32, they paid 90,000 ducats, in annual instalments of 15,000 ducats, towards his national wedding present (*servicio de casamiento*) for marrying Isabella of Portugal, and then, between 1533 and 1538, similar annual amounts towards the cost of the construction of the somewhat incongruous Renaissance palace which he had started building within the precincts of the Alhambra. One thing is clear, though. Manrique's firm policy, as expressed towards former Jews and Muslims, would receive an even sterner test from developments within the 'Old' Christian Church itself.[10]

The reigns of Isabella and Ferdinand (1474–1516) had seen a royally sponsored process of reform in the structures and personnel of the Spanish Church.[11] Efforts were made to improve the education and discipline of the clergy from the bench of bishops down to the humblest chantry chaplain, and also to bring the religious orders back to the full 'Observance' of their original rules of life. Especially after his appointment as archbishop of Toledo in 1495, Cisneros put considerable energy into reform and, as a prelude to Manrique's engagement in this area, it is useful to examine the spiritual and doctrinal, rather than the organisational, characteristics of what has been described by some as the *reforma cisneriana*. José Nieto has fairly categorised these as being an effort to revive 'medieval piety' (what Eamon Duffy has described in the English context as 'traditional religion') in the parishes by means of the translation and diffusion of foreign devotional works, as well as the continuation of the earlier programme of institutional reform in dioceses and religious orders.[12] The third aspect of Cisneros' reform programme was his foundation, between 1499 and 1508, of the University of Alcalá de Henares which, unlike the other Spanish universities of the period, was to give priority to theology, often with a humanist bent, rather than civil and canon law. The vernacular translations commissioned by Cisneros included the epistle and Gospel readings used at Mass, which, in a similar manner to parallel versions in other countries, enabled at least the literate to have direct access to the fundamental sources of the liturgy and of preaching.[13] Werner Thomas has argued, however, that part of the modern conception of Cisneros and his work is mythological, not least as a result of successful 'spin' by the Franciscan cardinal himself, so that the achievement of others has been falsely attributed to him.

Cisneros' troubles began in his own cathedral of Toledo, where he resorted to excommunicating canons who resisted his attempts at disciplinary reform, though they succeeded in scuppering his scheme to make them live the communal religious life, on the model of the Augustinian canons who staffed other European cathedrals and collegiate churches. In his sprawling archdiocese as a whole, he attempted, at the synods of Alcalá de Henares (1497) and Talavera (1498), to implement the programme of reform which had been on the agenda of the Spanish Church at least since the late fourteenth century. Clergy were to be 'resident': that is, present to do the jobs that they were paid to do, teaching the people the lessons of the Gospel, which was said or sung in portions each Sunday. In particular, parish clergy were to instruct children, using a simple catechism which Cisneros published for the purpose. None of this was new, but his development into a university of the existing archiepiscopal 'schools' in Alcalá was more original. Not only did the new foundation give an unaccustomed priority to theology of various types, including Thomism and Nominalism, but the founding statutes envisaged the endowment of chairs in Hebrew, Greek, Arabic and Syriac ('Chaldean'), all languages essential for the humanistic study of the text of Scripture.

The result, fully realised only after Cisneros' death in 1517, would be the great multilingual edition of the Bible known as the 'Complutensian Polyglot'.

Thomas argues, though, that the cardinal's greatest contribution was made not in his archdiocese or in his university, let alone in the Inquisition, but in the reform of his own Franciscan order. He had played an extremely active part in the attempt to bring the whole order in Spain, including male and female convents, into the Observance, though there was much resistance from the 'Conventuals', or traditionalists, who not only used a gentler interpretation of the founder's rule but also placed a greater stress on academic theology than did the Observants. Yet by the early 1490s only a minority of Spain's Franciscans had joined the latter movement. In 1496, Pope Alexander VI, at Queen Isabella's request, named Archbishop Cisneros as his visitor and representative in all the convents of both the first, male Franciscan order and the second, female order, the 'Clares' (*clarisas*). He met stiff resistance, though, which sometimes took dramatic forms. Thus in Andalusia no fewer than 400 Franciscan friars abandoned their habits and took the drastic step of converting to Islam, while in Cisneros' own see of Toledo their brothers marched out of their convent in that city in procession, singing the psalm of the Israelites' liberation from the tyranny of the Egyptian Pharoahs, *In exitu Israel de Aegypto* (Ps. 113/114: 'When Israel came out of Egypt'). In 1499, Cisneros was appointed to 'reform' all the mendicant orders in Spain, and perhaps his main achievement in this connection was to bring all the convents of Clares within the Observant movement. It was initially for the benefit of the religious orders that Cisneros ordered the translation and/or distribution of devotional works, for example by Vincent Ferrer, Catherine of Siena, John Climachus and possibly the controversial Florentine Dominican, Girolamo

Savonarola. Nevertheless, these books also spread among lay Christians, thus helping to create a stronger devotional life in the Church as a whole.[14]

Since 'modern' Catholic historiography developed, in Spain as elsewhere, in the late nineteenth century, it has become common – even orthodox – to ascribe to Cisneros the fact that the ideas of Luther and the other magisterial reformers took no permanent hold in the country. Reform had been achieved, the argument goes, under Ferdinand and Isabella and their successors within the existing structures of the Catholic Church, thus obviating the horror of schism. The next chapter will show that things were much more complicated than that, but it is still necessary, before considering the encounters of Alonso Manrique and his successor, Fernando de Valdés, with what would come to be known as 'Protestantism', to offer an overall assessment of the contribution of Francisco de Cisneros, as friar, bishop and Inquisitor General. In reality, while he was undoubtedly devout and austere in his personal life, retaining when in high office much more than just the dress of a Franciscan friar, circumstances severely restricted his ability to diffuse such values even among the lower clergy, let alone to the public at large. As Thomas puts it: 'there was a difference between the model cleric, as propagated by the reform[ers], and the cleric with whom the people in the villages [*pueblos*] came into contact'.[15] Thus bishops, including Cisneros, when attempting reform, collided immediately with their own cathedral chapters, which were normally dedicated to preserving at all costs their wealth and privileges, and then, when trying to implement policies set down in provincial councils and diocesan synods, met the inertia of both clergy and people. Cisneros' own archdiocese of Toledo was the most significant of numerous such examples. In addition, as the great historian of

Spanish 'Erasmians' Marcel Bataillon observed, Cisneros' most successful policy, the spread of the Observance in the religious orders, had an unfortunate consequence. This was to inflate the number of clergy and thus create 'a numerous spiritual proletariat, obliged to live on alms or by means of other expedients, which does not always offer an entirely edifying spectacle'.[16] As will become clear in Chapter 4, during the inquisitorial reigns of Manrique and Valdés Christian reformers generally shared a 'top-down' approach to what they saw as improvements in the Church, often with limited, or unfortunate, results on the ground. Cisneros' own diocese, both before and during his tenure, well illustrates the point. Archbishop Alonso Carrillo's 1473 provincial council laid down that the core of Christian doctrine, which should be taught to all the faithful, would consist of the fourteen articles of the faith, the Ten Commandments, the seven sacraments, the seven deadly sins, and the seven virtues, three theological and four cardinal. To this, Carrillo's 1480 Toledan council added the seven corporal works of mercy, the seven gifts of the Holy Spirit and the five human senses. Cisneros both added to this system and reformed it, including the commandments of the Church and placing the twelve articles of the Nicene Creed alongside the traditional fourteen articles of Catholic faith.[17] Would the Franciscan cardinal's approach withstand the ideas of Church reform which, even before his death in 1517, were beginning to emerge from lands to the north of the Pyrenees?

4

Heresy-Hunting: The Question of Church Reform

The traditional view of the impact of the European Reformation on Spain between about 1520 and 1560 has been well summarised by Joseph Pérez. As thus interpreted, things began with the reception in the Peninsula of the writings and ideas of the Dutch scholar Desiderius Erasmus (b.1466/7). In 1937, Marcel Bataillon published his pioneering and masterly study *Erasme et l'Espagne*, which until recently has defined the subject and for many still does.[1] According to this account, Erasmus' 'Christian humanism', in which an undogmatic faith was combined with rigorous philological scholarship and Classical philosophy, fell on fertile ground in Spain, thanks to the reform programme led by Cardinal Cisneros. Thus Erasmus was praised and respected by Spanish university circles, particularly for his views on the true nature of Christianity and the conduct of the Church. His criticism of the papacy found a ready echo in Spain, as did his desire for an end to dogmatism and external ritualism, and a return to the simple truth of the Gospel, which was to be absorbed internally. Erasmus' 1516 edition of the New Testament (known as the *Novum Instrumentum*), in his own translation from the Greek, was well received in Spain, and Cisneros and his collaborators initially hoped to involve him in the 'Polyglot Bible' project at Alcalá de Henares. In the event, the Dutch scholar refused to accept the cardinal's formal invitation and, although he subsequently had correspondents in Spain, he never visited the country, at least in part because of its 'Jewishness', which he found as repugnant as any Spanish inquisitor could have done. In any case, though, his work began to be more generally known in educated Spanish circles when, in 1520, his denunciation of war, the *Querela Pacis* ('The Complaint of Peace'), was translated into Castilian Spanish. At this stage, though, some Spaniards at least began to have direct experience of religious developments elsewhere in Europe, when Charles V and his court left the Peninsula for Germany.

Among those who accompanied the king-emperor was his chancellor Gattinara's Latin secretary, the Cuencan Alfonso de Valdés, who would become perhaps Erasmus' most devoted Spanish disciple. Never again would circumstances be so propitious for the adoption of the Dutch scholar's ideas in Spain. Charles and his Imperial court, faced by the disturbances caused by Martin Luther, were anxious to reform the Church without breaking it apart. Meanwhile, at home, various groups of Spanish Christians, particularly in

Castile, were independently seeking a purer and more 'internal' Christianity, purged of corruption and over-elaborate external ceremony. In or about 1524, the official printer to the University of Alcalá, Miguel de Eguía, published in the original Latin various of Erasmus' works, and Spanish translations of his *Enchiridion militis christiani* ('Handbook of the Christian soldier'), which advocated the internal adoption of Christ on the model set out in St Paul's epistles and also in his own *Paraphrases*, or commentaries, on the four Gospels. These were followed by a version in Spanish of the colloquy (dialogue) on Christian marriage. During the next five years, more of Erasmus' works were translated for a Spanish readership, spreading his criticism of the 'excesses' of the friars and of the 'superstitions' which he believed to be commonly associated with the Christianity of his day. In addition, some Spaniards began to produce works on an 'Erasmian' model, the most notable among them being Alfonso de Valdés, who wrote two 'Dialogues' containing astringent criticism of the practices of the Roman Church in general and the papacy in particular. Valdés, a Latinate layman in some respects more 'Erasmian' than Erasmus and with the king's apparent support, advocated a simplified and highly moral form of Christianity which he regarded as both closer to the spirit of the New Testament and better adapted to the strained circumstances of Europe at the time. According to the interpretation which was first advocated with both deep erudition and strong personal commitment by Bataillon, it was inevitable that these ideas, potentially corrosive both to the religious establishment and to popular assumptions, would produce an opposing reaction in the Spain of the late 1520s and early 1530s. By then, Erasmus' 'New Testament' had already been fiercely criticised by Diego López de Zúñiga (known in Latinate humanistic circles as 'Stunica'), on the grounds that it contained major errors in translation from the original Greek. In 1522, Zúñiga went further, publishing a collection of phrases and passages from the *Instrumentum* which he claimed to be impious and even blasphemous, and linking Erasmus directly with the 'new heresy' of Luther. Many Spaniards would in future be accused of a similar offence, but it could be said that Erasmus himself was the first *luterano* (Lutheran) in at least some Spanish eyes.[2] In this way, according to the interpretation which still prevails in Spain, the excesses of Erasmus and Luther led to the curbing of some native reformers by the Spanish Inquisition under Manrique. Essentially, though, the reforms over which Cisneros had presided rendered the country largely immune to what would become the Protestant Reformation.

Some scholars, including Gordon Kinder and José Nieto, have shown more sympathy for the foreign and native reformers of the period from 1520 to 1560, and rated less highly the achievements of Cisneros under the patronage of Isabella and Ferdinand. Thus Kinder comments that it is 'worth emphasising that, while these [latter] measures did to some extent sharpen morals, deepen piety and strengthen ecclesiastical discipline, they left untouched the structure of the Church and its doctrines, which were the two main pre-occupations of the reformers.[…] And, however successful [Cisneros'] reforms, they still left room in the country for a ready response to Erasmian satire against hypocrisy and low standards among secular and regular clergy, particularly the mendicant orders'.[3] More precisely, Nieto recognises Cisneros' achievements as having constituted 'a reform of the Spanish Church before Luther, and although it was not at all total or complete, it must be considered as Reform and not Pre-reform, although it preceded Luther'.[4] Inquisitor General Manrique's reaction to this situation illustrates the complexity of religious attitudes in the period, which fits poorly into the later

categories which are commonly used in current religious
and historical analysis of the period. Meseguer Fernández
comments that:

> The historiography has seen in this character [that of Alonso Manrique]
> and in what is considered to be his conduct in office, proof that Caesar
> [the Emperor Charles V] listened to the complaints of the Cortes or
> of public opinion, through the Erasmian talent which is attributed
> to him and that, on the other hand, in fact adorned the brother of
> Jorge Manrique.

He rightly adds that:

> ...it does not seem to us that Erasmianism ever constituted the unique
> key to Manrique's religious personality.[5]

Nevertheless, the ideas associated, rightly or wrongly, with
the Dutch humanist did constitute the main intellectual
challenge to the Spanish Church of the 1520s, and thus it
was inevitable that Manrique as Inquisitor General would
have to confront it. In the event, at the peak of Erasmus'
popularity in court and ecclesiastical circles, he decided on
a scholarly consultation.

In the summer of 1527, Manrique summoned thirty-three
of Spain's most distinguished theologians to a conference in
the northern Castilian town of Valladolid, which was one
of the kingdom's main legal and administrative centres and
where the Castilian Cortes had been summoned earlier
in the year. The intention was that the assembled scholars should examine numerous passages from the published
works of Erasmus and identify anything in them that they
judged to be dubious or even heretical. In the event, the
meetings were spread over more than two months, but they
resulted in much conflict, and were ended in early August

by an outbreak of plague in Valladolid before all the agenda
had been covered. The gathering was never reconvened.
Led by Bataillon, modern scholars have tended to charac-
terise the Valladolid conference as a confrontation between
'progressives' and 'reactionaries'. In the French scholar's
view, the initial stance of Manrique and the Suprema was
strongly favourable to Erasmus. As evidence for this, he
pointed to a letter which Charles V's chancellor, Mercurino
Gattinara, had written from Valladolid to the emperor's
agent in Rome, the royal secretary Gonzalo Pérez, asking
him to try to obtain from Pope Clement VII the authority
'to shut the mouths of those who are running a campaign
against the works of Erasmus'.[6] The document in question arrived after it was over but nonetheless, according
to this interpretation, the abortive conference in Valladolid
appears, in Homza's words, as 'only a momentary glitch in
the swelling Erasmian revolution'.[7] As this scholar argues,
things were not in fact so simple, and the full complexity
of the expert theological approach in Spain to Erasmus'
ideas is revealed in the surviving written responses of
individual scholars, which were compiled on Manrique's
orders.[8] The picture which emerges from Homza's comprehensive analysis of the surviving records of the conference
is one of great complexity, which cannot be fitted into
simplistic categories such as 'Renaissance' versus medieval
'Scholasticism'. In fact, they 'oscillated between scholastic
and humanist methods, and betrayed a potential gap between
textual criticism and pious counsel'. Thus the theologians
showed enthusiasm for emotional, affective spirituality, and
downplayed the importance of Greek in Biblical scholarship. They appealed to a wide range of sources from all
periods, including Church history as well as tradition, but
the overriding characteristic of their contributions was
what may appear, to more hidebound modern scholars who

demand tidiness, to be a lack of consistency in their treatment of Erasmus' works. Thus a complex interaction was
taking place between the differing subtleties of the author
and the reader, so that an 'Erasmian', if such a person self-
consciously existed, might be very different from Erasmus
himself. In these circumstances, the Inquisitor General was
forced to be equally subtle in his approach to a subject
which was causing some turbulence in the upper echelons
of Church and State.

In advance of the conference, on 24 April 1527, one of
Erasmus' Spanish supporters, Juan de Vergara, who would
himself later fall victim to Manrique's Inquisition, outlined
the purpose of the planned gathering in a letter to the
master himself. In reaction to the publication of the Alcalá
translation of the Dutchman's *Enchiridion*:

> [the monks] began to shout continuously from the pulpits, the
> market-places, the shrines, the basilicas (for shouters of this sort are
> distributed everywhere), 'Erasmus is heretical, blasphemous, impious,
> sacrilegious'. What more? More enemies for you suddenly arose from
> the vernacular translation of the book than from Cadmus's sowing
> of the teeth.[9]

According to Vergara, Manrique had reacted by telling the
superiors of the religious orders to restrain their members
from attacking Erasmus openly and leave the judgement on
his works to others. Nevertheless, if the monks and friars did
find anything unacceptable in these writings, they should
put their objections down on paper and submit them to
the consideration of a committee of theologians which
would be convened in the future. This was the origin of the
Valladolid conference and the gossip among Erasmus' supporters was that the friars in particular took up Manrique's
urging with such enthusiasm that they hardly had time to

hear the confessions of the faithful before Easter communion
that year, so busy were they with dissecting the humanist's
writings. Thus, according to Vergara's account, the religious
presented their comments and objections to the Suprema
on 5 April 1527. The context was a formal session, in which
Dominicans, Franciscans, Benedictines and Trinitarians
read out their submissions, but there was much duplication
between the offerings, and Manrique asked them to take
their papers away and produce a consolidated account of
their concerns. Vergara asserts that the Inquisitor General
would have preferred the objections to be sent for study
to the theological faculties of Salamanca and Alcalá, and
anticipated that any doubts would be referred to Erasmus
himself and to the Pope. Nevertheless, other evidence also
indicates the strength of Spanish opposition to those of
the humanist's works which were available in Spain. The
Provincial of the Dominicans, García Loaysa y Mendoza,
reacted furiously to the Latin text of the *Enchiridion*, on
the grounds of its conspicuous scepticism concerning the
doctrine of purgatory and the accompanying widespread
purchase of indulgences and its rejection of the notion that
monasticism was the supreme example of Christian piety.
In the previous year, the translator of the *Enchiridion*, Alonso
Fernández de Madrid, engaged in a furious argument with
a Franciscan who had attached to his pulpit in Palencia a
list of what he regarded as Erasmus' errors. Homza points
out, however, that objections in Spain to Erasmus arose not
so much from his attacks on monks and friars as from his
notorious and inevitable association with Martin Luther.

It used to be thought that Luther had little influence in
Spain during the earlier years of his conflict with Rome, but
it now appears that knowledge of the German Augustinian
friar and his controversial views reached at least intellectual circles in the country not long after his publication of

'ninety-five theses' in Wittenberg at the end of October 1517. Already, in 1520, the controversial Spanish theologian Zúñiga connected the two in his diatribe against Erasmus and repeated the assertion in a letter to Vergara written two years later. In 1527, the point was forcefully made once again in the response of the religious orders to Manrique's request for a co-ordinated commentary on Erasmus' works. The monks and friars sharply criticised the Inquisition for its slowness in identifying what they regarded as the obvious links between Erasmus and Luther. Thus the years up to the Valladolid conference seem, on closer inspection, not to have been the 'golden age of Spanish Erasmianism' which have sometimes been imagined. The meeting itself was postponed by the impact of the 'Sack of Rome' of May 1527, in which Imperial troops, including both Spaniards and 'Lutheran' Germans, looted the city and captured and imprisoned Pope Clement VII. Thus it was not until 27 June of that year that thirty-three theologians swore themselves to secrecy, under the rules of the Inquisition, before the Suprema and two prosecutors representing its Castilian and Aragonese sections. Formal proceedings started almost immediately, and the sessions would be spread over six weeks. Every Tuesday, Thursday and Saturday, the delegates would meet to consider further 'dubious' propositions from Erasmus' works. The system used was thematic, with passages for debate being culled from various texts. One of the theologians would introduce a topic, and the rest would then comment, but the method was slow and laborious, with the result that when Manrique sent the delegates away on 13 August only four of the planned twenty themes had been discussed.

It is not known who made the selection of subjects and passages for the conference, but it does appear that those responsible did not include Erasmus' most noted Spanish opponents, 'Stunica' and Sancho Carranza de Miranda. In any case, Homza notes that participants in the Valladolid conference did not simply copy earlier attacks on Erasmus, but developed their own arguments. Thus they provide clues to the intellectual character of the Church which Manrique was attempting to supervise. The compilers gleaned much of their evidence from the Dutch human-ist's written defences against the attacks of 'Stunica' and the English bishop Edward Lee, particularly stressing the points made by the former, who was highly respected by his colleagues in Spain. Whereas earlier criticism of Erasmus' work had tended to concentrate on his edition of the New Testament, mainly in its revised version of 1519, considering the text verse by verse, Valladolid copied Stunica's criticisms of 1522 in adopting instead a thematic approach. Also, the Spanish theologians included Erasmus' most recent works in their field of fire, with the implication that the author was obstinate in his 'errors'. From a more modern point of view, though, there appear to be methodological prob-lems implicit in the approach adopted by the compilers of the Valladolid dossier. Nowadays it might be expected that the texts under consideration would, if they were not complete, at least consist of lengthy passages, so that the propositions which excited controversy might be studied in context. This was not, however, the approach adopted by the Valladolid theologians, who nonetheless raised, or drew from Erasmus, fundamental questions about the relation-ship between Renaissance humanistic techniques of textual criticism and traditional Biblical scholarship and belief. In the records of the Inquisition, twenty-nine sets of responses to the dossier survive, and they show diverse approaches and often great subtlety.[10]

As the Valladolid conference of 1527 ended abruptly and inconclusively, it is impossible to draw from it any precise

view of Inquisitor General Manrique's approach to the
vital intellectual issues involved, concerning the text and
understanding of the Bible, in the light of the new Classical
knowledge which was being gained by Renaissance human-
ists in various countries, including Erasmus. The Valladolid
theological consultants are clearly shown by their own
writings for the conference, which were conserved by the
Inquisition, to have each contained in themselves a highly
individual collection of attitudes, 'conservative' or 'progres-
sive' (if such anachronistic and rather unhelpful terms can
be usefully employed here), on the issues of the authorship,
status and accuracy of the established Biblical text, the Latin
'Vulgate' traditionally attributed to St Jerome. Thus, at the
level of intellectual activity, Manrique, in the 1520s and early
1530s, was the supposedly orthodox guardian of a Spanish
Church in lively ferment. This ebullience was not, however,
restricted to the libraries and lecture halls, in the case of the
Church as a whole or in that of Manrique personally.

One incident shines a light on the religious attitudes of
the Inquisitor General which will be unexpected to those
who see the developments in the Church in this period in
terms of a misleading dichotomy between 'Scholasticism' and
'Renaissance humanism'. On 21 May 1527, a son was born
in Valladolid to Queen Isabella and King Charles of Spain.
The infant Prince Philip, the future Philip I of England and
II of Spain, was baptised six weeks later in the Dominican
convent of San Pablo in the same city, while the conference
on Erasmus' works was in session. Manrique proposed that
the child should be taken to the font in a cradle which had
been blessed by the then superior of the Franciscan convent
of Clares in Córdoba, Sor (Sister) Magdalena de la Cruz.
Magdalena was a highly influential visionary and spiritual
counsellor whom Manrique, in his capacity as archbishop
of Seville, had consulted in Córdoba before travelling north

to Valladolid on this occasion. It is precisely this dimension of Spanish Christianity in the period, and the fact that it was fully shared by Church leaders and even inquisitors, which renders concepts such as 'Spanish Erasmianism' so doubtful. Soon, Manrique, as Inquisitor General, would find himself presiding over a series of trials of Christian figures in Spain whose spiritual exuberance was deemed, like some of the more cerebral thoughts of Erasmus, to have crossed the line between 'orthodoxy' and 'heresy'. It is important to remember, though, that at least as late as 1527 the condition of Spanish Christian life was much less polarised than it would later become. A case in point is that of the preacher and evangelist Juan de Ávila, who would more than once be in trouble with the Inquisition and still later be canonised as a saint. In the 1520s, Manrique adopted Juan as a protégé, when he arrived in Seville with the aim of going to the New World as a missionary. The reformer and future saint was allowed to preach in Seville Cathedral on several occasions and his patron decided to appoint him as a licensed diocesan preacher, to help raise the quality of the Christian life in Andalusia. To understand the significance of this choice on the part of the then Inquisitor General, it is useful to look more carefully at Juan de Ávila's activities and writings in this period. Juan was born of Jewish convert stock in or around 1499, and studied at Cisneros' University of Alcalá. If the accusations made against him by inquisitors are correct, he uttered a series of controversial statements during his preaching career up to 1532, indicating a radical approach to Christian faith and practice, though one which evidently had a strong basis in Scripture. Thus he was accused of saying that heaven was for the poor and that it was impossible for the rich to achieve eternal salvation. Like Manrique, he recognised the authenticity of female visionaries such as Sor Magdalena of Córdoba, commenting that it was unsurprising that he appeared to such women when he came into the Eucharistic hosts consecrated by so many unworthy priests. He was also accused of asserting that the only authentic prayer was mental, that is to say internal rather than publicly recited. Probably at least in part because of the support given to him by Manrique, Juan de Ávila escaped sanction from the Inquisition in 1532, being permitted to found a small university at Baeza, in Andalusia, for the training of priests.[11] Not everything was allowed to go unchecked, though, in the varied religious life of Spain in the 1520s and early 1530s, and Manrique inevitably became involved in a certain degree of investigation and repression.

In the first two decades of the sixteenth century, certain groupings, which have by some been termed a 'movement', developed in an area of central Spain bounded by Toledo, Salamanca and Alcalá de Henares. A certain 'Friar Melchor' (Melchior) seems to have begun things by travelling about and preaching the reform of Franciscan houses, very much on the model which Cardinal Cisneros strongly supported. Melchior gained a considerable following, especially among friars and lay people, including converts of Jewish origin, not only for his sermons but also for his readings of passages of Scripture in Spanish, and of popular devotional works such as Thomas à Kempis' *Imitation of Christ*. Followers of such groups gradually became known as *Alumbrados* ('Illuminated' or 'Enlightened' ones), the term having probably begun as a code-word of recognition among members, but soon being adopted by the general public and eventually by the Inquisition. The exact nature of these groups, and of their religious life, remains obscure, but in general terms some of those who practised a 'recollected' form of mental prayer, which was approved of by the Church authorities, moved on to a more abandoned (*dejado*) approach, the exuberant aspects of which were frowned upon. Many have examined the question of whether the *Alumbrados* derived their ideas from Erasmus and Luther, as the inquisitors later suggested, but although there are some similarities, and there may indeed have been some direct links after 1525, this spiritual current seems to have had definite indigenous roots.[12] Things were about to tighten up, though, and Manrique was inevitably in the forefront of action against those who were held by some in authority to have overstepped the mark.

One significant feature of the *Alumbrado* groupings was the prominence in them of female leadership. Notable among these women was a Franciscan tertiary, Isabel de la Cruz, who in about 1512 began to preach in the district around Guadalajara, east of Madrid. At the time, another woman, Marí Núñez, was dominant in such worshipping groups in that area, and a power struggle ensued which Isabel eventually won, with the help of local aristocrats. In what turned out to be a foolhardy move, her defeated rival denounced Isabel to the Inquisition in 1519. At the time, with the largely uninterested Adrian of Utrecht still Inquisitor General, nothing came of the case, and Marí Núñez faded into obscurity, but a dangerous precedent had been set for the turbulent years which were to follow in the Spanish Church. In the meantime, Isabel de la Cruz had begun to attract followers, including Pedro Ruiz de Alcaraz, who was an accountant and lay preacher in the household of the Marquis of Villena in Escalona, and María de Cazalla, who would take over as leader of the Guadalajara group after Isabel was arrested by the Inquisition in 1524. Also prominent in *Alumbrado* circles at this time was Francisca Hernández, who was said to have absorbed the essence of the doctrine of the Holy Trinity by the time she was three, practised *dejado* prayer, a holy form of fortune-telling, and

apparently carried out miraculous cures in Salamanca and
Valladolid. Her main followers seem all to have been male and
many were Franciscan friars, most prominent among them
being Bernardino de Tovar, who was the older half-brother
of Juan de Vergara, the supporter of Erasmus and secretary
to the archbishop of Toledo and himself a highly prominent
future prisoner of the Inquisition. While Vergara pursued a
career in the service of the archbishop and the Emperor,
Fray Bernardino developed his links with *Alumbrado* groups
and their predominantly female leadership.

It is notable that pressure from the Inquisition on
Alumbrado groups began well before the 1527 Valladolid
conference. In 1524, both Isabel de la Cruz and Pedro Ruiz
de Alcaraz were arrested, and it is interesting to see the reasons why. The opening for Manrique's officials to investigate
seems to have been offered initially by a conflict within the
Alumbrado group which surrounded the Marquis of Villena
in Escalona. Because Franciscan friars were involved, this
came to the attention of the vicar general of the order, who
expressed concern at the goings-on there, and not least the
female leadership of the group. There was also a supposed
connection with Luther, who had been condemned by
both Charles V and Leo X in 1521. After that, the Suprema
instructed Spanish inquisitorial officials to confiscate all
'Lutheran' books which came into the country. Castilians
were forbidden to sell or read the works of Luther, or preach
them from the pulpit, and in the autumn of 1521 books
in this category were indeed seized by the Inquisition in
Aragon, Valencia and Navarre. What seems to have happened in the early 1520s is that Inquisitors who still had a
fairly vague notion of Luther's 'evangelical' ideas became
alarmed at what they saw as *Alumbrado* excesses, and tarred
native Spanish Christians, who had probably developed
their ideas quite independently, with the 'Luterano' brush.

Whatever the truth, a meeting of theologians summoned in 1525 under the Inquisition's auspices decided to its own satisfaction that Isabel de la Cruz and Pedro Ruiz de Alcaraz did indeed have links with Luther and his supporters, these being demonstrated by their disparaging attitude towards Catholic teaching on auricular confession and the veneration of the saints. After this, Manrique and the Suprema promptly issued an edict of faith, the preliminary to an inquisitorial investigation, against the *Alumbrado* 'heresy'. It contained forty-eight propositions derived from the trials of Isabel and Pedro, and was ordered to be read out in Castilian churches on Sundays and feast days. As in previous cases involving 'Judaisers' and 'Islamicisers', the purpose of this measure was to provoke confessions from those who imagined themselves to have offended and, indeed, María de Cazalla denounced herself to the Toledo Inquisition and was released with minor penances.

Manrique's 1525 edict did not, however, end the kind of religious activity which the authorities would come to regard as unorthodox. Thus, in that year and in 1526, *Alumbrado* 'apostles' preached in the lands of the admiral of Castile, Fadrique Enríquez, in and around Medina de Rioseco. The Valladolid conference, together with the repercussions of the 1527 Sack of Rome, seems to have diverted the attention of Manrique and the Suprema for a while but in 1529 further arrests took place of prominent *Alumbrado* figures: Francisca Hernández was arrested in March 1529, and Bernardino de Tovar in the following year, though the records of both these trials are lost.[13] Another case involved Francisco Ortiz, a Franciscan friar in the royal foundation of San Juan de los Reyes in Toledo where, on 6 April 1529, he preached a sermon, supposedly in thanksgiving for the gift of rain. In fact, Ortiz made an attack on the Inquisitor General for the 'sin' he had committed in arresting Francisca Hernández. The preacher had previously had two interviews with Manrique in an attempt to stave off such action, claiming that on the first occasion his interlocutor seemed sympathetic while on the second he seemed 'changed'. For this Ortiz blamed his own superior, the Guardian of San Juan de los Reyes, Friar Barnabás. Once in the prison of the Toledo Inquisition, Ortiz wrote two letters to Manrique, the first being delivered on 9 April 1529. In it, the friar set out his defence, stating that he had had to say what he did for conscience's sake. He had warned Manrique previously not to 'fall into sin induced by the voices of the friars [of San Juan de los Reyes]' and claimed that the Inquisitor General had agreed with him during their first conversation that 'there was no offence [of heresy] in the spouse of the Most High God [Francisca Hernández] for which she should have been arrested thus'. Ortiz claimed that he himself was entirely orthodox: 'If I did not preach Catholic doctrine, why has [the Guardian] had me here in Toledo [preaching sermons] during five Lents?' The friar indignantly denied Manrique's claim that his preaching was inspired by the Devil, and begged the inquisitor to: 'have it [...] examined among scholars [*letrados*] whether it is possible to reach a most high purity of perfection without being a friar or nun'. Ortiz evidently thought so, and his approach would very naturally have made Manrique think of Erasmus and Luther in connection with his words, given their strong assertion of the sins of the monastic life and the postive virtues of the secular married state. Friar Francisco, on the other hand, claimed that he had not taken such a black-and-white stance on the subject and had indeed preached more than once *against* Erasmus' views. Nonetheless, he (rightly) claimed that it was heresy to assert that Christian perfection may only be reached through the religious life, and that many general Councils of the Church had pronounced accordingly. Daringly, Ortiz described Francisca Hernández as a 'new St Susanna' (she being a third-century Roman martyr) with whom the Inquisition had no business, and begged Manrique to repent of his 'sin' in arresting her, so as not to find himself 'mocked at the hour of death'. He ended the letter with a flourish: 'See that my words in the pulpits are not habitually vain – and I know well that if you do not listen to me, this writing will burn with your Lordship on the Day of Judgement!'. Ortiz wrote three more letters to Manrique during April 1529, but none were answered, and the friar was eventually condemned, mainly, ir seemed, for his defiant assertion of liberty of conscience, to five years' incarceration in a convent.[14] His direct defiance of the Inquisitor General may seem surprising to the modern reader, but it gives some indication of the prevailing atmosphere in the Spanish Church of the 1520s.

Alonso Manrique seems to have been reluctant to face up to such challenges, and the suggestion is that he was more than sympathetic towards those whom his office forced him to confront. The most conspicuous sign of his weakness in defending them was the case of Juan de Vergara, the half-brother of Friar Bernardino de Tovar. Vergara's political and ecclesiastical connections might have been thought likely to preserve him from any entanglement with the Holy Office of the Inquisition, but his efforts to help Bernardino made such an outcome inevitable. He smuggled messages into the Toledo Inquisition's prison, written in 'invisible ink' on the wrapping paper of some raisins meant for his half-brother, but the ruse was discovered, in April 1533, by the official responsible for distributing food to the prisoners. As a result, the inquisitors began to suspect Vergara, despite his position as confidant to the archbishop and primate, but nearly three months passed before they finally felt able to arrest him as an aider and abettor (*fautor*) of his 'heretical' brother. A lengthy investigation followed, during which Vergara used all his skill and former authority and connections in order to resist such charges, but finally, in December 1535, he was condemned to do public penance in an *auto de fe*. He duly did so on the 21 December, wearing a *sambenito* and carrying a large candle, as was the custom for penitent heretics. Standing in the Plaza de Zocodover in Toledo, with other convicted prisoners of the Inquisition, he was told in his 'sentence' that he had been proved to have supported the views of Martin Luther and to have mocked the bulls on the subject issued by Popes. He had also mocked the doctrine of purgatory and the resulting purchase of indulgences by those who wished to help their departed relatives to rise from there to heaven. He had owned 'Lutheran' books after their possession had been banned in Spain, and had devalued vocal, as opposed to mental, prayer; he had denied the value of the fasting prescribed by the Church, mocked the cult of the saints, supported *Alumbrados* and publicly sympathised with Erasmus. Thus Vergara had been convicted as an aider and abettor of heresy, and as a corrupter of employees of the Inquisition, through words, actions and promises. His punishment, though, was relatively mild: he was confined in seclusion in a monastery for a year, and made to pay the large fine of 1,500 gold ducats.[15] The message of doom was clear but, as things turned out, it was no more hopeful for Manrique's own future as Inquisitor General.

By failing to protect as prominent and sympathetic a churchman as Vergara, Archbishop Alonso had demonstrated his weakness to all, and his tenure in charge of the Spanish Inquisition went into terminal decline. He was summoned by Vergara as a witness in his trial, but refused to appear, and the point appeared not to be lost on his subordinates in the Holy Office. One of his protégés, Juan del Castillo, who had been a professor at the University of Louvain and an evangelist, along with Bernardino de Tovar, in the lands of Fadrique Enríquez around Medina de Rioseco, was arrested by the Inquisition in 1535, alongside his brother and sister, while Vergara's trial was still in progress. Manrique failed to protect Castillo, who was burned as an unrepentant heretic. It was at this point that the Inquisitor General fell out of favour at court and was banished from it by Charles V. He returned permanently to Seville, dying there on 28 September 1538 and being subsequently buried in the Manrique family chapel at Santa Clara de Calabazanas near Palencia, in Old Castile.[16] In the meantime, and as an omen for the difficult years the Spanish Church would pass through in mid-century, he had, as archbishop, supported the introduction to the staff of Seville Cathedral of three former students of the University of Alcalá: Dr Francisco de Vargas, Dr Juan Gil [Egidio], and Dr Constantino Ponce de la Fuente.[17] When Manrique's earthly troubles ceased, theirs began.

The archbishop of Seville's immediate successor as Inquisitor General was Juan Pardo de Tavera who, like his uncle Diego de Deza, came from Toro. His term of office lasted from 7 November 1539 until his death in Valladolid on 1 August 1545, at the age of seventy-three. Miguel Avilés has assessed his 'reign' as one of active consolidation of the somewhat controversial achievements of his predecessor. He reorganised and clarified Manrique's guidelines on the treatment of converts from Islam (moriscos) and strengthened the existing edict of the Inquisition against the reading in Spain of the works of Luther and his followers. In a series of further administrative measures, he endeavoured to clarify the treatment by the Holy Office of such varied subjects and social groups as banned literature, the property of moriscos, which was not to be confiscated in Aragon, and the sentencing of convicted prisoners to the royal galleys. Emperor Charles V evidently appreciated Tavera's administrative efficiency, being recorded as commenting, on hearing of his death:'A little old man has died on me who kept my kingdoms of Spain peaceful with his walking-stick'.[18] In terms of Spain's religious identity, though, it was Tavera's successor, Fernando de Valdés, who had the greatest impact.

Fernando de Valdés y Salas, who became Inquisitor General on 20 January 1547, had been born into the minor nobility, at Salas in the northern principality of Asturias, in 1483. He studied at Salamanca, becoming a professor of canon law, and rector of the university in 1514–15. Later, he was dean of Oviedo Cathedral in place of his uncle, Jordán de Valdés, and also held several other prominent ecclesiastical posts as a non-resident. On this issue, he was to come into conflict with perhaps his most prominent inquisitorial prisoner, Friar Bartolomé Carranza. As a member of the Suprema from 7 April 1524, Valdés was involved in the Valladolid conference of 1527, and he was also politically active during the 1530s, eventually becoming president of the Royal Council of Castile, from 1 July 1539 until 1547. In August 1546 he was elected archbishop of Seville and in the following year, on 19 February, Pope Paul III named him as Inquisitor General of Spain, a post which he would occupy until September 1566, dying in Madrid on 29 December 1568, and being subsequently buried in his home town of Salas. Before his activities against heresy are examined, it is worth noting that he was generous in the foundation and endowment of educational, ecclesiastical and charitable institutions. In education these included the college of San Gregorio in Oviedo (1534), the University of Oviedo (1566) and the college of San Pelayo in Salamanca (also in 1566). He also endowed eight chaplaincies in the parish church of Salas, founded hospitals in various places, including Cangas de Onís and Seville, and rebuilt the castle and bishop's palace at Sigüenza.[19] Fernando de Valdés' biographer, González Novalín, while admitting that his subject was 'a figure lacking in personal and human attractions', asserts that he gave to the Spanish Inquisition 'the character which forms the basis of its greatness and of its ruin'.[20] This is a strong and significant statement, and the justification for it requires closer examination.

Valdés, who was a fairly distant relative of the 'Erasmian' Alfonso de Valdés, became closely involved with Charles V at an early stage. He accompanied him to Flanders and Germany in 1520, with his fellow canon Juan de Vergara, whose later Inquisition trial has already been noted, as a representative of the cathedral chapter of Toledo in the matter of finding a successor for Cardinal Cisneros as archbishop there. The favoured candidate was the Netherlander Guillaume de Croy, but there was much resistance to the appointment of a foreigner as ecclesiastical primate of Spain and, ironically in view of the later bitter controversy between Valdés and Carranza, both he and Vergara demanded that their new archbishop should be resident in his extensive diocese. The canons were also concerned at the time that new dioceses of Alcalá de Henares and Talavera might be carved out of traditional Toledan territory. In the event, the death of Guillaume de Croy, on 7 January 1521, solved the immediate problem of a 'foreign prelate', but the issue of his promotion and that of others among Charles' Netherlandish courtiers to prominent positions in Spain would soon precipitate a major rebellion (the 'Comunidades') against the king's government in Castile, in which Toledo was actively involved. Right up to his nomination as Inquisitor General in 1547, Valdés showed a clear preference for political activity, helping in 1522 to negotiate Charles' marriage to Isabella of Portugal, and to bring

Navarre back to the Castilian allegiance in 1523–4. He served as a member of the Suprema for ten years after 1524, but in 1532 he became president of the High Court (Chancillería) in Valladolid. He was discontented with this situation, though, expressing a desire for more political power and more ecclesiastical benefices. His wishes were apparently fulfilled in his appointments to the Castilian Royal Council and then the leadership of the Spanish Inquisition.[21] It was during his time in the latter post that he faced what appeared to be a significant crisis in the 'Reform' of the Spanish Church, one which involved, among others, his predecessor Alonso Manrique's protégés in Seville.

Although Inquisitor General Tavera had attempted to stiffen the attitude of the Holy Office towards the more radical among Spanish Church reformers, Valdés inherited a situation in which many differing flowers were still allowed to bloom. In particular, Francisco de Vargas, Juan Gil [Egidio] and Constantino Ponce de la Fuente were still engaged in an active ministry based at Seville Cathedral. Vargas was monitored by the Inquisition but died unscathed, leaving no surviving written works. 'Dr Egidio', though, as official preacher at the cathedral from 1537, gave rise to house-groups ('conventicles') in Seville and eventually, in 1552, was brought before the Inquisition and told to recant various 'heretical propositions'. Even then, it did not appear that Valdés had ordered any systematic investigation of 'evangelicals', though a printer, Gaspar Zapata, and three priests from one of the city's hospitals thought it prudent to leave Seville at this point. The latter group, Juan Pérez de Pineda, Luis Hernández del Castillo and Diego de la Cruz, headed for Paris, where they joined forces with Juan Morillo, an Aragonese who had previously worked, at the General Council of the Church at Trent, with Cardinal Reginald Pole, who will reappear in this story. There, they

welcomed other Spanish reformers who had felt the pressure of Valdés' inquisitors. Dr Egidio also left no known
publication and died, unmolested by the Inquisition, in 1556,
after visiting Valladolid to confer with the leader of the
reforming group there, Agustín Cazalla. By 1559, though,
Juan Gil was being tried posthumously and his bones were
disinterred and burned along with his effigy, while his followers were investigated. He was succeeded as cathedral
preacher by Constantino Ponce de la Fuente, who had been
an enthusiast for the ideas of Erasmus since about 1530, and
had corresponded with him.

Constantino served at Seville Cathedral between 1533
and 1548, then becoming a royal chaplain. In 1543 he
published in Seville a summary of Christian doctrine,
together with a dialogue entitled *Sermon of Christ our
redeemer on the Mount*. His work shows the influence of the
prominent reformer Juan de Valdés, brother of the Imperial
secretary Alfonso, who had fled to Italy from the threat of
the Spanish inquisitors, and it appeared in several editions,
both in Seville and in Antwerp. The same applied in the
case of his commentary, in the form of six sermons, on
Psalm 1, which was first published in Seville in 1546. The
first part of his 'Catechism' appeared in 1547 and his doctrinal treatise *Doctrina cristiana*, together with a commentary
on the Creed and a further work entitled *Confession before
Jesus Christ, redeemer and judge of men*, came out in 1548.
Ominously, in the prevailing climate of Fernando de Valdés'
inquisitorial regime, the tribunal's censors condemned some
passages in Ponce de la Fuente's *Doctrina* as demonstrating
Alumbrado influence. He was evidently being watched, not
least because he gave Bible classes to the boys in the orphan-
age in Seville, the 'Teaching College for Boys' (*Colegio de los
Niños de la Doctrina*) from which his fellow priests, Pineda,
Hernández and de la Cruz, had previously fled. It would not

be until 1558, though, that Constantino was finally arrested
by the Inquisition, as part of a general panic in the kingdom
about supposed 'Protestant' infiltration. In the event, he died
before he could reach trial, but a search of the house of
one of his female supporters, who had also been arrested,
revealed many more of his writings. These were destroyed,
but Inquisition records suggest that they had a more strongly
'Protestant' flavour than his published works.

Fernando de Valdés evidently came to the conclusion
that there was a large 'evangelical' group in Seville, and it
does appear that Dr Egidio's former followers had recruited
numerous new members, possibly as many as 800, from
all social classes. Intriguingly, apart from illegal imports
which they obtained on their own account, these reformist
Christians also succeeded in abstracting confiscated material
from the Inquisition itself. The source for this daring enterprise was a monk called Antonio del Corro, whose uncle of
the same name was an inquisitor. Ironically, the Inquisition
under Valdés probably had the best 'Protestant' library in
Spain. When the books belonging to the Seville group were
confiscated, they turned out to include works by all the
major reformers, including Luther and Calvin, as well as
some minor ones and authors on the fringe of Catholic
orthodoxy. Kinder suggests that what had been a reforming group entirely within Catholicism had become more
clearly 'evangelical' when one of its members, Rodrigo Valer,
underwent a personal conversion and challenged the leaders
to develop a more profound faith. Not all these leaders were
clerics, one being a physician named Cristóbal de Losada.
The movement also affected Seville's religious communities, including the female convents of Santa Paula and Santa
Isabel, as well as Dominican and Jeronymite houses outside
the city. At the Observant Jeronymite friary of Santiponce,
the prior, García Arias, allowed the community to desert

the choir liturgy, which was traditionally the heart of the order's life, in favour of Bible study. Arias would eventually be burned by the Inquisition, in 1562.

During these years a parallel, though socially more exclusive, group of reformists seems to have developed in the northern city of Valladolid, under the leadership of Agustín Cazalla, who was a canon of Salamanca and acted as chaplain and preacher to Charles V between 1542 and 1552. Cazalla had accompanied the emperor to Germany and the Low Countries in 1543 and 1548, thus acquiring experience of Protestantism. The Valladolid group met in the house of Cazalla's mother, and went so far as to celebrate the Lord's Supper in a reformed manner. There were also meetings in the Cistercian nunnery of Belén (Bethlehem), and the group's members maintained contacts with the Seville group, though they seem to have had access to fewer Protestant books than their Andalusian contmporaries. Traditionally it has been assumed that the rest of Spain, outside Seville and Valladolid, contained very few, isolated, 'evangelical' sympathisers, but it is now known that there was another organised group in Aragon. In fact, the Inquisition's investigations in Seville, which resulted from the denunciation of individuals in 1555, revealed a quite sophisticated network of contacts throughout Spain, but its very complexity brought the inevitable danger of a fatal lapse in security. This eventually occurred in 1557, when a religious refugee abroad, Julián Hernández, returned to his homeland on one of his regular clandestine visits, with the aim of contacting sympathisers in Seville and bringing them new books from the Calvinist capital, Geneva. By this time, the Inquisition had guards posted at the city gates, so that Hernández was forced to operate at night, with the help of sympathisers. The contraband material was hidden in packets containing innocent items but, while texts were being distributed, one parcel containing copies of a violently anti-papal tract entitled *Image of the Antichrist* fell into the hands of a hostile cleric with the same name as the intended recipient, who reported the find to the authorities. The Inquisition quickly became involved, first in Seville and then in the rest of Spain. Hernández managed to escape from Seville, but was detained at Adamuz in the Sierra de Córdoba, on the road north, and on 7 October 1557 he entered the prison of the Seville Inquisition in the riverside Castle of St George (*Castillo de San Jorge*). Before formal investigations began, the Jeronymite friars of San Isidro de Santiponce and Nuestra Señora de Écija were tipped off, perhaps by Antonio del Corro, and about a dozen of them fled abroad, together with some lay people, mainly heading for Geneva or Germany, though some were arrested before they could leave Andalusia. Those who reached Germany included Antonio del Corro and Casiodoro de la Reina, who would achieve great prominence in the Reform. Large numbers of suspects were moved into San Jorge, including various priests, the head sacristan of Seville Cathedral and some nuns from the Jeronymite convent of San Pablo. In all, more than 180 people, from Seville itself, Cádiz, Jerez de la Frontera and other parts of Andalusia and Extremadura were arrested, while an unknown number escaped, though some of them were later burned in effigy by the Inquisition. Charles V was informed and one of his last acts as ruler was to instruct his son Philip to crack down, adding that he wished he himself had dealt more firmly with Luther in the 1520s. At the same time, the existence of the Valladolid 'evangelicals' was also discovered by the authorities. In this case, no doubt in part because of the central and landlocked location of the city, many, including Cazalla himself, made no attempt to flee, and those who did were all, apart from one, arrested before they could reach the border. It seems clear that the discovery of these two groups caused panic among the authorities, which was only increased when the Aragonese group was discovered during an investigation into the rector of Zaragoza University, Miguel Monterde, who had been corresponding with Spanish religious exiles abroad. The main entry to this group, however, was the ill-timed return of Jayme Sánchez, who had been brought up as a Protestant in Paris. He was already known to the Inquisition and was identified when he foolishly attempted to ward off action by the tribunal through a false, voluntary confession. With strong royal support, Valdés took the hardest possible line with the dissidents, personally co-ordinating action against them, and the incipient Spanish Protestant movement was effectively eliminated by a series of *autos de fe* and burnings in person or effigy, at Valladolid on 21 May and 8 October 1559, and at Seville on 24 September 1559, 22 December 1560 and 26 April and 28 October 1562. Werner Thomas comments that 'in the succeeding years, Valdés exploited the affair of the Spanish Protestants to prolong his political career, at the same time as he used the Holy Office to eliminate his enemies at court'.[22] The classic case in point was the trial of Friar Bartolomé Carranza de Miranda, an archbishop of Toledo accused of 'Lutheran' heresy by an Inquisitor General.

Of Vizcayan (Basque) descent, Bartolomé was born in the small Navarrese town of Miranda de Arga, near that kingdom's capital Pamplona, probably in 1503. Both his father and his uncle were recognised as minor nobles (*hidalgos*) by Charles V, the latter being the Canon Sancho Carranza who took part in the Valladolid conference of 1527 on the works of Erasmus. Bartolomé studied at the University of Alcalá de Henares, where his uncle was a professor and acted as his patron, envisaging for him a brilliant academic career. At the age of sixteen, though, his nephew announced that he wished to join the Dominican order and, despite Sancho's heartfelt opposition, he duly professed and continued his philosophical studies, in the Thomist tradition, as a friar. In 1525, he was chosen by his order to join its convent and college of San Gregorio in Valladolid, being therefore present in the city during the 1527 conference on Erasmus. Carranza held various teaching posts at San Gregorio, including those of Regent of Arts and Regent of Theology, and in 1539 received the signal honour of the award, in Rome, of the Dominicans' own degree of Master of Theology. From then until 1539, he continued teaching Thomist philosophy and the Bible at San Gregorio, having been involved, since 1533, in the work of the Valladolid Inquisition as an adviser on potentially heretical material. He refused ecclesiastical preferment in the case of the Peruvian bishopric of Cuzco, but did agree to act as a theological adviser to Charles V during the first session of the Council of Trent, from 1545 to 1548. During this period, he intervened in discussions on doctrinal and disciplinary matters, preached sermons to the Council, and published several works in 1546 and 1547. These were a short history of the previous Councils of the Church, four 'Controversies' or tracts directed against various Protestant tenets, and a treatise on the desirability of bishops residing in their dioceses. This last is worth noting in view of Carranza's later clash with Fernando de Valdés, but it is quite clear that in the 1540s the Dominican was regarded as an able theologian and defender of orthodoxy.

When he returned to Spain, in 1548, he was elected prior of the Dominican friary in Palencia, where he continued to teach Scripture and refused a request from Charles V and his son Philip to become the latter's confessor. Instead, in 1550 Carranza was elected as Dominican Provincial for Castile and devoted himself to visiting and reforming the order's convents in that province. At this time, he refused another bishopric, that of the Canary Islands. In 1551 he returned to Trent for the second session of the Council, taking part

in and concluding the debate on the sacrifice of the Mass,
and when the session finished in January 1553 he went back
to San Gregorio in Valladolid, where he was appointed as a
preacher to the royal court. Soon after this, his career took a
more disturbed and controversial turn when, in the summer
of 1554, Prince Philip, who was soon to become Philip II,
chose him as an adviser to accompany him to England
for his marriage with Mary Tudor, which took place at
Winchester on 25 July of that year. Carranza's arrival in a
turbulent England was eventually to precipitate his arrest
by the Spanish Inquisition, on the orders of Fernando de
Valdés, but his route to seventeen years of imprisonment
was to be tortuous and complex.

Philip's choice of Carranza as one of his team of advisers was directed at the restoration of Roman Catholicism
in England, after the reforms of the Church there which
had taken place under Henry VIII and Edward VI. In this
enterprise, which was passionately supported by Queen
Mary, the granddaughter of Isabella of Castile, Carranza
had a prominent role which is at last being recognised by
historians. Not only did the Dominican theologian advise
his royal master, and by implication the queen as well, but
he also had a commission from the vicar general of his
order to restore its English province, and a close friend-
ship with the new Catholic archbishop of Canterbury,
Cardinal Reginald Pole, whom he had come to know
during the Council of Trent. Particularly as a result of
this last connection, Carranza played a prominent role
in the synod of the English Church in London in 1555.
Specifically, he was commissioned to write a new catechism of the Christian faith, which would be used to
root the somewhat wayward English clergy once more in
Catholicism. With his immense theological and pastoral
experience, including a prominent role at Trent, he was

the ideal man to bring to the far corners of the English Church the latest ideas of reforming Catholicism which, from 1563, would be binding on the Roman Catholic Church as a considerable part of the Tridentine catechism. By then, Carranza would be in an Inquisition prison, and this extraordinary fact demands explanation. First, though, it is necessary to look at the Dominican's years in England and the events which followed, in the Low Countries and in Spain.

While in Tudor England, Carranza preached frequently, took part in the visitation and reform of the universities of Oxford and Cambridge, and worked to restore traditional liturgical practices, in particular the devotions associated with the feast of Corpus Christi. As a long-standing theological adviser to the Inquisition, he also took a hard line on heresy, especially in the case of lapsed friars but also in that of the former archbishop of Canterbury, Thomas Cranmer, who was both tried for treason against the queen, at the beginning of her reign, and burned as a relapsed heretic. As political demands on the Continent increased, and it became increasingly clear that Mary would not produce an heir to the Habsburg and Tudor thrones, Philip left for Flanders, and soon asked Carranza to join him. There, he continued to act against the supporters of Reformed ideas, some of whom were of course Spaniards. He was scandalised to find heretical works being distributed even in the royal palace at Brussels, and urged the head of the royal household, Francisco de Castilla, to pursue the refugee and book-distribution networks which connected the Low Countries and Germany. While he continued his preaching and heresy-hunting, though, an event took place in Spain which was to change his life forever.

In the autumn of 1557, the archbishop of Toledo, Juan Martínez de Silíceo, died. Philip, who expected to play

a major part in the appointment of his successor, immediately lighted upon Carranza, thus, in the words of the
greatest scholar of his life and work, Ignacio Tellechea, 'raising at a stroke a simple Dominican friar to the first see of
Christendom after Rome, leaping over the requirements of the
promotion-ladder and leaving aside existing bishops and archbishops, some of them of high birth'. Carranza was named to the
primatial see of Spain in the Roman Consistory of 10 December
1557, and consecrated bishop in the Dominican church in Brussels
on 27 February 1558. It was in the same year that his catechism,
which had been commissioned in England and written in great
haste in Spanish, with a view to future translation into Latin
and English, was printed in Antwerp by Martín Nucio. Though
dedicated to Philip, and complete with his licences for publication and distribution in Castile and Aragon, it would be the
pretext of his ensuing conflict with Inquisitor General Valdés.

Between November 1558 and April 1559, Carranza
occupied his see as archbishop of Toledo and by all accounts,
not only his own, he devoted himself wholeheartedly to
putting into practice all the precepts which he had previously urged on clerical leaders in Spain, England, the Low
Countries, and at the Council of Trent, which was still
suspended at that time. In his inaugural sermon at Toledo,
which was discovered in the Vatican Library by Tellechea,
he made explicit reference to the religious controversies
of his own day. He daringly discussed both the *Alumbrado*
beliefs of the 1520s and 1530s, some of which he praised,
in particular mental prayer, which he described as being
'better' than vocal prayer. He then went on to the teachings
which were described in the Spain of that time as 'Lutheran',
more than implying that, in such conditions, any devout and
conscientious Christian was liable to be called a 'Lutheran'
just as, twenty years before, he would probably have been
called an *Alumbrado*. This was brave, even foolhardy, stuff,

but in the succeeding months Carranza devoted himself to his liturgical, disciplinary and social duties as a bishop. He made formal visitations to his own cathedral chapter and to convents; he attempted to ensure that his parish clergy stayed at the posts; and he occupied much of his time in alms-giving and other charitable work. He also admitted the Jesuits to work in his archdiocese (something his friend Pole had refused to do in England) and one of that 'Company', Bartolomé Bustamente, told the Society's General, Ignatius of Loyola's successor Diego Laínez, that Carranza was 'a portrait of the good prelates of the primitive Church'.[23]

On 25 April 1559, Archbishop Bartolomé left Toledo to carry out a formal visitation of his extensive archdiocese. He would not return until his remains were brought back to his primatial cathedral in 1993. In what happened to him in the meantime, Fernando de Valdés played a significant role. A few days after Carranza departed from Toledo, the Suprema voted to arrest him, though the plan was not put into effect at once. In the event, Valdés acted deviously, not speaking directly to his episcopal superior (Toledo being senior in status to his own see of Seville), but arranging for Princess Juana, who was governing the kingdom on behalf of Philip II, to summon him to his old haunt of Valladolid to give her advice. Philip's favourite, Rui Gómez de Silva, warned Carranza that there was a plot and he dawdled on his journey, but he was nevertheless arrested by the Inquisition at Torrelaguna, near Madrid, which was the birthplace of a former archbishop of Toledo, Cardinal Cisneros. Valdés had taken time and care in preparing his trap for Carranza. Some of those accused in the trials of 'evangelicals' in Seville and Valladolid had asked for the archbishop of Toledo to be called in their defence, thus suggesting guilt by association, even though, in September 1558, Carranza had visited the entirely orthodox ex-Emperor Charles, in his retreat in the Extremaduran monastery of Yuste, and had been with him when he died on 21 September. It was, however, the catechism which proved to be Carranza's nemesis, after this major work by a leading Catholic theologian had been examined, at Valdés' request, by a committee of other theologians which included his fierce Dominican rival, Melchor Cano. Traditionally, canon law had dictated that no diocesan bishop could be arrested by the Inquisition but, on 7 January 1559, the Spanish Inquisitor General had obtained permission from Pope Paul IV (a bitter enemy of both Carranza and Pole), to make an exception in the case of the archbishop of Toledo. What followed was a trial which continued, at intervals, until a few weeks before Carranza's death, on 2 May 1576, in the Dominican community of Santa Maria sopra Minerva in Rome, where he had received his degree of Master of Theology back in 1539. Just before his death, the then Pope, Gregory XIII, almost rehabilitated him, and appeared to show his true feelings by writing the text of his epitaph, which is still displayed in the Carafa chapel of La Minerva.

At this distance, it is hard to see, bearing in mind the voluminous evidence which has been assembled over more than five decades by Tellechea, how Carranza could ever have been thought, even by the standards of his own day, to be a 'Lutheran heretic'. The archbishop himself, though, had no hestitation in placing much of the blame for his arrest and trial, first by the Spanish Inquisition and then by the Roman one, on Fernando de Valdés. Indeed, early in proceedings, Carranza took the remarkable step of suing successfully for the Inquisitor General to be removed from his case. Having been arrested in Torrelaguna and taken to Valladolid, the primate of Spain disappeared effectively from public life, though he received strong support from the cathedral chapter of Toledo, his own Dominican order and numerous fellow bishops. Paul IV's permission for Valdés to arrest Carranza did not authorise his trial by the Spanish tribunal. On the contrary, orders were that the prisoner and the relevant papers should be sent at once to Rome. Nevertheless, although the archbishop was kept in comfortable conditions and was allowed to choose his own servants, proceedings against him were begun in Valladolid. It was on this basis that Carranza made his *recusación* against his chief judge. As Escudero has pointed out, the process was full of irregularities by normal inquisitorial standards, and the archbishop completed, on 17 October 1559, a lengthy document in which he exercised the traditional right of any prisoner of the Inquisition, which was to denounce and have removed from the case any witness or judge who was known, or could be proved, to be his long-standing enemy. Carranza could demonstrate that Valdés and he had crossed swords during many years over the governorship (*adelantamiento*) of Cazorla, which had belonged to the Inquisitor General's deceased friend, the former royal secretary Francisco de los Cobos, and which Carranza claimed by right as archbishop of Toledo. Even more personally, the residence of bishops in their dioceses had been a crusade of the latter for many years, apparently with the support not only of Charles V but also of the Council of Trent, and by that standard Valdés, with many lucrative benefices which he held as an absentee, including the extremely wealthy archdiocese of Seville, was a conspicuous and vulnerable target. The result of the duel of the prelates was a draw, in the sense that Valdés eventually lost the case to Rome, but his adversary spent nearly all of the rest of his life in prison there.[24] The abuses which might be committed by the Inquisition, and often were, would never be more spectacularly demonstrated.

5

'A Covenant With Hell': The Inquisitors and the Witches

Inquisitors in Spain, as elsewhere, although they often appeared to act as politicians, lawyers and bureaucrats, were primarily intended to be agents of God's grace, with the aim of reconciling those who erred to the Church. Thus they were always concerned with the supernatural, and in particular with those who appeared to reject God, and even to collaborate with the powers of the Enemy, who was traditionally known as 'Satan' or 'the Devil'. Indeed, it is generally assumed that in early modern Europe these were the common beliefs of the population. Yet in 1612 the inquisitor Alonso de Salazar

Frías wrote the following: 'There were neither witches nor bewitched until they were talked or written about'.[1] How can such a rationalistic approach be squared with the traditional general impression of European society in the period as 'superstitious' and even 'fanatical' on this subject?

In truth, things had not always been so in the Spanish Inquisition's dealings with the powers of evil, and the tribunal's treatment of the subject needs first to be placed in the context of the relevant Catholic theology of the fifteenth and sixteenth centuries. The normal Spanish word for 'witch', then as now, was *bruja*, its derivation being uncertain. The word is normally found in its feminine form, but occasionally as the masculine *brujo*. If this term concerned 'witchcraft', Castilian Spanish also had the general concept of *magia* ('magic') and the notion of *hechicería* ('sorcery'). Although these terms are commonly, and perhaps inevitably, confused, it may be useful to attempt to define 'magic' as the basic concept of methods used by humans to achieve dominance over nature by extraordinary means, exploiting the 'natural' mutual sympathy or repulsion between things. More specifically, 'witchcraft' (*brujería*) is defined in the relevant literature as the attempt to achieve such ends in a negative way by means of a pact with the Devil, while 'sorcery' (*hechicería*) has the same aim but without the use of 'devilish' co-operation.[2] Late medieval theoretical work on the general subject of witches and sorcerers was based on the acceptance by the Church of Greek and Roman pagan concepts which had taken place in the early Christian centuries. Many Roman writers held it as a commonplace that women, in particular, were naturally inclined towards witchcraft, and this belief was still to be found in medieval European 'penitentiaries' or handbooks, and canonical legislation aimed at the identification of sins and sinners and the reconciliation of the latter to the Church (this also being the basic task of the Inquisition).

NOS EL RECTOR, CONSILIARIOS Y Colegio mayor de Fonseca de la ciudad de Santiago.

A los Señores Corregidores, Alcalde mayor, Juez ordinario ó su lugar-Teniente, que jurisdiccion Real ordinaria egerza en ....

Salud en nuestro Señor Jesucristo.

Hacemos saber, que habiendo provisto el Rey nuestro Señor una Beca vacante en este Colegio mayor de Fonseca, perteneciente á la facultad de .... y en atencion á lo prevenido por su Real decreto de arreglo de Colegios, en que manda que preceda, para tomar la posesion, informacion sumaria de cinco testigos examinados de oficio por V. como Juez ordinario de dicho pueblo, donde es natural el Colegial electo, ó lo han sido su Padre y Madre, con asistencia del Procurador sindico general, y ante Escribano Real y público, por la cual se justifique la limpieza de sangre de dicho Colegial electo; la de sus Padres, Abuelos paternos y maternos, y demas circunstancias que comprenden las preguntas siguientes:

1.ª .... Primeramente, si conoce á dicho Colegial electo, y si es natural de .... y á sus Padres, Abuelos paternos y maternos, como se llaman, ó llamaron unos y otros, y de donde son ó fueron naturales originarios, y si el testigo es pariente, amigo ó enemigo de dicho Colegial electo; si ha sido llamado ó inducido; si le han dado ó ofrecido alguna cosa para que diga en favor ó en contra, y qué edad tiene; diga lo que sepa.

..... Si sabe que dicho Colegial es hijo legítimo, y de legítimo matrimonio de los referidos sus Padres, que lo han educado y criado, y ha sido, y es tenido, y comunmente reputado por tal; diga &c.

..... Si saben que los Padres del dicho Colegial electo son igualmente hijos legítimos y de legítimos matrimonios, y por tales han sido criados y educados, tenidos y comunmente reputados; diga &c.

..... Si sabe que, asi dicho Colegial electo, como sus Padres, Abuelos y Bisabuelos por las respectivas lineas han sido y son tenidos, y reputados por Cristianos viejos, sin raza ni mezcla de Judio, Moro ó Converso; y que no han sido condenados, ni penitenciados por el Santo Oficio de la Inquisicion, como Hereges ó sospechosos en la Fé; diga &c.

..... Si sabe que dicho Colegial electo no es casado, ó desposado con palabras de presente: que es de vida arreglada y de loables costumbres; que no está infamado de caso grave ó delito feo; diga &c.

..... Si sabe que del origen ó naturaleza de dicho Colegial electo no hay otro Colegial en el mismo Colegio, ni sabe que alguno de los actuales sea pariente del referido Colegial dentro del cuarto grado de consanguinidad ó afinidad; diga &c.

..... Si sabe que todo lo que lleva dicho, es público y notorio, pública voz y fama, sin cosa en contrario; y si sabe que á los testigos que han de jurar, ó han jurado, se les da entera fe y crédito en juicio y fuera de él, y por lo mismo se persuade

1 and 2 'Purity of blood' questionnaire, Colegio Mayor Fonseca, University of Santiago de Compostela. In the early nineteenth century it was still necessary to meet Inquisition criteria in order to obtain a scholarship. Paragraph 4 translates as 'If he knows that the said member of the College, as well as his Parents, Grandparents and Great-Grandparents, through their respective lines, have been, and are, held and reputed for Old Christians, without race or mixture of Jew, Moor or Converso, and that they have not been condemned, nor given penance by the Holy Office of the Inquisition, as heretics or suspicious in the Faith'.

3 A Toledo inquisitor rested drinks for himself and his friends on this ceramic tray. The sessions, after all, were often long.

4 No one portrayed more vividly than Goya the distress and shame suffered by Inquisition penitents. In this case, the cross on the *sambenito* indicates 'reconciliation' to the Church, which still meant humiliation and punishment.

ISABEL ĐHERERA MVJER ĐJVAN Đ BILBAO VE3INA ĐCORDOVA·HEREJE JV DAI3ANTE RECONÇILI ADA· AÑO· 1504·

5 Isabel de Herrera, wife of Juan de Bilbao, was 'reconciled' to the Church as a 'Judaising' heretic in 1504, when the tyrannical inquisitor Lucero was active in Córdoba.

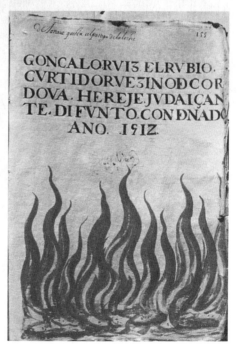

GONCALORVI3 ELRVBIO· CVRTIDORVE3INODCOR DOVA· HEREJE JVDAIÇAN TE· DIFVNTO·CONĐÑADO AÑO· 1512·

6 Gonzalo Ruiz 'el Rubio' (Blond), a tanner, was convicted after death as a 'Judaiser' by the Inquisition, and his bones were burnt in 1512.

Above: 7 An Inquisition scene by Goya. The painter regarded the Holy Office, in its last days, as one of the many horrors and nightmares of a war-torn Spain.

Left: 8 A fifteenth-century representation of the supposed 'martyrdom' by crucifixion of the 'Holy Child of La Guardia'.

9 An imaginary version by Pedro Berruguete of a late-fifteenth-century *auto de fe*, with St Dominic, whose Order of Preachers supplied many inquisitors, in charge. In reality, all these actions would not have taken place in the same scene. The painter meant to show the terrifying power of the Holy Office.

Above: 10 Bernard Picart's engraving of an *auto de fe* in the Plaza Mayor in Madrid in 1723.

Below left: 11 Goya shows the humiliating procession of a convicted prisoner, wearing a *sambenito* and escorted by Inquisition familiars and a hostile crowd, probably to his death.

Below right: 12 Goya shows a convicted penitent at an *auto de fe*, listening either to a sermon or possibly to the reading of his sentence.

On the face of it, this incorporation of older concepts of witchcraft into Christianity was odd and inconsistent. At the intellectual, or theological, level, the new religion was based on its ancestor, Jewish monotheism, in which there are just two spheres of action in human life: the 'Good', which is pursued by those who submit to God, and 'Evil', which is the area controlled by the Devil and his subordinate demons. Thus the ethics of Christianity assert that all that is morally wrong — beliefs, sins and violent passions — comes from the Devil. Medieval and early modern Christians, of all social and educational levels, believed that this 'devilishness' was represented not only by the pre-Christian gods and goddesses of Europe, but also by the Jewish and Muslim 'infidels' of their own day. Thus the whole of humanity had been plunged into error and sin until the birth of Christ on earth, and this continued to be the 'diabolical' state of those who subsequently rejected the Christian faith In this scheme of things, theologians and other writers attributed 'devilish' powers to both male and female witches and sorcerers — indeed, to everyone involved in the huge range of 'magical arts'. Yet, and this will be crucial for the consideration of the conduct of the Spanish inquisitors in the sixteenth and seventeenth centuries, there was an alternative current of thought in the medieval period, which appeared to contradict absolutely the theory of the 'diabolisation' of the world. According to this latter view, the Devil deceived his disciples by convincing them that they possessed powers which they did not in fact possess. In general, earlier Christian theologians had enthusiastically adopted the arguments of pagan rationalists who had mocked the excesses of Classical mythology. On this subject, later medieval theologians took St Augustine as their guide. Speaking, he claimed, from personal experience, he declared that it was unbelievable that demons could affect the soul or transform the body, though he admitted that such things could in principle happen if God permitted them. In the central Middle Ages, most theologians maintained a sceptical approach to such phenomena, but lawyers and judges, who handled many 'witchcraft' cases, were more inclined to believe that such phenomena existed, presumably because they reckoned that they saw the consequences on the ground. The theologians (including inquisitors from the thirteenth century onwards) indeed admitted the theoretical possibility of diabolical action, but believed its existence to be unlikely. Thus they were inclined to downplay the power of the Devil, and even mock those, such as elderly 'sorceresses' (*hechiceras*), who 'deluded' themselves in this way. Yet, by the time of the introduction of the 'new' Spanish Inquisition, in the late fifteenth century, powerful images of the Devil, or the 'Fallen Angel' or Antichrist, had been developed in western Europe, not least by artists. The Church could not prevent the general mass of believers from accepting the reality of the diabolical inspiration of witches and wizards. Nevertheless, up until the fourteenth century the religious authorities used as a basis for their treatment of the subject the so-called *Canon episcopi*, which first appeared in the early tenth century. It adopted an Augustinian approach, stating that 'it must be loudly proclaimed that those who believe such things have lost the faith and no longer belong to God, but only to him whom they believe, that is the Devil'.[3]

Nonetheless, the 'Scholastic' thought of the thirteenth and fourteenth centuries, which was still highly respected, for example at the University of Alcalá de Henares, in the sixteenth century, came in practice to accept the absolute reality of diabolically-inspired practices. Indeed, much play was made with the statement by the doyen of Dominican theologians, St Thomas Aquinas, who also retained immense influence in early modern Spain, that: 'The Catholic faith

declares that demons are able to do harm by their operations, and to impede sexual congress'.[4] Thus witchcraft and
sorcery were held directly to affect the body, and the violent
persecutions of the Europe of the fifteenth to seventeenth
centuries were set in train, with the intellectual and legal
backing of the Church. A significant canonical basis for the
trial of 'witches' was a bull issued in 1326 by Pope John
XXII, which referred to the existence of many so-called
Christians:

> ...who ally themselves with death and make a covenant with Hell,
> who sacrifice to demons, making and causing to be made images,
> rings, mirrors, phials and similar objects intended as magic bonds to
> hold fast the demons whom they interrogate and from whom they
> obtain answers, having recourse to the same demons to satisfy their
> depraved desires.[5]

Thus the whole paraphenalia of witchcraft was already
firmly established in the official as well as the popular mind,
when Torquemada and his colleagues started their work.[6]

Although it is clear that the new inquisitors were primarily concerned with converts from Judaism and their
descendants, with their equivalents in Islam to follow after
1492, their new tribunals were confronted with a society
which, and not only in rural areas, accepted the reality of
the Devil's intervention. In the early years, although the
inquisitors themselves seem not to have been interested in
pursuing such cases, members of the public did supply them
with information on 'magic' under the terms of the 'edicts
of faith' which required them to confess their own faults
and/or those of others, on pain of their immortal souls.
Thus, for example, some Castilians in the north-eastern
diocese of Burgo de Osma and Soria, in the 1480s and
earlier, felt constrained to tell the local Inquisition about

some dabbling in love-magic by neighbours. Catalina de Violante, a stall-holder in Soria, was said to have told Catalina Sánchez, from the same town, who later betrayed her to the inquisitors, that in order to discover whether her lover, Pedro Fernández de Berlanga, parish priest of Santo Tomás, who was away on a visit to Rome and liable to the temptations of that 'Babylon', was still alive, she had made an image of him out of stone or oak (*sic*), in the fairly explicit form of a boy holding a rod. This she placed in a pan, and saw there that 'her beloved was alive and coming along the road'. The witness also told the inquisitors that, presumably by the use of magical arts, the accused had escaped from officials who were seeking out clergy mistresses, something that was undoubtedly a concern of Ferdinand and Isabella's government. In another case, according to the testimony of several women, Marina, wife of a doctor in nearby Gumiel de Mercado called Juan de Toledo, claimed that she could tell in advance the look and physique of guests who were coming to the house, by the expedient of examining the shape and condition of the loaves in the oven at home. The allusion again seems fairly explicit, and it seems unlikely that the inquisitors took an interest in such cases, for which no trial records have been found. Nonetheless, this evidence probably gives a fairly good indication of the kind of 'white magic' which was commonly practised in that society and period, as does the rather pathetic case of Juana de Cabrejas, from Burgo de Osma. For many years, she had been the 'housekeeper' of one of the canons of the cathedral there, Bartolomé Martínez. In about 1490, Juana was living in nearby Santisteban de Gormaz, 'and being under the power of a cleric and because of his jealousy for her, he gave her a bad life'. Marina Sánchez, a friend of hers who was a widow, offered to help her. She took away some of the hair of the clergyman in question, and told the unfortunate Juana to keep some bread which she had previously chewed, as well as a piece of the cassock of the clergyman in question, which she should also chew, and some wax. Juana, on her own admission with 'little common sense', followed these instructions, but confessed to the inquisitors that the 'charm' had had no effect.[7]

There were no doubt hundreds of such cases in early modern Spain, a society in which faith-healers and purveyors of herbal and other 'alternative' remedies, many of whom were female (*curanderas*), were omnipresent, while university-trained medical practitioners were rare and largely ineffective. As has been suggested by the late-fifteenth-century cases in Soria and district, the 'healers' were locally based and offered a wide range of services, not only repairing of relationships between spouses or partners, but also curing sick people and animals, and finding lost people and objects. Particularly in country districts, such activities, with their attendant prayers and charms, even found their way into the local church, often in the Biblically-approved practice of exorcising evil spirits. It was not a large step from driving such 'demons' out of people, on the model demonstrated by Jesus himself, to adopting a similar approach to 'haunted' animals, places and objects. Yet overall, between 1480 and 1600, Spanish inquisitors showed a marked reluctance to pursue witches, sorcerers or *curanderos*. Early Trastamaran parliaments (Cortes) in Castile had passed two laws, in 1370 and 1387, which followed current European practice in declaring that sorcery was a crime which involved heresy. As in other cases, laymen guilty of this offence were to be punished by secular tribunals and clergy by ecclesiastical courts, and this was still the position after 1480. Thus a law of Ferdinand and Isabella, issued in 1500, ordered an investigation into sorcery, but entrusted it to local city governors (*corregidores*) and the secular courts. This situation would continue into the sixteenth century, when the Inquisition was otherwise widening its scope of operation beyond the initial target group of converts from Judaism and their descendants. It is true, as Henry Kamen suggests, that the inquisitors, in accordance with earlier theological thinking, were not entirely sure whether sorcery and magic were in fact heretical, in the normally-understood terms of false doctrine and practice. Some such techniques, along with astrology, which was a university subject at Salamanca throughout most of the sixteenth century, were even practised by the clergy. Nonetheless, the establishment of Torquemada's Inquisition coincided with an increased ecclesiastical interest in the repression of 'diabolical' magic.

In 1484, Pope Innocent VIII issued a bull which constituted the first papal recognition of witchcraft as a 'disease', a term which was traditionally used as a metaphor for heresy. As a result of this connection two Dominican inquisitors, Heinrich Krämer and Jakob Sprenger, were despatched to investigate such activities in northern and central Germany. The result of their work was the publication in 1486 of what was intended to be a comprehensive handbook of the 'black arts', entitled *Malleus maleficarum* ('Hammer of the [female] witches'). This was a massive collection of German case-histories set in the context of the central argument that, far from being a delusion, as much Church tradition had suggested, witchcraft not only existed but involved direct intercourse between supposedly Christian people and the Devil. Thus 'witches' really did eat children, copulate with demons, fly to 'witches' sabbats, do damage to livestock, conjure up storms and direct lightning to specific targets. Kamen rightly comments, with reference to Europe as a whole, that: 'No book did more in its time to promote a belief it was allegedly fighting'.[8] The *Malleus* won subsequent ecclesiastical support in the form of papal bulls and other canonical legislation, but it remained to be seen how the new papal policy would be received in Spain, in the midst of the purge of 'false' Jewish converts and the military campaign against Islam in Granada.

In general terms, many bishops and other leading church-men in both Spain and Italy seem to have remained highly dubious about the more lurid of Krämer and Sprenger's sup-posed findings, particularly in so far as they concerned flying through the air and copulation between humans and the Devil or demons. Nevertheless, the Spanish Inquisition began to punish convicted 'witches' in 1498, the year of Torquemada's death. Following previous practice in the secular Spanish courts in such cases, one was burned by the Zaragoza tribu-nal in that year, another in 1499 and three in 1500. During Cisneros' reign as Inquisitor General, such trials continued, for example in Toledo in 1513 and Cuenca in 1515. In the latter case 'witches' were blamed for bruising and otherwise injuring children and, from 1520 onwards, under Adrian of Utrecht and Manrique's authority, offences such as magic, sorcery and witchcraft began to feature routinely in inquisito-rial 'edicts of faith' in both Castile and Aragon. Nonetheless a theologian in Zaragoza still felt able to declare, in 1521, that the 'witches' sabbat was a delusion and could therefore not amount to heresy. It should be noted that, in parallel with the activities of the Inquisition in this matter, cases of the kind supposedly found, for example, in Navarre continued to be investigated by secular courts, which took a severe view. In 1525, up to thirty 'witches' were burned there, on the orders of the prosecutor for the Royal Council. Not for the last time, violent action of this kind in Navarre provoked a crisis of conscience, or at least of policy, in the Suprema.

The events in the northern kingdom provoked Alonso Manrique, as Inquisitor General, to summon another of his expert committees, this time including the noted jurist

Hernando de Guevara and the future Inquisitor General
Fernando de Valdés, to meet in Granada, where the future
of the *moriscos* was also under consideration. On the agenda
was a discussion paper which asserted that most lawyers in
Spain did not believe in the reality of witchcraft, because it
was not possible for witches to do the things they claimed
to do, such as flying to sabbats and having sexual intercourse
with the Devil or his ministers. The meeting eventually
voted on the central question, six agreeing that the witches
really did go to sabbats, while the other four, who interestingly included Valdés, declared that they went only in their
imagination. The meeting also agreed that, since the murders
that witches sometimes claimed to have committed were
probably also illusory, the supposed 'offences' were a matter
for the Inquisition rather than the secular courts. If, however, the latter could produce solid evidence of a crime, the
matter should remain in their hands. The witchcraft meeting went in parallel with the consideration of the *moriscos*,
and the inquisitors' pre-occupation seems to have been to
attempt the further 'education' of those susceptible to belief
in the power to harness Satanic evil for human ends. Thus,
during the Granada meeting, Antonio de Guevara, Bishop
of Mondoñedo in Galicia, urged that preachers should be
sent to his diocese to convince the faithful that the so-called
'witches' had in fact been deceived by the Devil. After the
1526 Granada meeting, the persecution of 'witches' continued in Spain, but the inquisitors were little involved in such
action. In Navarre though, in 1527–28, Inquisitor Avellanada
does seem to have prosecuted witches, fifty of whom were
executed on the authority of the kingdom's Royal Council.
There were cases in other parts of Spain as well, though in
Zaragoza there were such protests from the Suprema when
a 'witch' was burned that the tribunal in that city never
burned another in its entire history.[9] The issue remained a

controversial one, though, and in 1538 a new and important contribution was made by Pedro Ciruelo, under the title *Reprovación de las supersticiones y hechizerías* ('Reproof of superstitions and sorceries').

Pedro Sánchez Ciruelo, known as 'Maestro Ciruelo', was born in the Aragonese town of Daroca in 1470, and studied and taught in three universities, Salamanca, Paris and Alcalá de Henares. In the academic disputes of his lifetime he tended strongly to the 'humanist' side and away from the 'scholastic'. He took part in the 1527 Valladolid conference on the works of Erasmus, where he was the only Alcalá theologian to come down on the side of colleagues from his old university of Salamanca in condemning the Dutch humanist. Thus he demonstrated the complexity of the Spanish academic world of the 1520s, and he was also to do this in his works on 'superstitions'. In 1521, while holding the senior, 'Prime' chair in Thomist theology (*cátedra de Prima de Santo Tomás*) at Alcalá, he produced a 'Defence of Christian astrology' (*Apostelesmata astrologiae christianae*) in which, on the basis of the Ancient Greek works of Ptolemy, he justified the use of that science, particularly in legal matters, against the criticism of the Italian humanist Pico della Mirandola. In the same year, he published his first 'Work on magical superstition' (*Opus de magica superstitione*), a subject to which he would later return at greater length. Having left the college of San Ildefonso in Alcalá, Ciruelo spent four years in a teaching canonry (as *magistral*) in Segovia Cathedral, before returning to Salamanca in 1537 to take up a similar office. A year later he published his *Reprovación* ('Reproof') against superstition and sorcery, which quickly became a basic text for all those working in that particular field, and offered a comprehensive guide to the magical practices of early modern Spain. There were numerous subsequent editions, no doubt because readers agreed with the author that its subject matter constituted a major current problem in Spain. In the prologue to the work, Ciruelo places his discussion in the context of the first commandment of the Law of Moses, fully binding on Catholics: 'You shall have no other God before me'. He goes on to identify four 'species' of the 'idolatry' which follows from disobeying this commandment, the first, necromancy, being an open form of disobedience, while the other three 'hidden' forms are 'superstitions', 'vain ceremonies' and 'sorceries'. He states that he has written the book 'to warn all good Christians and fearful servants of God to keep away from [these superstitions] more than from serpents and vipers, because they are very poisonous things and dangerous to the health and spiritual life of souls'.[10]

Having begun by praising the first commandment, Ciruelo goes on to set out four general principles of his subject. Firstly, as Scripture indicates, there are both good angels and wicked angels, or demons. Secondly, the demons keep up a ceaseless enmity against men, so that a Christian must never make any kind of pact with the Devil. If he does so, he becomes an apostate and renegade. The author's third principle is that the Devil is the teacher of 'all superstitions and vain sorceries'. In the beginning idolatry reigned on Earth, but God sent his son to end it by means of his sacrifice of himself. Sorcery and superstitions, both overt and hidden, are thus the means by which the Devil seeks to regain his former rule over humans. Fourthly, if a man achieves something by means of words which have no natural or supernatural virtue, this is the work of the Devil. If these words are ones which are otherwise properly employed by the priest in the administration of the sacraments, they are of course good in themselves, but their use by other Christians may come from evil, fallen angels. Ciruelo asserts that the authorities should impose much more severe penalties in such cases

than on murderers or adulterers. While the latter disturb
the peace of society, the former commit the much graver
offence of sinning against the first commandment: the love
of God above all other. The author goes on to argue that
the unregulated desire to obtain certain goods in this world
and to avoid certain ills is at the root of all sins. On the basis
of this general principle, he analyses the two main categories of 'superstition'. The first, the 'divinatory arts', exists 'to
know some of the secrets of things, which by the course
of natural reason cannot be known, or as quickly as [these
people] desire'. In such cases, if there is an explicit pact with
the Devil, this is 'necromancy'. If the pact is implicit, this
is one of the divinatory arts, which consist of divination,
geomancy, chiromancy and pyromancy. The second category
of superstition, according to Ciruelo, seeks either to obtain
certain goods or to avoid certain evils. It consists of two
types, one of which is curing illnesses by means of charms
or invocations, and the other is using sorcery in the form of
games of chance. After this, Ciruelo goes into greater detail
concerning specific 'black arts'.

The first to be considered is necromancy, which arises out
of a pact between man and the Devil, who reveals secrets
to him and helps him to gain certain ends. The techniques
used include special words, and ceremonies which included,
for example, sacrifices and herbs, and the Devil may appear
to the necromancer as a man, who speaks to him or gives
him signs, in the form of a soul in torment or as an animal,
such as a dog or cat. He may also speak through a corpse,
through dreams or by means of various signs, in the air, in
fire or in the entrails of animals. Devotees of such activities are *brujas* (witches), also known as *xorguinas*, who rub
themselves with certain ointments while saying particular words, and fly by night, travelling to far-away places to
carry out evil spells (*maleficios*). In one of the most quoted

passages of his text, Ciruelo affirms that all these things are illusions, going on to describe the two ways in which they may happen, 'really' or by the inducement of the Devil – in other words, 'in fantasy'. The Devil makes these women go into a trance and manipulates their tongues so that they speak of 'secret knowledge'. The writer urges inquisitors, if they know of a case of necromancy, to act with firmness because, even though it is not a heresy, it is very close to being one. He goes on to list various domestic happenings, such as strange noises, objects which move for no apparent reason, and mysterious feelings of being touched. He comments that the Devil particularly plagues monasteries and convents with these matters, where all the inhabitants are devout Catholics and he has no followers, and outlines the Church's traditional methods for dealing with such things, these being rites of exorcism and special Masses. Ciruelo then discusses 'divination' (*adivinación*), stating that man cannot know, either by science or by art, the secrets of the hearts of other people or what Fortune may cause to happen in the world. Such things may only be communicated by God through revelation. He asserts that it is possible that man may, through effort and experience, succeed in knowing by the light of natural reason the effects which follow from certain causes, such as stars, stones, plants and animals. But 'diviners', in their efforts to bring the future forward into the present, themselves seek to be like God – hence their names in Spanish: *divinos* or *adivinos*. Like necromancers, they are apostates from Christianity, since they have a secret pact with the Devil. If this knowledge is not given to them by way of natural reason, nor is it revealed to them by God, one may be sure that it is given to them by the Devil.

Interestingly, given that the subject was a respectable academic discipline at the time and taught at university, Ciruelo

then goes on to discuss astrology. He claims that there are
two kinds, one 'true' and the other 'false', although their
aim is the same: to judge future happenings by means of the
observation of the heavens. True astrology, in his opinion,
achieves this aim by means of its proper methods, which
consist of the relationship between cause and effect. The use
of this method renders the subject 'scientific', in the same
sense as other 'natural sciences', since the stars are capable of
affecting not only the air and the earth, but also humans and
animals. Ciruelo, along with most or all of his educated contemporaries, believed that the stars are the cause of various
human character traits, including passions, as well as illnesses,
desires and even arts and sciences. This kind of astrology,
unlike many of the other arts discussed in the treatise, is good
and virtuous. But there is also a false astrology, which is not
based on the principles of cause and effect and is therefore
not, in the strict sense, a science, but rather a superstition.
False astrologers claim to be able to use the stars to determine
things in the world which occur merely by chance, and
Ciruelo equates this activity with necromancy.

He then goes on to discuss other divining arts, beginning with geomancy, which he derives from astrology. This
involves the prediction of things which happen in the world
by means of the interpretation of lines or points either
on the earth itself or on paper. Hydromancy, on the other
hand, involves divining by means of figures seen in water
(this being the technique allegedly used by Catalina de
Violante of Berlanga in the late fifteenth century, see above),
while aeromancy claimed to see the future in signs in the
air which blows through trees or into houses. Pyromancy
involved divination through the smoke and flames of fire,
and spatulancy (from the Latin for a shoulder blade) claimed
to achieve such a goal by monitoring the reaction of such
bones to contact with fire. Chiromancy employed the bones

of the hand in divination, while other methods included *sortiaria*, which involved the use of lots, darts, playing cards and other such things, *consultoria*, which required direct consultation of God, and *divisoria*, which involved the sharing out of things between individuals.

Ciruelo then goes on to consider the subject of omens (*agüeros*), among which he includes the interpretation of the sounds of birds and animals, the sneezes and other bodily movements of humans, and what he calls *omen*, this being the prediction of the future on the basis of words and phrases overheard by chance. After this, the author discusses the subject of dreams, identifying three distinct kinds: natural, moral and theological. He states that their natural causes are the bodily humours, which are intrinsic, and changes in the air, which are extrinsic. 'Natural' dreams normally concern the past and the present, and if they do refer to the future, this is normally only to predict changes in the weather. The causes of 'moral' dreams are to be found in the imagination of men who are busy when awake, and when asleep come to understand their problems better or take better decisions. As in the previous case, Ciruelo is referring to the past and present, rather than the future. 'Theological' dreams, on the other hand, come from God, usually through a good angel but sometimes through a bad one. Interestingly, given that he was writing in a country where the Inquisition habitually burned those who were convicted of heresy and also that such things had been much respected in the early and central Middle Ages as methods of determining guilt and innocence, Ciruelo continues by discussing oaths (*salvas*) by ordeal. In this process people might, to prove their innocence of an offence, pick up burning iron or put their hand in boiling oil, or else engage in single combat with their accuser in some country place. Clearly habits had changed between the twelfth century and the sixteenth, as Ciruelo condemns those who use such practices as fraudsters who deceive the poor. Now, though, the author turns to the role of the Devil in the subjects which he is treating. He states that Satan and the wicked angels, when they fell from Heaven, retained their former abilities, which they can now use against God's plans, particularly in the spheres of astrology, philosophy and medicine. They reveal their secrets to their devotees, the necromancers and diviners, largely concerning the past and the present, rather than the future.

In the third part of his treatise, Ciruelo announces a 'dispute' against those who practice witchcraft (*hechicerías*) to achieve some good end, or else to free themselves from bad circumstances which are outside the normal course of nature. He begins, as a professional academic well might, by attacking those who claim to be able to gain knowledge without study or teaching. According to this 'black art', by acquiring powers which properly belong to God, it is possible to arrive at knowledge and wisdom without the expense of time or money. Ciruelo rejects the notion that the legendary 'wisdom' of King Solomon was achieved by such means, asserting that it came entirely as a gift from God. He refers to 'false' books, then available in Spain, which contained prayers and lists of practices, such as fasting, alms-giving and receiving Holy Communion, which were claimed to help bring about such 'evil' results. Such works also contained accounts of cases in which the Devil was claimed to have entered people's bodies and made them suddenly wise. In the following chapter the author goes on to discuss the 'superstitions' and 'vain things' which some people indulge in so that they may achieve success. He states that some people attach written documents (*cédulas*) to their door-hinges with the aim of getting rich, while others place them in fields and vineyards in the hope of

a better harvest. Others would make type-characters out
of various metals, forged under the influence of certain
constellations. None of these things, Ciruelo stated, had any
natural or supernatural virtue. After this he attacks some of
the humbler practitioners of the magical arts, the common
quacks (*ensalmadores*), not professionally trained but nonetheless ubiquitous in the towns and villages of Spain, who
employed these techniques in the area of personal health.
When faced with sick patients, an *ensalmador* would adopt
one of two approaches: either resorting to help and advice,
with or without a medical basis, or else urging them to
commend themselves to God by means of attendance at
Mass, prayers and works of charity. Ciruelo condemns these
practitioners if they attempt to cure illness by means of evil
rather than good words, or evil rather than good practices.
He then turns to the written word.

For incurable illnesses, among which he included lep-
rosy, gout, blindness and deafness, the author recommended
that a person should turn to God not with charms but
in Masses and pilgrimages, with the Christian hope of a
miracle. Ciruelo praised the then common practice, for
people in such circumstances, of carrying around with
them a copy of the Gospels as a protection. Interestingly,
though, he condemns the equally general custom of using
the relics of saints in this way, not presumably because he
regarded them as inefficacious, but because they would
thus be out of the control of the Church authorities, and
in danger of irreverent treatment. After this he sets out and
comments on ten rules about the use of charms and invocations, which allows for uneducated people but not for the
lettered. For him, the best invocation (*nómina*) is: 'Lord have
mercy, Christ have mercy, Lord have mercy' (*Kyrie eleison,
Christe eleison, Kyrie eleison*), followed by 'Our Father, Hail
Mary, I believe in God, and Hail Queen [of heaven]' (*Pater*

noster, Ave Maria, Credo in Deum, Salve Regina). Ciruelo then turns to the subject of active black magic against one's neighbour, beginning with the evil eye (*aojamiento*). All such means of harming a neighbour come from the Devil, and such 'infection by sight' may arrive either by natural means or as the result of a specific curse. Among 'natural causes' Ciruelo includes a small child being spoken to, or just looked at, by a sick person or a menstruating woman. As for curses, the victim should call a priest to administer exorcism.

The author's next theme is that of 'bad' or 'evil' days (*días aziagos*, the term supposedly being derived from Egypt). According to Ciruelo, it was the custom in the sixteenth century to print, in religious books, verses about the days and hours of ill-fortune. He condemns such practices on the grounds that the constellations change their position from season to season, and hence are an unreliable guide to events on earth. In any case, the actions of men's free will are not influenced by the constellations. Ciruelo's next target is the healers (*saludadores*) who claim to be able to cure rabies by means of words and ceremonies. He understands the causes of rabies poorly, but is right to say that the origins of the disease, which is commonly fatal for humans, are natural and it should therefore be treated by medicine. In this respect his approach is scientific and entirely 'modern'. He particularly disapproves of the use by such pretended healers of the names and emblems of the saints, notably St Catherine and her wheel, as supposed methods of cure. However, under the heading 'Advice' (*Consejos*), the author appends a list of remedies which he regards as effective against 'rabies and poison'. This includes a wide range of plants which still appear in the prescriptions of 'alternative' medicine, but also the blood and hair of dogs, honey, fat, fresh cheese, dead birds, raw bacon and various vegetables, including garlic, onions and cabbages,

as well as wine and vinegar. The border here between scholarly 'science' and popular beliefs seems virtually invisible.

The last five chapters of Ciruelo's treatise target further
categories among those who claim to perform functions in
relation to human illness and danger which properly belong
to Christ and His Church. Thus he condemns unofficial
exorcists, who, in his view falsely, claimed to be able to deliver
sufferers from evil spirits, and also those who claimed that
demons could influence the weather and cause hailstorms
with the aim of destroying crops. He also opposed the use
of religious ceremonies such as exorcism in an attempt to
drive away plagues of locusts, and also the not uncommon
medieval practice of putting supposedly 'criminal' animals,
such as straying livestock, on trial. To do such things was, in
Ciruelo's view, to make a mockery of the Church. Finally, the
author spoke harshly of those who used legitimate Christian
prayers for nefarious and diabolical purposes, and stated, in
the last chapter of his treatise, that, contrary to what was
asserted by many Spaniards in his own day, it was always a
sin for a Christian to employ the techniques which he had
outlined in the preceding chapters.[11] Ciruelo's *Reproof* was,
of course, written in the context of Alonso Manrique's 1526
Granada conference on witchcraft but, even so, it is notable
that throughout the length of the work he never mentions
a role for the Inquisition in the repression of the beliefs and
practices which he so strongly condemns. Here, he seems to
have been in line with successive Inquisitors General who,
for the rest of the sixteenth century, continued to show a
marked reluctance to intervene in such cases.[12]

Nonetheless, the records of regional tribunals indicate that
some inquisitors, at least, did believe in the reality of diabolical possession and activity, and were prepared to take action.
This was so even in what is now, thanks to the researches
of Gustav Henningsen, the most famous case of all, that of

the inquisitor Alonso de Salazar Frías and the 'witches' of
the Basque country and Navarre, in north-eastern Spain.
Virtually nothing is known of Salazar's life before he became
an inquisitor in the tribunal of Logroño in the first decade
of the seventeenth century, apart from the fact that he was
a university graduate. The significance of what happened
in that area between 1608 and 1614 is that, although many
accusations of witchcraft were made, after the latter year
the Spanish Inquisition never burned another witch.[13] This
is a remarkable fact, seeing that Salazar's fellow inquisitors,
Alonso Becerra Holguín and Juan de Valle, appear to have
believed implicitly in the reality of sorcery and witchcraft
writing, as late as 1613:

> We are still completely convinced that when the Council [Suprema]
> reads our report with the thoroughness and consideration which are cus-
> tomary, it will be bound to realise as a clear and obvious fact supported
> by unassailable arguments, that this sect [of witches] is a reality.[14]

Although the records of the early-seventeenth-century
witch trials in Logroño were destroyed during the French
invasion of Spain in 1808, those retained by the Suprema
have survived, and form the basis of Henningsen's magisterial study of the last days of the Inquisition's violent
persecution of witches, in 1610–1614.[15]

The context of the inquisitors' activities at that time in
the Basque country and Navarre was events on the French
side of the border. In the first decade of the seventeenth
century, a councillor-judge at the high court (*Parlement*)
in Bordeaux, Pierre de Lancre, prosecuted numerous
individuals in Labourde for supposed witchcraft, and had
about eighty of them burnt. There being no Inquisition in
early modern France, though there had been one in the
Middle Ages, the responsibility for trying such offences

rested with the secular courts. By 1608–1609, similar stories were emerging in large numbers from Navarre and the Basque provinces of the Crown of Castile, and the Logroño tribunal was beginning to take action, by means of formal visits to the affected areas and the collection of confessions and other evidence from witnesses. In 1610, an *auto de fe* took place in Logroño and was followed by the burning of 'witches'. In the following year, one of the inquisitors based there, Pedro de Valencia, published a pamphlet in Burgos entitled 'Concerning the witches' stories', in which he pointed to the dangers of publicity in such cases, which might lead the weak-minded astray, and also harm the reputation of the Inquisition. Valencia's work was firmly in the tradition of the 1526 Granada conference and of Ciruelo's treatise of 1538, in that it allowed for some such stories being true, while others were false. He generally favoured flogging of offenders over more severe punishments and observed that those involved were generally the weaker or more anti-social members of the community. Traditionally, both the authorities and the general population accepted a distinction between 'witches', who were clearly bad, and 'sorcerers', who might be either benign or malevolent. In Henningsen's view, the problem with the 1610 trials and *auto* in Logroño was that the inquisitors there did not follow the procedures which had been laid down in Granada in 1526 and subsequently adopted by the Suprema. Pedro de Valencia and his colleagues obtained most of their evidence from two Navarrese villages on the north side of the Pyrenees, Zugarramurdi and Urdax, where the local communities had tried to sort things out for themselves, until the Inquisition was informed and took over the investigation.[16]

When the first reports of 'witchcraft' at Zugarramurdi reached Logroño, in January 1609, the inquisitors there, with Pedro de Valencia, were Becerra and Valle. In March of that year they duly obtained from the Suprema in Madrid a suitable list of questions (*interrogatorio*) to put to witnesses and accused, whom they proceeded to interrogate in two batches. What resulted was, in Henningsen's view, exactly what they wanted to hear, in other words that there was indeed a full-scale diabolical cult in Zugarramurdi and nearby Urdax, which contained all the elements which had been so painstakingly described in the *Malleus maleficarum*. Pedro de Valencia was not content, however, with what he believed himself to have discovered about just two villages, and he proceeded to order a 'trawl' (this being a common practice of the Holy Office in the later sixteenth and seventeenth centuries), in the hope of finding similar activities in other parts of northern Navarre and the neighbouring Basque province of Guipúzcoa. The customary 'edict of faith' was issued to persuade witnesses to come forward. After what he had already achieved, Valle was reluctant to take part in the new *visita*, but he eventually did so and, with Zugarramurdi and Urdax once again the main targets, more people were arrested and tried. A second *auto* of 'witches' (*el de las brujas*) took place in Logroño on 8 November 1610. On this occasion thirty-one 'witches' were processed, along with others who had been convicted of 'Judaising', 'Mohammedanism', 'Lutheranism' and blasphemy, as well as two who had apparently impersonated agents of the Inquisition! Far from putting a stop to the supposed activities of black magic, though, the second *auto* merely served to precipitate a new witch-craze, which sprang up in places which had been visited by inquisitor Valle in the summer of 1610. It was at this point that Salazar Frías began to become concerned that an injustice was being done to the overwhelmingly female group of 'witches' (*brujas*).

By June 1611, Salazar was complaining to his colleagues that they (and he) were spending too much of their time on witch investigations and trials. He was concerned that the rules set out by Manrique's Granada conference of 1526 were not being properly followed, especially in the fact that witnesses were being allowed, contrary to the Inquisition's practice, to talk to each other, thus muddying the waters of evidence. Thus a person who had absorbed the full apparatus of black arts, as set out in the 1486 *Malleus* and believed in by some of the inquisitors, might contaminate the mind, and the evidence, of another witness or prisoner. In March 1611, Valle admitted in writing that he now regarded Salazar as an enemy, and the latter decided that it was necessary to undertake a visitation of his own, in order to examine the situation in the countryside at close quarters. He did so at the end of that month, armed with the authority of the Suprema, and it was at this point that the Logroño inquisitors made the crucial decision to ban discussion of witches and witchcraft in the affected area. Vitally, this policy was supported by the Inquisitor General, Bernardo de Sandoval y Rojas, and the Suprema. The senior inquisitors in Logroño, Becerra and Valle, were ordered to cool their heels in Logroño, while their junior, Salazar, did the field-work. A new edict of faith was issued, allowing the unusually long interval of six rather than four weeks for the guilty to confess and witnesses to come forward. Even though the publication of this document by Becerra and Valle, before Salazar left Logroño, seems to have been intended as an official 'leak' to pre-empt his investigation, the supposed cases of complex and sinister witchcraft began rapidly to collapse. Salazar nonetheless reported that on 24 July an attempt had been made to poison him, though he survived without difficulty. By then, though, he was beginning to receive recantations from individuals who had earlier confessed to being witches. On 4 September 1611, he sent a letter to the Inquisitor General in which he stated that 'When I left Logroño, only 333 confessions had been made. But by now, with God's help, I have dealt with 1546 cases on my journey'. The great majority of these were children under the age of responsibility, by which he meant girls under twelve and boys under fourteen. He had even had to deal with a large number of children under the age of five. Salazar's approach was not to force confessions and arrest people, but to hear genuinely spontaneous confessions and recantations. Thus his method was diametrically opposed to that of Becerra and Valle. As he put it to Inquisitor General Sandoval: '[...] people of all ages have had a share in the comfort and consolation which has been anticipated by them and by their children and relatives, and this has served to generally reassure the whole district'. In his fourth report on this visitation, Salazar was scathing about the effects of the previous conduct of his colleagues in Logroño:

A great deal of terrible injustice had already been imposed in the name of Christian zeal on those who were suspected of belonging to this sect [of witches], and this was done even when the suspicion rested only on the allegations of children. Banning the suspect from the sacraments of the Church, which has been practised quite openly and been very extensive, has also caused great harm.

At this point the whole affair began to unravel.

When the Castilian-speaking Salazar went into rural areas, he took with him two friars as Basque interpreters, whom he succeeded in converting to his view that most or all of the supposed witchcraft was in fact a delusion. But while Salazar was being praised for his efforts by the Suprema, his colleagues in Logroño were keeping hold of seventeen prisoners who they were convinced were witches. Salazar, however, made a second journey, this time in the country-side of Vizcaya and Guipúzcoa. He was particularly shocked when he came upon a case of suicide in Atarri (Álava). María Pérez killed herself in remorse for having given false evidence to the inquisitors against more than thirty people. Meanwhile Salazar went on interrogating over 100 suspects, now excluding girls under twelve and boys under fourteen, in an effort to discover whether there was any reality at all in the allegations of witchcraft. During this process, he performed a subtle and daring experiment on a sample of thirty-six people from all parts of the suspect area. He used a set of instructions which had been sent from Madrid by the Suprema on 26 March 1611. A selection of the 'most intelligent' among those who claimed to have visited sab-bats (*aquelarres*) were to be asked a set of eight questions: where exactly they had met; where the Devil had sat and they had made sacrifices and danced; whether they escaped to go to the sabbat through locked doors or windows and if so how they travelled to it (was this by air, how long did it take and was the Devil involved?); whether the witches travelled together and could recognise each other easily; whether they saw others while on the way there or back and spoke to them; how they returned to their houses (with times of departure and return); whether there were clocks or bells which they could hear while at the sabbat; and, finally, whether they could provide any solid proof to sub-stantiate their answers. In its forensic skill and rationalistic approach to a heated and emotional subject, the document in question is quite remarkable. As in a modern professional poll, this set of questions was put to a carefully selected sample of thirty-six people from nine different places in the northern part of Navarre, who were deliberately prevented from contacting each other. The investigation resulted in the immediate exposure of various falsehoods included in earlier testimony which had previously been accepted without question, these including all the more picturesque fantasies of black magic and sabbats with the Devil. With some pride, Salazar subsequently made a full report of the results to the Suprema, which he later referred to in a memorandum to Inquisitor General Sandoval, which is worthy of extensive quotation as an example of the better moments of the Spanish Inquisition.

> In a letter which I addressed to Your Highness, from Fuenterrabía, on 4 September [1611]. I reported how, as a sequel to the Edict of Grace [...] 1546 persons of all ranks and ages came forward to avail themselves of it.[...] I now report that, during the period from 22 May 1611, when I set out on the visitation, to 10 January this year [1612], when I concluded it, a total of 1802 cases have been despatched. [...] The figure can be broken down into the following groups: 1384 children of twelve or fourteen years of age [girls and boys respectively] were absolved *ad cautelam* [with a caution]. Of those older than twelve or fourteen, 290 were reconciled, 41 absolved *ad cautelam* with abjuration *de leve* [under only light suspicion], 81 retracted the confessions which they had made to the Holy Office [...], and finally 6 confessed to having returned to the sabbats [*aquelarres*]. Among the 290 whom I reconciled [as guilty], there were a hundred persons over 20, [...] many of them being 60, 70, 80 or even more years old.

Salazar stated that the 'trouble' about witchcraft had been less serious in Guipúzcoa, Vizcaya and Álava than in the mountains of Navarre, and that a great deal of the panic had been occasioned by the receipt of news from other places. He also commented to the Inquisitor General Sandoval on the conflict which had broken out among the inquisitors then working in Logroño. In an attempt to resolve it, both sides had shut themselves up with the trial papers, but their views proved to be irreconcilable. Later, in a document dated

7 January 1614, Salazar states fully and accurately the view
which his colleagues Becerra and Valle had taken of him:

> We marvel that he [Salazar] tries to insinuate that the majority of the
> witches' confessions and everything that emerges from the visitations
> are dreams and fantasies, for it is clear that the tricks, intrigues and
> contrivances of the Devil have been powerful and strong enough
> to blind the understanding of many people. All of this, naturally, has
> allowed the Devil better to protect his witches.

In this document, Salazar accuses his colleagues of taking
everything they heard at face value, while they complained
about his writing privately to Sandoval and to the diocesan
bishop, Venegas. Salazar states his objections to the methods
of Becerra and Valle in this way:

> All of this they reduce to accepted conclusions, as if the doctors
> and authorities [on witchcraft] had enjoyed revelations or had suc-
> ceeded in limiting the Devil to a uniform pattern of activity without
> variations in time, place or occasion, with the result that a gathering
> of witches in Zugarramurdi should be exactly the same as one in
> Fuenterrabía or in France.

To simplify matters, Becerra and Valle had adopted three
crude categories of 'good', 'bad' and 'indifferent' believers (*confitentes*), according to the degree of accuracy and
completeness with which they showed themselves able to
reproduce the set account of diabolical possession and
witchcraft which these inquisitors had in their heads. Also,
in Salazar's view, the categories they used were arbitrary:
'Thus the name of "bad" *confitente* is given to someone
whom another might call "good"'. His third objection to
his colleagues' approach and methods was as follows:

Thirdly, they assume that the Devil exercises great astuteness and constant vigilance in concealing his sect and in avoiding the danger that he fears will result if it should become known, lest his detestable designs for corrupting the Christian religion should fail. All this flies in the face of the copious testimony from over two thousand suspects which led to the discovery of the [supposed] sect. Similarly it does not seem that the Devil's machinations, the product of an angelic sagacity and a nature far superior to the human, could be exposed so easily by children of such tender years – eight and under. More than 1500 of the witnesses have not reached the age of twelve.

Salazar concludes his diatribe with a final shot directed against Becerra and Valle:

My colleagues make a forced comparison with seafarers who, without knowing how to use the compass or pilot chart, nevertheless find their way to the Indies, or to the ports they are seeking. I see no basis for a comparison here, since these two cases are completely unrelated to one another. In the former case, the seafarers, while on the high seas, are prepared for any eventuality by day or by night, but in the latter case, when the witches are travelling to the *aquelarre*, it is only the witch, or at the most the novice and the mistress, who see the way. Further more, no-one can be found to confirm this, nor can anyone outside the sect reveal anything about it.

The one thing on which all three inquisitors in Logroño could agree was that only the Suprema could resolve their dispute.

Finally, on 29 August 1614, the Council duly did so by issuing instructions for the hearing of witchcraft cases which came down firmly on the side of Salazar. He was sent a new colleague as inquisitor, Antonio de Aranda y Alarcón, and by the end of September 1614 the 'crisis' in Navarre and the Basque country was rapidly winding down. Crucially, instead of the traditional edict of grace, or faith, which was intended to elicit testimony, an 'edict of silence' was issued for the area, which followed Salazar's recommendation in forbidding public discussion of such matters as pacts with the Devil and sabbats. Yet, despite this moral victory for Salazar, the Inquisition, as an institution, was typically reluctant to admit that its prisoners had been wrongfully arrested, or that they should be absolved of their remaining debts to the tribunal. Once again, Salazar took up the cudgels on their behalf, in a further letter to the Inquisitor General, Sandoval de Rojas:

> These poor mountain people of Navarre, who are still suffering from the persecution and chastisement they have been subjected to, would be alarmed and distressed if we now forced them to produce what they neither possess nor have the possibility of paying. It thus seems preferable to apply the mercy that your Eminences [of the Suprema] may be inclined to show them.

On this point, though, Sandoval, who was the son of one of the Emperor Charles V's intimate servants and the archbishop of Toledo, refused to budge, replying that those who had the necessary funds should be forced to pay. By this time, Inquisitor Valle was away on a health cure, but he returned to his post in order to work once again alongside Salazar and Alarcón. He tried to obstruct his colleagues' proceedings under terms of the new instructions, but could not prevent a continuing flow of recantations by witnesses and prisoners, which was still under way in 1617.

As in the case of Lucero at the beginning of the previous century, there was no automatic connection between failure or controversy in the field and career prospects. Thus, despite the controversy, Alonso Becerra became a prosecutor (*fiscal*) for the Suprema on 10 October 1613 and was sworn in as a member of that Council on 28 August 1617, dying two years later. In his last years he devoted his energies not to witches but to counterfeiters. Nonetheless, the crusading Alonso Salazar Frías also had his reward. On 30 March 1617 he was appointed inquisitor of Llerena, in Extremadura, and on 3 August 1618 to the equivalent post in Murcia. At that time, he was also elected to a lucrative canonry of Seville Cathedral and, like his old adversary Becerra, he eventually became a prosecutor for the Suprema on 27 July 1628, retaining this post when he was elected to the Council itself on 5 July 1631.[17] The version of rationalism which he had practised, and the strength of the opposition which he experienced, together illustrate the prevailing character of the leadership, at least, of the seventeenth-century Inquisition. After 1700, the institution would face a similar test but on a much larger scale.

6

Censored:
The Battle of the Books

In modern histories of the Spanish Inquisition, the eighteenth century has generally been seen as a time when the institution began to come under sustained and corrosive criticism, both at home and abroad. For many, this change has been symbolised by the career of one of Philip V's leading government ministers, the layman Melchor Rafael de Macanaz, who managed to combine the roles of strong opponent and equally powerful defender of the Holy Office.

The accession to the Spanish throne, in 1700, of the French-born and French-speaking Bourbon Philip had the effect of initiating this controversy. Like his Habsburg predecessors,

Philip I and Charles V, Philip arrived in Spain with an already well-developed antipathy towards the Inquisition, which was quickly demonstrated when, in May 1701, he refused to attend an *auto de fe* in Madrid which had been specially staged by the local tribunal in order to celebrate his arrival in his new capital.[1] Following this opening gesture, the Spanish Inquisition could not fail to become embroiled in the tortured domestic and international politics of the period and, as so often, the conflict over more general issues came to be symbolised by an acrimonious dispute between Macanaz and his contemporary as Inquisitor General of Spain, the Italian Cardinal Francesco Giudice. Macanaz's adversary, though not a Spaniard (something that would later come to be of great importance), was born in Spanish Naples on 7 December 1647, inheriting the titles of Prince of Cellamare and Duke of Giovenazzo. However, he went into the Church, first becoming bishop of Ostia and Vercelli, and then receiving a cardinal's hat, with the title of San Sabino, on 13 February 1690. During 1696 and 1697, he was resident Spanish ambassador in Rome, and on 29 November 1699 Charles II of Spain made him a member of his Council of State. In 1702 he was appointed as archbishop of Monrreale in Sicily, becoming secular viceroy of the island in 1705. His involvement with the Inquisition began at the top, when on 2 June 1711 Pope Clement IX appointed him as Inquisitor General of Spain.[2]

Giudice (often known in Spain as 'Judice') took up his post at a fraught and difficult time in the relationship between the Spanish Crown and the Holy See, and Clement intended that he should become a member of the committee (*junta*) which had been set up in an attempt to resolve the disputed issues. Much of the motivation for conflict came from Philip V and his ministers and advisers. As John Lynch has commented: 'Bourbon absolutism tolerated no alternative allegiance and no resistance'.[3] Thus the Spanish Church, including the Inquisition, quickly felt the 'smack' of firm Bourbon government after 1700, especially since it gradually became clear that, with the help of his French allies, Philip would succeed in defeating the Habsburg challenge of the Austrian archduke, Charles. While its authority in matters of faith and morals was not at this stage questioned, the Church was forced to disgorge resources to the Crown, and was put under acute pressure to take Philip's side both in the succession conflict with the Austrian Habsburgs and their British and Dutch allies and in his dispute with the papacy. This was not the first time that attempts had been made to exclude papal jurisdiction from Spain, but the Bourbon monarchy went further than its Habsburg predecessor had done by claiming complete legal and financial control over all ecclesiastical institutions in the country, including the Spanish Inquisition. This claim was based on supposed legal and historical precedents and provided the background for the conflict between Macanaz and Giudice. A crucial issue in dispute was the traditional one of the provision of clergy to senior posts such as bishoprics and canonries. Philip V wanted the two-thirds of these benefices which were traditionally in papal hands to be transferred to the Spanish Crown, together with the revenues of vacant Spanish bishoprics and the fees charged by higher ecclesiastical courts. It was in this context that Macanaz, who came from Hellín in the kingdom of Murcia, began to make himself indispensable to his royal master.

In 1712 the Cortes was asked to ratify a new law of succession, which would have made it impossible for the future children of Spanish princesses who had married into the enemy royal houses of Savoy and Austria to inherit the Spanish throne. In the process, Philip was introducing into Castile the Salic law prescribing male succession, which had applied for several centuries in the Crown of Aragon. The new succession law, which became effective on 10 May 1713, initiated a general reform programme, known as the *nueva planta*, in which the leading roles were taken by a French minister of Philip V, Jean Orry, and also Melchor de Macanaz. One of the targets of this programme, which was put into law on 10 November 1713, was inevitably the Church, and Macanaz was asked to draw up a position paper covering the matters which were currently in dispute between Church and state. The resulting *proposiciones* (the term also commonly used by the Inquisition to refer to statements which it regarded as heretical) were published on 19 December 1713. In this document, Macanaz adopted as a basis the 'regalist' proposition that the Crown should have complete control over everything that happened in Spain, and hence that royal jurisdiction should have priority in every case over that of the Church. Macanaz asserted, in a manner of which Henry VIII of England and his secretary Thomas Cromwell would entirely have approved, that the papacy should have no power to tax Spanish subjects and that there should be no right of appeal from any Spanish court, whether secular or ecclesiastical, to Rome. Church courts should be deprived of all temporal power; the Crown should have sole responsibility for choosing and appointing bishops; the Church should by law have to pay any tax which the state might choose to levy upon it; and the numbers of monks, friars and nuns should be reduced to the levels current in the time of Cardinal Cisneros, around 1500.[4] It was as a result of this paper that Macanaz first came into conflict with the Inquisition.

This particular issue came to the fore when Louis XIV offered to mediate in the dispute between Spain and the papacy, which had been going on since 1709. It was for the relevant talks, held in Paris at the end of 1713, that Macanaz produced his 'regalist' paper on Church-state relations. Its approval by the Council of Castile precipitated a crisis in which both Macanaz and Giudice took centre stage, though the Inquisitor General of Spain was in fact based in France from April 1714, as Philip V's ambassador to his grandfather Louis. Perhaps inevitably, on 15 August of that year, Giudice had ordered to be published in Spain an *ex officio* condemnation of Macanaz's December 1713 paper, and the Spanish king's reaction was furious and decisive. He called his ambassador home, sacked him from all the positions which he held from the Crown and, in a manner which would have amazed Ferdinand the Catholic and Philip II, ordered the Suprema to suspend its condemnation of the document in question. He also instructed Macanaz to produce a counterblast to the Inquisition's condemnation of his, and his royal master's, views. This the former intendant of Aragon duly did, presenting the resulting document to the king on 3 November 1714. In his preface to the work, Macanaz noted that while he was still in Aragon Philip had called him in to give advice on 'the aggravations which the Spains and their Churches have been suffering for a long time from the Tribunals of Rome [including the Inquisition]'. According to this account, he had then obtained the relevant documents from Giudice, on whom he proceeded to launch a personal attack, claiming (without much danger of contradiction) that the Neapolitan inquisitor had used his influence in Rome to propel his nephew, Abbot Giudice, into the post of papal nuncio to Spain, and was himself aiming at securing the country's primatial see, the archbishopric of Toledo. This was indeed true and would prove to be a source of further conflict, involving the Spanish Bourbon monarchy, the Inquisition and the papacy. Macanaz called in aid both Trastamaran and Habsburg laws, from the reigns of Henry II and Charles V respectively, to support his proposition

that a non-Spaniard might not occupy this post. More personally, he accused Giudice of himself holding 'suspicious
doctrine' and of being willing to sacrifice true religion for
the sake of his own ambition. The Inquisitor General had
tried to obtain the see of Toledo by means of a brief from
Clement XI, but by then Philip V had placed his enemy
Macanaz in his Royal Council and made him Fiscal General
to the Crown. The Murcian author determinedly defended
his own religious orthodoxy and placed his argument with
the Inquisition entirely in the context of legal precedent.
He accused Giudice of abusing processes in Rome in order
to condemn him and Philip V, adding that 'the whole of
Spain' was appalled when the Inquisitor General was made a
cardinal. What follows this polemical preface is a meticulous
effort to demonstrate that the Spanish Church had been
under royal rather than papal control for many centuries.
From this, Macanaz concluded that in future the Inquisition
should be confined to spiritual rather than temporal matters.
This meant that the latter jurisdictions, and in particular the
power of the Holy Office to ban and censor books, should
be returned to the Crown.[5]

The year 1715 saw a complete reversal of roles, however, in
which the current administration fell and, despite the king's
support for his views, Macanaz was dismissed from office
and sent into exile. Giudice, on the other hand, was welcomed back to Spain in February of that year, and appointed
as minister of state for ecclesiastical affairs. A month later
he became tutor (ayo) to the heir to the throne, though his
triumph in Spain was short-lived, as he was dismissed from
these offices on 22 January 1717 and resigned his post as
Inquisitor General on 11 February of that year, returning to
Rome in June to become a diplomat in the service of the
Habsburg emperor, and dying in 1725.[6] His defeated rival
would, on the other hand, live until 1760, still trying to

regain his lost reputation. As Lynch rightly states: 'Macanaz was an orthodox Catholic, [...] and a defender of the very Spanish Inquisition which prohibited his works, kept him out of Spain and persecuted his family'.[7]

The accuracy of Lynch's observation is demonstrated by a treatise which Macanaz published in 1734 in defence of the Inquisition against 'the Calvinist, Lutheran and other heretics, and not a few Catholics deceived by them, [...] who with horror and shock and with such uncontrolled fury have fought against the Inquisition since [its foundation in] the thirteenth century [...]'. Macanaz's text is an explicit reply to French 'Enlightenment' views, as expressed in a history of the French monarchy which was published in 1734 by the Academician Abbé Die. Clearly, if the Murcian ex-minister and reformer was to be a guide, any Spanish 'Enlightenment' (*Ilustración*) would have a very much more 'Catholic' character than its foreign equivalents, and the author illustrates this point in his 'second preface' to his *Critical defence of the Inquisition*, which he concludes with the words: 'Everything will be for the greater glory and honour of God. Amen'. In the work which follows, the author demonstrates the permanent need of the Church to find and defeat heresy, correctly observing that this task had been carried out in other ways for centuries before the specialised, institutional Inquisition was founded in the 1230s.[8] In 1744, Macanaz returned to his standard theme of Spanish ecclesiastical independence in a detailed commentary on a history of Spain between 1713 and 1733, which had been written by a discalced Franciscan friar called Nicolás Belando.[9] In lengthy notes on Belando's text, the former minister defends the author against the attacks of the Inquisition. Interestingly, in supporting Belando's view that the Spanish monarch traditionally had overall control of the Holy Office, Macanaz refers, among other precedents, to the Carranza case (see Chapter 4):

According to the apostolic [papal] bulls, the King is Papal legate and principal Inquisitor, having the power to place and remove from the highest to the lowest minister of the Inquisition, to call cases in to himself and enquire into them whenever he pleased. He had done so on many occasions, as Philip the Second did in the case of Archbishop [Bartolomé] Carranza, even though this conflicted with Pontifical authority and that of the Council of Trent.[10]

Between his fall from grace in 1715 and his death, surrounded by his family, in his home town of Hellín on 5 December 1760, Melchor de Macanaz received shameful and vindictive treatment from his old master, Philip V, from the king's son and successor (in 1746), Ferdinand VI, and from a series of Inquisitors General. The story has been powerfully told, on the basis of solid scholarly research, by the historian and novelist Carmen Martín Gaite.

On 28 June 1716, from the pulpit of San Sebastián, Madrid, which was the latter's parish church, a commissioner of the Inquisition announced the arrest of Melchor de Macanaz and the confiscation of his property. The addressee was, of course, not present in church to hear the edict and was told about it, in Pau in French Navarre, by a relative. He immediately made an attempt to have the case remitted to Rome, writing to Cardinal Gualteri:

> I declare and protest that I believe and confess whatever Holy Scripture, the Councils, Holy Fathers and Supreme Pontiffs believe and confess and have commanded the faithful to believe and confess and that I condemn and have condemned and will always condemn what they have ordained and condemned and that if I have up to now spoken, written or acted against this directly or indirectly, or should do so in future (which let God not permit), from this moment I retract it.[11]

Given his policies in government, though, Macanaz also felt it necessary to assure the papal curia that he was not in reality hostile to Rome, either. As for the Inquisition in Spain, it declared itself totally unconvinced by his protestations of orthodoxy and loyalty. In reality, Giudice's triumph would not last long, but his dismissal and departure did not release Macanaz from his toils. The family property was duly confiscated and administered by the Holy Office and Philip V proved to be distinctly lukewarm in his defence of his former protégé. Thus, on 4 October 1716, the 'impenitent' accused was condemned by an official of the Inquisition, from the pulpit of San Sebastián in Madrid, to excommunication as a 'rebel' against God and the Holy Office. The sentence was confirmed as 'definitive' in the following year. In these circumstances, Macanaz naturally felt unable to return to Spain, remaining in exile in Pau, while the political upheavals of his native land repeatedly failed to work to his advantage. He remained in exile throughout the rest of Philip V's reign and when he attempted to return to his homeland, in 1748, he was arrested in Vitoria, in northern Spain, on the orders of Ferdinand VI's government, and the Inquisition pursued him to his grave. In January 1761, though, the Holy Office at least agreed not to harry his family further, as the law, both ecclesiastical and secular, entitled it to do.[12] Yet, although Macanaz's intellectual and political challenge may have been successfully weathered by the Spanish inquisitors, it remains to be seen whether, if at all, their conflict with the Crown affected the day-to-day work of Inquisition tribunals throughout the country. There has been a tendency, in general histories, to suggest that the inquisitors of the eighteenth century were influenced by French 'Bourbon' thinking, and reduced the intensity of their pursuit of traditional quarry, such as 'Judaisers' and witches. Evidence from scattered parts of Philip and Ferdinand's realm suggests,

though, that the Holy Office by no means lost its power
and zeal in this period, even if Inquisitors General appeared
to lack the personal power and charisma of their predecessors in the fifteenth and sixteenth centuries.

All too typical of the Inquisition's business in this period
was the procession of penitents which emerged from the
Dominican priory of San Pablo in Córdoba on 24 April
1718. It consisted of four 'Jews' (two brothers and two sis-
ters), two female bigamists, a 'Lutheran', and a *beata*, or
devout woman, who was convicted as a 'heresiarch', together
with four of her male disciples, who were all Franciscans.
It is clear from the surviving records that the *beata* was
the main focus of this effort by the Cordoban inquisitors, who felt that they had identified a late successor to
the *Alumbrados* with whom the Inquisitor General Alonso
Manrique had contended in the sixteenth century. She was
said to have possessed a 'Child Jesus', who through diabolical arts controlled her and her disciples, the group being
accused of sexual licence as well as heretical statements.[13]
However, in the other *autos* recorded in Córdoba in this
period, 'Judaisers' were the main target. On 20 April 1721,
twenty-six were processed either in person or in effigy,
one forty-year-old woman being burned while showing
'signs of the greatest repentance', while others were flogged
and imprisoned. In the following year, on 12 April, four
more 'Judaisers' were burned and others reconciled, and
a similar pattern was followed in *autos* on 13 June 1723,
23 April 1724, 2 July 1724, 12 May 1726, 15 May 1728, 3
May 1730 and 4 March 1731. A further ceremony was held
in Córdoba on 5 December 1745, but this time without
any burnings.[14] Similar assaults on 'Judaising' are recorded
in other areas of Spain in this period, including Logroño in
the north (1700–30) and the Extremaduran town of Llerena
in the south-west (1700–46).[15] All this activity indicates

clearly that inquisitors in the eighteenth century were still interested in the category of 'heresy' which had mainly preoccupied Torquemada, just as the tribunal at Logroño continued to pursue 'witches' in the Basque country and Navarre, though without the violence which Salazar Frías had successfully restrained in the early seventeenth century.[16] It remained to be seen how the Holy Office would fare after 1759, in the Spain of Charles III.

From its very foundation, the Inquisition in Spain and its dependencies had been subject to fierce internal criticism, primarily from defenders of the *conversos*. External attacks, on the other hand, began to loom large in the mid-sixteenth century, at the time when the Inquisitor General and his staff first came into conflict with identifiable Protestantism derived from north of the Pyrenees. For the foreign criticism which followed, and would survive the final abolition of the Spanish Holy Office in 1834, Edward Peters coined the phrase 'the invention of the Inquisition', which has since been taken up by other historians, in particular Henry Kamen and Doris Moreno.[17] The opportunity to use this stick to beat Spain, the European superpower of its day, was provided by the uniquely ecclesiastical nature of this instrument of oppression, unlike those so freely wielded by other states. In the sixteenth century, the Inquisition thus became the main symbol of Spanish 'cruelty' and 'tyranny', both in the country itself and in the foreign territories which it ruled and conquered. This stereotype developed further during the European debates over religious toleration in the seventeenth century, and more especially in the thought and writings of the French *philosophes* of the eighteenth century. One of the focuses of such criticism and attack was the question of religious and literary censorship, which would provide ammunition for attacks on the Inquisition until the very end of its days.

It was not always so. As soon as printing arrived in Spain in the late 1470s, Isabella and Ferdinand's government in Castile and Aragon had become concerned with the uses, or misuses, to which the presses might be put, and invoked the authority of the state in order to control their activities. This was not, however, done through the medium of the Inquisition. Instead, in Castile, the licensing of printed books was on 8 July 1502 placed in the hands of the high courts of justice (*chancillerías*) in Valladolid and Granada, and of the archbishops of Toledo and Seville and the bishops of Burgos and Salamanca, with responsibility for the matter in their respective areas of jurisdiction. In the Crown of Aragon, where local jurisdiction was more fragmented, such powers were reserved to the 'regent' of the high court (*audiencia*) and to bishops' administrative deputies (*vicarios generales*). It is interesting to note that these arrangements gave a much greater role in licensing, and hence in censorship, to secular authorities than was customary at the time elsewhere in western Europe, where successive Popes, Innocent VIII, Alexander VI and Leo X, claimed ultimate control. In any case, the Inquisition was not involved in the process, and this remained the case when, in 1554, censorship was tightened in Castile. The granting of licences to print was henceforward centralised in the Council of Castile, the supreme governing body of the kingdom, while in 1556 the Council of the Indies took charge of works published in Spanish America. However, religious books, which still constituted the vast majority of publications in this period, had also to be approved by local diocesan bishops, and if they concerned matters involving the Inquisition (which meant casting the net fairly widely), inquisitors, too, had to review the material in question. Although in 1569 the Council of Castile reasserted its control over all printing licences, it continued to tap the expertise of bishops, inquisitors and the universities. Thus the Inquisition was comparatively late in gaining a prominent role in the licensing and censorship of books, and when Melchor de Macanaz unsuccessfully argued, in 1714, that such powers should revert in their entirety to the Crown, his view was soundly based in historical terms, even though Giudice and the bishops succeeded in defeating him.

Ever since the reign of Alonso Manrique as Inquisitor General, the Holy Office had been concerned with preventing the importation into Spain of books which it regarded as heretical. This logically led to the notion of compiling lists of books which Spaniards should be forbidden to read. Between 1520 and 1545, Luther and his allies were naturally the main target of such efforts, the works of the former being condemned in their entirety by Adrian of Utrecht, Manrique and Fernando de Valdés. After 1536, when his *Colloquies* were condemned, the works of Erasmus began to be added to the list of 'forbidden books'. It was not, however, until 1551 that Valdés' Inquisition issued its first formal 'Index of forbidden books', which was modelled on a 'catalogue' of such works which had been issued by the University of Louvain (Leuven) in 1546. In late 1550 or early 1551, while he was on what turned out to be his only visit to his archiepiscopal see of Seville, Valdés sent a letter, with a copy of the Louvain catalogue, to the Suprema, which quickly went into action. All this effort seems to have been precipitated by a papal bull, issued in early May 1550, which instructed the inquisitors to gather in all the versions of the Bible which were condemned by the University of Louvain or else in the list which was printed in the then current Roman missal. The result was that the Spanish Inquisition authorised the publication in 1551 of four editions of the new Index, in Valladolid, Toledo, Seville and Valencia, there being minor variations between them. During the 1550s, in which official worries about evangelical groups in Spain were steadily growing, the Louvain-based list remained in force but finally, in 1559, Valdés issued a new Index, in a context of increasingly xenophobic fear. As an accompanying measure, in July 1559 Philip II issued his notorious decree which ostensibly forbade his subjects in future to study in foreign universities, apart from Coimbra in Portugal and Bologna and Naples in Italy. By the time that the Index was published in August of that year, the evangelicals of Seville and Valladolid were under trial and Archbishop Carranza was about to be arrested. In this context it is noticeable that among those consulted by the Inquisitor General concerning works which should be included were two of his closest confidants, Francisco Sancho, a professor at the University of Salamanca, and Melchor Cano, who, as well as being prior of the Dominican convent and college of San Esteban, also in Salamanca, was by this time one of Carranza's bitterest enemies.

The Spanish Index, which was immediately preceded by the Roman one, issued by Pope Paul IV, was put together at great speed, and was mainly directed against versions of the Bible which were regarded as textually inaccurate in relation to the Latin Vulgate, and annotated in an anti-Catholic or anti-papal, way. Also condemned in it were earlier authors such as the late-fifteenth-century Florentine Dominican reformer Girolamo Savonarola and Erasmus, as well as contemporary Spanish spiritual writers such as Juan de Ávila and Francisco de Borja, who would both later be canonised as saints, as well as Luis de Granada. Inevitably, the writings of the more notorious Spanish evangelicals, such as Juan de Valdés, Juan Pérez de Pineda and Constantino Ponce de la Fuente were condemned, as well as the *Commentaries on the Christian Catechism* by Bartolomé Carranza, a work which was soon to be approved by the Council of Trent and to form a considerable portion of the Tridentine Catechism that remained in force for Roman Catholics until replaced by Pope John Paul II in 1992. Despite the rapidity of their operations, Fernando de Valdés and his advisers delved deep into the literature of Christendom, indiscriminately condemning not only pagan writers, such as Aristotle, Ovid, Demosthenes, Hippocrates, Seneca, Plato and Dioscorides, but even some of the 'Books of Hours' which were pillars of the devotion of so many lay Christians in the period. The inquisitorial net also spread to Italy, with the condemnation of sometimes salacious authors such as Giovanni Boccaccio and Pietro Aretino, who were merciless towards the ills and abuses of the Church, as well as those of society in general. The Inquisition also cut swathes through recent and contemporary Spanish literature, much of which has since become part of the canon for academic study. Thus books that might be regarded as obscene as well as humorous came under the ban, but Fernando de Valdés was particularly severe in his treatment of spiritual works of which he disapproved. Some authors, notably St Francisco Borja in his *Works of Christianity*, attempted to avoid inclusion in the Index by denying authorship of the offending passages, but without success. The equally saintly Luis de Granada travelled from Lisbon to Valladolid to talk to Valdés, but his effort simply resulted in the inclusion of an extra work of his in the second edition of the 1559 Index.

Subsequently, several further Indices were published, beginning in 1571 in Antwerp. The list in question was more subtle in method than its predecessor, in that it allowed works to be read on condition that certain offending paragraphs were expunged. However, the most comprehensive sixteenth-century Index was that of Inquisitor General Gaspar de Quiroga, which was published in 1583, though work on it had begun as early as 1569. Whereas Valdés had included 699 works in his Index, and the 1564 Roman Tridentine Index condemned 1,012, that of Quiroga contained no fewer than 2,315. Also, it was composed on different principles in that, whereas Valdés had launched directly into the general condemnations of authors' entire output, or else of single works, Quiroga followed the example of the Tridentine Index by initially setting out fourteen general criteria for what followed. Fundamental to the future of the Spanish Inquisition's efforts at censorship was the first of these principles, which broadened the definition of what constituted heresy to include any work which contained doctrine that had been condemned by the Roman Catholic Church, as well as errors even in the works of authors who had not been condemned in general. Also considered heretical, under the Quirogan principles, were works seen as scandalous, suspicious or erroneous in that they attacked good customs and behaviour. Doubt or ambiguity were enough to attract condemnation, as were things which the humourless inquisitors regarded as 'vain and ridiculous'. A hierarchy of heresy was established, which was headed by 'heresiarchs' such as Wycliffe, Hus, Luther, Calvin and Zwingli, but also included native Spanish reformers such as Antonio del Corro and Cipriano de Valera. Particular condemnation was attracted by vernacular Spanish translations of the Bible. Indeed, an authorised translation of the Vulgate would not be produced in Spain until 1790.[18] Rule 8 of Quiroga's Index went further than book censorship, prohibiting debates and discussions on religious matters between Catholics and Protestants, and even condemning attempted refutations of the Koran in vernacular languages. Rules 10 and 12 spread the net even wider, to include any images, portraits, figures, satires, songs, verses, and even coins and medals which might be deemed to show any disrespect to the Catholic faith. This multi-media approach aimed, of course, at preventing rather than assisting the diffusion of opinion and information. In addition, rule 14 forbade the translation of works on the Index from one vernacular language into another. A particular worry was manuscript writing, which might circulate outside the system of governmental and inquisitorial control that applied to printing presses. Even so, unlike their colleagues in Rome, the Spanish inquisitors did at least permit the circulation of handwritten university examination mark-sheets and lecture notes. They completely banned Jewish and Muslim books, though, as well as the vernacular Books of Hours which had enabled so many fifteenth-century Christians to participate more fully in the Latin services of the Church. In many of these respects, Quiroga followed the precedent of Trent, but he and his advisers appear to have been less concerned than the compilers of the Roman Index about straightforwardly licentious and erotic works. For them, irreverence towards God and His Church was a greater threat and a more serious offence.[19]

The next 'Index of forbidden books' was drawn up in 1612, in the midst of the witchcraft controversy in north-eastern Spain, by Sandoval y Rojas as Inquisitor General. It was influenced, even more than that of Quiroga, by contemporary practice in Rome. In an advisory memorandum, the Jesuit Diego Álvarez introduced the requirement that anything which encouraged 'bad habits' should be regarded as heretical. This widened further Quiroga's all-embracing categories, bringing many works of Spanish and foreign literature onto the list of forbidden books. A new departure was the inclusion of controversial political works, of which there were many in the early seventeenth century, as debate grew about the perceived 'decline of Spain' as a great power. Twenty years later, in 1632, the then Inquisitor General, Luis Zapata, returned to the matter of censorship with a new Index, which was quickly replaced in 1640 by that of his successor, Antonio de Sotomayor. For much of the remainder of the seventeenth century, the Roman curia exercised a strong influence over the control of publications and reading in Spain. During this period, there was a growing concern to censor sexual references, beginning with the Zapata Index and continuing with that of Sotomayor, which banned 'jokes and witticisms published to the offence, prejudice and against the good standing of ones neighbours'. As García Cárcel rightly observes: 'Puritanism is imposing itself [here]'.[20] Another feature of the indexes of the mid-seventeenth century in Spain was a growing fear of 'novelty', leading to an attack on new authors. Thus the 1640 index included in its list of heresies that of urging any change or innovation in the beliefs and rites of the Roman Church which would lead the souls of the faithful astray. Sotomayor's index also introduced the new principle of 'cautious reading' (caute lege), 'which is not censorship, but caution aimed at defending books from the less respectful censorship which they would [otherwise] receive, so that the ignorant may not unwittingly fall, and the malicious may not twist the understanding [of the reader] into supporting their errors'.[21] This approach led inevitably to self-censorship by the reader, in which the inquisitor was effectively inside his head, thus saving staff time. The 1640 index also contained an intriguing reference to the need to defend the Church against a particular category of 'heretical proposition'. Not only were the liberty, immunities and jurisdiction of the Church to be defended, but also to be expurgated were those passages in books 'which support tyrannical political government which is falsely called "reason of State", opposed to the Evangelical and Christian law'. Thus, long before Melchor de Macanaz entered his struggle, the first signs of the future battle between religion and secularism were beginning to appear. As part of its counter-offensive against modern science, natural as well as political, the 1640 Index condemned wholesale the works of Copernicus.

It was on this basis that the Spanish Inquisition would enter the eighteenth century. Between 1679 and 1707, a new Index was slowly prepared and Philip V had no hesitation in allowing its implementation. Its criteria were those of the seventeenth century and older works continued to be examined and condemned, as a whole or in part. There was little sign that the Bourbon king had brought any French 'Enlightenment' ideas with him to Spain, and this impression was confirmed in the 1747 Index, which was drawn up by two Jesuits, Lasani and Carrasco. They closely followed the Roman Index of 1744, and their particular concern was the reforming movement which had originated in France in the previous century, under the leadership of Cornelius Jansen (see Chapter 7), who had been opposed from the start by the Society of Jesus. The 1747 Index also launched a direct assault on the thinkers of the Enlightenment, condemning wholesale the works of Grotius, Pufendorf and Bayle, as well as the early output of Voltaire. After the publication of this list, though, there was no further Index until 1790. Instead, decrees were issued from time to time against specific works, but the second half of the eighteenth century saw a major realignment of the upper reaches of the Spanish Church, with the development of a systematic attack on the Jesuits, who were eventually expelled from Spain in 1767. The Inquisition was losing its authority, though, under the pressure of events over which it had no control. Thus, when the Holy Office returned in 1790 to the matter of indexes of forbidden books, it was reacting to the powers unleashed by the French Revolution of the previous year. New criteria were adopted for considering published works and for presenting the results. Thus the list was presented in alphabetical order rather than in analytical categories, and numerous contemporary works, both Spanish and foreign,

were included. A supplement would eventually be published, covering the years 1805 to 1819, but that would be
born into a very different world from that of Valdés and
Quiroga.[22] The inquisitors had 'lost the plot' and the end
of their ministrations was nigh.

7

The Death of the Holy Office

The Spain which Charles IV inherited in 1788 appeared to be strong. In John Lynch's words: 'Spanish imperial power had never been greater, American trade was free and protected, revenues were high, defences were secure'.[1] Initially, it seemed that it would not be difficult for the new king to pursue his predecessor's policies of modernising Spain and increasing its power and influence, but external events soon rendered both policies problematic. They would also drastically affect the nature, and even the existence, of the Inquisition. In considering the fate of the Church and the inquisitors it is necessary, though, to bear in mind the overall political context in which Spain

found itself at the end of the eighteenth century and the
beginning of the nineteenth. The country was run on an
absolutist system, to some extent modelled on the Bourbon
monarchy in France, which needed an effective working
ruler to lead its administration. Charles was not, unfortunately, a man of great ability, but he had a high sense of his
own position and prerogative. To begin with, he retained
his father's first secretary of state, José Moniño y Redondo,
Count of Floridablanca, who was efficient but somewhat
abrasive. Floridablanca appeared to be a reformer, but the
French Revolution of 1789 exposed his innate conservatism,
and king and minister worked together in an unsuccessful
attempt to keep Spain free from the contagion of French
libertarian and secularist ideas.[2] In the intellectual battle, the
Inquisition inevitably became a crucial participant.

Charles III had pursued with great vigour Philip V's
'regalist' policy of bringing the Church in general, and the
Inquisition in particular, under tighter royal control. He
had twice tried to reform the latter institution in the 1760s,
though with limited success, but in 1774 he went so far as
to dismiss an Inquisitor General, Manuel Quintano Bonifaz,
Bishop of Farsala, for disobeying him in a matter of book
censorship. Quintano's replacement, Felipe Beltrán, Bishop
of Salamanca, who held the office from 1775 to 1783, and
Agustín Rubín de Ceballos (1784–1793), Bishop of Jaén,
were effectively domestic servants of the king. Thus, when
Charles IV came to the throne in 1788, the Inquisition did
not appear to be in good shape to defend its role in Spanish
society. Nevertheless, the outbreak of revolution in France,
with the storming of the Paris Bastille in 1789, changed this
situation radically. Suddenly, an institution which had been
routinely mocked by Spanish supporters of the rationalist
Enlightenment (in Spain, *Ilustración*), as well as foreign commentators, was seen once more as a bulwark in the defence of

the nation, as it had been in the reign of Philip II. Under the orders of Charles and Floridablanca, the compliant Ceballos attempted to establish an ideological *cordon sanitaire* round the country, to keep out the French contagion. The repression went to the highest level, with the removal from office of distinguished reforming politicians such as Gaspar Melchor de Jovellanos and Pedro Rodríguez de Campomanes. At this time, a fierce intellectual battle broke out in Church and state, with writers such as Manuel María de Aguirre, a military man, advocating religious tolerance, while the inquisitor of Seville and bishop of León, Pedro Luis Blanco, took a line so conservative and traditionalist as to be effectively reactionary in the context of the years around 1800. This polarisation was to prove ominous for the history of Spain in the nineteenth and twentieth centuries.

In the event, successive Inquisitors General in this period, first Rubín de Ceballos and then Manuel Abad y La Sierra, Bishop of Astorga (1793–94), proved inadequate for the task which had been assigned to them by the monarchy. The promotion to the presidency of the Council of Castile of another leading reformer, the Count of Aranda, appeared to shift government away from traditionalism towards what was coming to be known as 'liberalism', thus creating the modern division between 'conservatives' and 'liberals'. In reality, though, the Spanish *Ilustrados*, supporters of the ideas of the French *philosophes*, were divided among themselves, and the need to defend the country against the threat of France was paramount. The French *Encyclopédie* (1751), compiled by D'Alembert and Diderot, had defined the Inquisition as 'a fanatical tribunal, an eternal obstacle to the progress of the mind, to the culture of the arts, to the introduction [to the world] of happiness'. Many Spanish supporters of French ideas were sympathetic to this view, and to the attacks and ironies of Montesquieu and Voltaire, but the inquisitors fought back, knowing that even in the decade of the 1790s, which was so dangerous to Spain's integrity as an independent nation, they too had their allies, at court and in the country. In 1792, Mariano Luis de Urquijo, another liberal, was tried by the Inquisition for having translated Voltaire's *The death of Caesar* into Spanish, and four years later the Suprema even attacked certain paragraphs of Jovellanos' reforming Agrarian Law. The Inquisition was evidently trying to find a new role in the contemporary world, but this was a difficult task. Both Abad y La Sierra, after just a year in office, and his successors Francisco Antonio Lorenzana, Archbishop of Toledo, in 1798, and Ramón José de Arce, Archbishop of Burgos and then Zaragoza, resigned the office of Inquisitor General, the latter in 1808, a momentous year. It was in the late 1790s that reforming circles, led by Jovellanos as 'Minister of Grace and Justice', began to propose a radical restructuring of the Inquisition. In essence, the proposal, which had earlier been advocated by Macanaz, was that the detection and punishment of heresy should cease to be dealt with by specialised tribunals, and that the task should revert to diocesan bishops and their delegates, as had been the case in the western Church up to the early thirteenth century. Supporters of the scheme, which they would pursue throughout the first few decades of the nine-teenth century, believed that this approach, rather than the outright abolition of heresy laws, would attract at least some of the Spanish clergy.[3]

In order to explain why Jovellanos and his allies may have thought this, it is useful at this stage to examine fur-ther the character of the Spanish Church in the reign of Charles IV. The French influences which came into Spain after the accession of Philip V had included the theologi-cal tendency or movement known as 'Jansenism'. It was

thus named after the Netherlandish bishop Cornelius
Otto Jansen who, between 1628 and his death ten years
later, had read the complete works of the fourth-century
theologian Augustine of Hippo. In his resulting book, the
Augustinus, which was published posthumously in 1640,
he made two major theological propositions. These were:
firstly, that without God's grace it is impossible for people
to keep his commandments and, secondly, that the operation of God's grace is irresistible. The consequence of these
conclusions was to render humankind the passive recipient
of a natural or divine determinism, and the theological
pessimism of Jansen's clerical and lay followers generally
led them to adopt a harsh moral and physical way of life.
The *Augustinus*, not least because of its marked resem-
blance to the views of Martin Luther and other Reformed
theologians who had used the same source, was first condemned on publication by the Catholic theologians of the
University of Paris, and then, in 1653, by Pope Innocent X.
Despite this widespread rejection, though, Jansen's theology continued to attract numerous followers, and when
they found conditions in France increasingly difficult
many, including clergy, moved to the Netherlands and parts
of Italy, especially Tuscany.[4] Thus Jansenism continued to
be influential in Europe throughout the eighteenth century, and Spain was also affected. Foreign works written
by Jansenists had some influence there, alongside the more
secular criticism of Montesquieu, Bayle and Voltaire, and
one target of other French writers such as Abbé Jacques
Marsollier (1693) and Louis-Ellies Dupin (c.1715–19) was
the Spanish Inquisition.[5] During the Bourbon monarchy
up to 1788, a climate of opinion was developing among
some Catholic clerical and lay circles in Spain which saw
a need for drastic reform of the Church in general and the
Inquisition in particular.

In 1787, the dramatist Antonio Valladares de Sotomayor, who was also an important thinker and commentator, began to publish a review entitled *Semanario erudito* ('Learned Weekly'). In his prospectus for the new publication, he reminded his readers that in earlier centuries (notably the sixteenth and seventeenth) Spain had been the intellectual leader of Europe, and he blamed its subsequent decline mainly on the religious orders, whose clergy 'always forms within the State a state apart, governed in its own private interest'.[6] In particular, the friars and other religious had succeeded in gaining control of numerous university chairs, and hence of the formation of Spain's future leaders. Valladares' *Semanario* was issued with a caution to the reader by the Council of Castile, but nonetheless helped to open up the new debate about the role of the Inquisition in Spanish society. In particular, there began to be, for the first time since the late Middle Ages, a discussion about the proper relationship between inquisitorial tribunals and diocesan bishops.[7] Even so, as Cuenca Toribio has pointed out, the clerical leadership of the Spanish Church, in its reaction to the outbreak of the French Revolution, was in a position to adopt a more coherent attitude than some other sectors of society, such as the nobility and the king's government. Even the most 'enlightened' clergy had no illusions about the nature and likely consequences of the events in Paris, especially from 1793 onwards, and the natural reaction was to seek self-defence and survival. Many clergy, at all levels, blamed the Spanish government for having, through prejudice or blindness and apathy, allowed an unhealthy intellectual and moral climate to develop in the country, and the Inquisition, as the designated guardian of these very matters, was inevitably vulnerable to criticism. Nonetheless, whatever their doubts and disagreements with secular politicians, a significant proportion of the Spanish clergy readily joined forces with Charles IV's government in its effort to defend the country, both politically and spiritually. The alert was sounded by the storming of the Bastille on 14 July 1789, and the inevitable result was a dialectical clash between 'revolutionary' and 'counter-revolutionary' modes of thought which brought conflict into every part of the clerical hierarchy.[8] Typical of the initially predominant loyalist tendency was a pastoral letter published at the end of 1793 by Victoriano López Gonzalo, Bishop of Cartagena, who was one of the leading thinkers among the Spanish bishops of the period. His words, addressed to the parish clergy, were well expressed and evidently deeply felt, giving a vivid impression of the state of the Church at the time:

> The painful and bitter circumstances of some most disagreeable times, which are going to close the blackest and darkest of centuries [the eighteenth], now more than ever render necessary your vigilance and application in the ministry of preaching to and teaching your parishioners, without omitting any means or diligence which may contribute to inspiring in them the most just, clear and worthy ideas of our holy religion. Now more than ever, we repeat that atheism, libertinism and insubordination seem to have emerged from the abysses to make disbelief and anarchy predominant, now that materialism, dissoluteness and scandal attack in its foundations the religion [which is] the only school in which the Christian must learn his duties towards the one God, towards himself, and towards others; and now finally those malign forces aimed at drawing Christians away from the Doctrine of the Gospel are such as have never been seen before, and go accompanied by a fury and a vehemence which tear down everything like a violent hurricane.[9]

The bishop goes on to refer to the initial spread of Islam, in the seventh century and after, and asks whether even this can compare with the 'diabolical astuteness and poisoned discourses of the *philosophes* of our century'. The self-proclaimed religious reformers of the eighteenth century have in fact worked with considerable success to undermine the whole doctrinal edifice of the Roman Catholic Church. What is more, another consequence of their efforts is the widespread outbreak of political and social upheaval in Spain as well as the rest of Europe. The urgent need now is for a vigorous teaching effort to place Christians once again under the 'gentle yoke of religion'. For, 'if unbelief succeeds in taking control of their hearts, and inspiring in them contempt for revealed truths, there will be no authority or brake in the world to contain it'. After more in the same vein, Bishop Victoriano goes on to offer detailed pastoral advice to his priestly colleagues. Perhaps surprisingly, in view of the doom-laden tone of the earlier part of the document, he appears to think that the parish priest may not in fact find that his task, though immense, is a completely hopeless one. It is not *yet* the case, the bishop says, that Heaven has decreed the complete abandonment by the laity of the Catholic faith. Instead, the priests are instructed:

Work, then [...], with the activity proper to your charge, to prevent these evils. Fix *in the hearts* [the bishop's italics] of your flock the principal maxims of the doctrine of religion. They are accustomed to listening, in the things which lead to their eternal salvation, to another voice than that of the Church, something [salvation, that is] which will be achieved if they are with frequency made to hear yours. [They are] taught with particular force the submission and obedience which they must give to the two powers on earth, the spiritual and the temporal; that anyone who strays from the first is a schismatic, and that he who resists the latter is a rebel, that one day the Lord will unsheath the sword of justice, and will use it against the impious who blaspheme against His holy name. Preach, urge, in season and out of

season; you need not be burdensome, because as you employ your
efforts in cultivating the spirit of your flock, our good God will make
your work fertile, and will give the increase, which can be hoped for
only from His hands.[10]

How different Spain was in 1800 from the country which
Valdés and Quiroga had been able to dominate psychologi-
cally more than 200 years earlier.

In these circumstances of Spanish weakness and French
expansionism, the Church was beleaguered, and yet seems
not, at least at the level of the episcopate, to have sought help
from conservative members of the aristocracy, who might
objectively seem to have been its natural allies. Cuenca
Toribio points to acute weakness and lack of leadership
among the Spanish bishops in this time of emergency, which
left the local parish clergy and members of religious orders
to fight their own battles with revolutionary enthusiasts, and
frequently to succumb to their essentially anti-Christian
ideas. Also largely failed by the leadership of the Spanish
Church were the French clergy and religious who took
refuge in Spain, and who knew exactly what awaited the
country when eventually, in 1808, the pretence of alliance
with the Spanish monarchy was abandoned and French
armies advanced across the border. In truth, it appears that
French revolutionary ideas already had considerable cur-
rency and acceptance among at least some of the Spanish
episcopate. It was not until Spanish 'liberalism' became
openly visible and comprehensible for what it was, in the
Cortes of Cádiz in 1812, that senior clergy would begin to
formulate a strictly 'reactionary' Christian ideology, and set
up a conflict within the country which still has resonance
even in the twenty-first century.[11]

A flavour of this kind of ecclesiastical leadership, in the
years before and after 1800, is given by events in Córdoba. A

characteristic feature of the Spanish bishops in the late eighteenth century, influenced as they were by the ideas of the
Enlightenment, was a deep distrust of, not to say contempt
for, the religion of the mass of the people, of all social classes.
Like so many scholars since, they dismissed such traditional,
but ever adaptable, beliefs and practices as 'popular religion',
which had to be distinguished from their own 'correct', 'spiritual' version of Christianity. While dangerously complacent
about the French political and military threat, senior clergy
were zealous in attempting to root out what they regarded
as at best semi-Christian practices and devotions among
their flock. This process went on even when the French
revolutionary army was at the gates. A case in point was the
issue of Holy Week processions in the small Andalusian town
of Benamejí, south of Córdoba, which was then governed
by the military order of Santiago. There as elsewhere, the
1700s had seen the development of elaborate observances
which, because of their evening and night-time schedule, the
clergy not unreasonably suspected of providing an occasion
and cover for illicit activities. The priests of the district, or
vicariate, were strong supporters of the Enlightenment, and
in 1794 the *vicario central*, Juan Antonio Aguilar y Luque,
sent a highly critical letter to the parish priest of Benamejí,
Juan Linares Artacho, which appeared to be aimed at banning the processions in Holy Week of that year. However,
Fr Linares and the senior chaplains of the town reported the
matter to the royal Council of the Military Orders, which
acted as their 'lord' in jurisdictional matters, both secular
and ecclesiastical. They demanded that the processions
should continue, arguing that they stimulated the faith of
the people by means of the visible signs of the Passion. They
regarded the traditional popular devotions as an expression
of a profoundly Christian feeling and understanding, not a
manifestation of paganism, as some Enlightenment thinkers

suggested. The abolition of the lay confraternities' processions, they said, would also have the unfortunate effect of
preventing the traditional prayers for beneficent rain which
were a part of the Holy Week devotions. The Council of the
Military Orders accepted these arguments and authorised
the processions, but Aguilar y Luque immediately began
a legal counter-attack, composing a memorandum which
outlined, in a thoroughly disparaging manner, the history of
Holy Week processions in Spain. This was quickly supported
by other reforming clergy some of whom, as Cuenca Toribio
observes, 'were born in the place [Benamejí] and enthusiasts,
in their youth, for the spectacular confraternities and rep-
resentations [of the story of Jesus' Passion]'. The Benamejí
dispute became a microcosm of the issues which were then
convulsing the Church nationally. A detailed questionnaire
was drawn up, which indicates elaborate observances of the
kind which are still popular in the present day, especially
in southern Spain. Witnesses were required to confirm that
there was indeed a confraternity of Jesus of Nazareth in the
town which, during Holy Week, represented the successive
episodes of the Passion dramatically and in procession, acting
the parts of Jesus, Mary and other figures in dramatised tableaux or *pasos*. They were asked whether the local vicar had
ever forbidden such processions, what kind of clothing was
worn by participants and, in particular, whether the mother
and maid of Pilate were played by men dressed as women,
whether members of the clergy took part in the processions,
and whether make-up was worn. There was also concern
(and this was central to the concerns of the 'enlightened'
(*ilustrados*) among the clergy) as to whether any kind of disorder or disturbance took place during the processions, thus
showing disrespect to the Saviour and Redeemer. Witnesses
were also asked to state whether individuals had begged for
alms during the processions and, if so, whether any account

of the money collected had been provided to the vicar or
to the ecclesiastical visitors of the district. This document
shines a bright light both on religious life in the Spain of
Charles IV and on the increasing bitterness of the intellectual
dispute at all levels of the Church between reformers and
traditionalists.

At the heart of all these questions was the concern that
disrespect should not be shown to the mysteries of the
Passion, and witnesses' responses tended to concentrate on
this issue, rather than the more detailed complaints about
the organisation and conduct of the processions. The opponents of traditional observances, influenced by the ideas of
the French Enlightenment, added these Holy Week observances to their list of 'backward' Spanish customs, along with
bullfights. The seriousness and concern of the 'enlightened'
clergy are well represented by the reply of one priest, José
de Lara y Torre, to the fifth question, which concerned
women's parts being played by men in the Passion represen-
tations. He focused on the fundamental question of whether
the processed *pasos* (dramatic tableaux) in reality assisted
the devotion of Christians to the sacred images of Jesus of
Nazareth, Our Lady of Sorrows and Our Lady of Solitude,
and roundly asserted that they did not. In his opinion:

> ...by the *pasos* those most holy days are profaned, with many offences
> committed against Jesus Christ and His Most Holy Mother, because
> in the years when there are *pasos* [evidently the processions were not
> annual], confessions and communions on Maundy Thursday are very
> rare, because while the *pasos* are being performed, Jesus in the Blessed
> Sacrament remains alone in the church.

Father de Lara had learnt about the goings-on in Benamejí
while acting as procurator fiscal for the regional Church
court (*Audiencia eclesiástica*). In that capacity, he had been

into the town's parish church and had observed 'many irreverences' by the soldiers who escorted the *pasos*, these including keeping their hats on in church, taking their boots off and even sleeping there. It should be noted that these were not 'atheist' French revolutionary forces but Spanish troops. This hostile witness confirmed in detail that men were indeed dressed as female New Testament characters and that, in a manner which had been common in the English 'mystery' plays before the Reformation, some actors played their parts for laughs. The characters involved included Barabbas, the future evangelist Mark, and Simon of Cyrene, and the priest's complaint about the bad taste and irreverence involved may well seem to many to be justified. There also seems to have been a general concern among the witnesses about the destination of the charitable offerings made during Holy Week, the suspicion being that they ended up in the pocket of the local parish priest.

As far as the official investigation was concerned, once the witnesses had responded to the questionnaire, the vicar, Aguilar y Luque, temporarily suspended the process while he gained the support of royal officials, resuming it on 27 July 1795. Given the gritty determination of Spanish royal and ecclesiastical administrators, even on the eve of the French invasion, the result was inevitable. Passive resistance in Benamejí, involving the parish priest and the head of the local administration, the *corregidor*, proved fruitless. The *pasos* were banned and, just to make sure, the script of the play about the death and resurrection of Christ was confiscated by the authorities. The triumphant, not to say triumphalist, statement of the Council of the Military Orders at the end of the case vividly illustrates the 'enlightened' view held by the authorities of the 'popular' devotion of the period. In the view of the councillors, the ending of the *pasos* at Benamejí represented the victory of:

...the spiritual cult over the ruins of superstition. The majestic ceremonies of the temple [parish church] are more spiritual, more sublime and more worthy of Reason than the *pasos*, with which we succeed in fooling the simple people.

[...] The frequency of the sacraments, attendance at church, common prayer at home, the visiting of places of mercy [shrines and sanctuaries], zeal for works of mercy [charity], modesty of dress, attendance at the sacred mysteries [Mass], the sanctification of souls, respect for the laws of the Church.[...] The observance of the holy mysteries which are respectable in their origin, for the faith of all the ages, for the piety of all the just, and for the rules of Religion. [...] An internal, fervent, unanimous devotion, which manifests itself in the intelligible exercises of the holy temple, consoling itself with these mutual signs of faith and of religion, offering all together to the Lord a sacrifice of praises with hymns and spiritual songs. [12]

This remarkable passage succeeds in expressing, with one breath, the spirit of the Reformation as well as the Counter-Reformation, of the idealistic French Revolution as well as the Enlightenment of the *ancien régime*. The words of Charles IV's Council of the Orders would undoubtedly have reeked of heresy in the nostrils of Inquisitors General such as Manrique, Valdés and many of their successors. The Spanish Church had evidently changed and the Inquisition would have to adjust.

A good example of the characteristics and tensions of senior clerical bodies of the period is the chapter of Benamejí's cathedral city, Córdoba, which must have had at least an indirect effect on the dispute over Passion observances which has been discussed. Among the canons of Córdoba as elsewhere, the first ten years of the reign of Charles IV saw the beginnings of an explicit conflict between reforming ('liberal') and conservative tendencies which would take over Spanish society completely once the

French were expelled and the king's son, Ferdinand VII, was restored in 1814. The growth of French influence, especially after the invasion of 1808 which led to the imposition of Joseph Bonaparte on the throne of Spain, had begun in the reign of Charles III, and supporters on the Córdoba chapter of the reforming views of the period before 1788 would turn out to be the readiest to welcome the Bonapartist regime. They were, however, a minority in a body which was generally characterised by quiet conservatism. The energy and activity of this small group of reforming canons did, however, compensate for their lack of numbers. They were monarchists and naturally they were strongly opposed to the ideological extremes of the French Revolution. Yet they, and their number included the dean, the senior teaching canon (*canónigo doctoral*) and the canon penitentiary, seem to have co-operated remarkably easily with the French occupiers of the city, and this unexpected attitude may well have been due to concealed intellectual sympathy. Most of the clergy, though, both in the cathedral and in the diocese of Córdoba as a whole, were traditionalist supporters of the Bourbon monarchy, who deplored both the French invaders and the increasingly strident and influential Spanish liberals. During the reigns of Charles IV and his son Ferdinand VII, the Córdoba Cathedral chapter, like other Spanish ecclesiastical institutions, employed much of its energy in an increasingly unsuccessful defence of its economic assets and social influence. In addition, though, many of the canons and other senior clergy, influenced by the reforming ideas of the eighteenth century, viewed popular manifestations of religious devotion, such as Holy Week processions and visits to shrines, as highly suspect and of dubious Christian value. Thus the power of Catholicism as a unifying factor in the nation began to diminish, not only because of secular attacks on the Church but also because of activity by the clergy themselves.[13] How, though, was the Inquisition able to function in this new environment?

One example of the work of a local tribunal is that of Córdoba which, like its equivalents in other cities, had to endure the succeeding crises of French invasion and its own abolition in 1809, restoration in 1814, a second abolition in 1820–21, another restoration three years later, and final abolition in 1834. In these turbulent times, the archives of the Inquisition, both nationally and locally, suffered severely, but it is nonetheless possible to gain just a glimpse of the activity of Córdoba's inquisitors, in the last years of what was the second tribunal to have been established, back in 1480. The first example vividly illustrates the contrast between the initial violent assault on the Jewish *conversos*, in the late fifteenth and early sixteenth centuries, and the matters which preoccupied the Inquisition in the early 1800s. On 15 January 1805, the inquisitors, Dr Juan de Vargas, Dr Miguel Celestino de la Madrid and Dr Ramón Pineda y Arellano, issued a report on the theft of oranges from the gardens of the Alcázar of Córdoba, which had been the headquarters of the tribunal since it began work in 1482. The tenant of the gardens, Juan Josef Nieto, reported that during the night of 14 January some 'aggressors' had jumped over the wall, entered the castle orchard and garden, and stolen a large quantity of oranges and other fruit and vegetables. The remaining traces of their activity indicated the thieves' method of entry, and indeed they had evidently picked so many oranges that some of them had to be left behind. Nieto asked the inquisitors to act and they duly did so, instructing their secretary and porter, Josef Merlo, to visit the site and to detain and interrogate any suspect persons. That morning, 15 January, the two officials duly inspected the scene and reported back to the inquisitors that they had identified a particular house as the point of entry to the castle gardens. They duly interrogated the housewife (*casera*), one Barbara Segovia, wife of Pedro Chacón, who was absent at the time, having noted that the house contained far more fresh oranges than one household could consume. Barbara was duly sworn and interrogated by the inquisitors, as were four other local inhabitants. After this, on 25 January 1805, the three inquisitors sat in 'morning audience' and declared that, as a result of their inquiries earlier in the month, they had decided that those guilty of the theft were Juan Saucedo and Antonio Márquez. The two men were ordered to give Nieto sixty-four *reales* in compensation, and also pay the costs of the investigation. In addition, Barbara Segovia was formally instructed to ensure that her house should not in future be used as a route for thieves. One wonders whether Torquemada or Lucero would have troubled themselves so formally with such a matter.

After the restoration of the monarchy and the Inquisition, an effort was made to rectify accounts concerning the period of French occupation. On 31 October 1814, four former officials of the Córdoba tribunal, the 'secret sec-retaries' (*secretarios del secreto*) Fernando Calvo and Ignacio Bonrostro, the treasurer and receiver of confiscated goods, Diego Negrete y Arias, and the accountant, Baltasar Vázquez y Saravia, petitioned the Suprema to be compensated for their losses during the suspension of the tribunal. In the process they gave a valuable insight into conditions during the French 'domination', as they described it. They stated that, in that period, 'they saw themselves persecuted by their Government [that of the French and their puppet king Joseph Bonaparte] and in the greatest misery, for having remained loyal, not wanting to accept the postings and jobs to which they were repeatedly named and invited'. The four officials claimed to have received the personal support of the people of Córdoba during the 'Movimiento Popular' of 9–10 May 1814, which overthrew the liberal government with which the restored Ferdinand VII at first ruled after the defeat of Joseph Bonaparte and the French:

> [...] they merited being called and conducted by the People to the Town Hall [*Casas de Ayuntamiento*] to be put in possession of their posts, with the exclusion of other ministers [servants of the Inquisition] who had notoriously been supporters of the intruding government [of King Joseph Bonaparte], from whom [the latter] received commissions for the suppression of convents and sale of their goods, apart from other odious charges, and had facilitated the subsistence of the armies, for which they were generally regarded with the utmost execration.

The four reported that, when the Inquisition was restored in Córdoba on 13 August 1814 they had been treated with 'honour and deference', while the pro-French officials had initially been removed from their posts. But they had appealed, and the inquisitors had allowed them to remain, 'without that delicate examination which the former circumstances demanded'. At this stage, all the Inquisition staff, both pro-French and loyalist, were awaiting the implementation of the political 'purification', which had been ordered by Ferdinand VII on 30 June of that year. The Córdoba inquisitors, though, appeared to be satisfied when it came to the matter of compensation if officials had remained in the tribunal's area of jurisdiction during the French occupation. They took no interest in what the individuals concerned had actually been doing during that time. In the view of the petitioners, speaking as self-proclaimed loyalists, the pro-French (*afrancesado*) officials should be removed from office, like their equivalents in 'other branches [of government] of lesser esteem', to avoid 'scandal among the people and paralysing the service of the Inquisition'. Calvo, Bonrostro, Negrete and Vázquez claimed not be seeking sanctions on their political opponents in the Inquisition, but rather compensation for their own self-sacrifice in refusing offers of employment from the 'intruding Government' of King Joseph.[14]

Unfortunately, as is so often the case with Inquisition records from earlier periods, the outcome of this petition is not known. However, there is evidence from the following year that the Córdoba tribunal did at least attempt to resume its activities in the traditional manner. Thus on 28 April 1815, the two inquisitors, Dr Joseph [sic] Casal and Dr Francisco Peláez Campomanes, responded to the general order of 7 April for the edict of grace which had been issued by the new Inquisitor General, Francisco Javier Mier y Campillo, Bishop of Almería, to be published within their jurisdiction. The edict targeted those guilty of 'heresy or [other matters] within the cognizance of the Holy Office', and had been published on Sunday 23 April in the Mezquita-Catedral of Córdoba, in the collegiate church of San Hipólito and in all other parish churches and convents in the city. It was subsequently being circulated throughout the diocese and in the neighbouring kingdom of Jaén.[15] How, though, did the Cordoban tribunal function during the years before its second abolition by a new liberal government in 1820–21?

Some additional evidence comes from 1819, by which time there was a new Inquisitor General, in fact the last, Jerónimo Castellón y Salas, Bishop of Tarazona, an apparently colourless character who held the office from 1818 until the final abolition of the Spanish Inquisition in 1834.[16] On 20 September of that year, Casal and Peláez, as inquisitors of Córdoba, referred to the Suprema, for their decision on censorship, a 'romance' in which 'there is reference to what some Jews did using certain sacred rites, and the story and unfortunate death of a young girl for having sworn falsely'. Possibly the Jewish reference was to the ancient accusation, already well established in the time of Torquemada, the first

Inquisitor General, that Jews murdered Christian children and put them to torment, in order to extract their blood for use in the making of Passover matzos. In any case, the last Cordoban inquisitors appear to have been engaged in fairly trivial pursuits. None the less, they also concerned themselves with political censorship, on the same day referring to the Suprema a recently-published history of the 'Spanish revolution', meaning the recent war against the French.[17] At the same time, Casal and Peláez had returned to the initial business of the Inquisition, which had been to prepare cases of convicted heretics for sentence and *auto de fe*. On 30 October 1819, the two inquisitors despatched to Madrid seven sheets of paper containing accounts of the cases (*relaciones de causas de fe*) pending in Córdoba. The cases had been drawn up by the prosecutor of the tribunal in accordance with an order from the Suprema dated 25 September 1819. There was a backlog because 'the old verdicts (*acordadas antiguas*) were destroyed in the past revolution'. The document in question does survive, however, being dated 30 October and drawn up by the licentiate Marcelino Mayoral de la Cueva.

No fewer than fifty-two individuals were indicted, and one case is strongly reminiscent of the campaign against *Alumbrados* which was led by Inquisitor General Manrique in the early sixteenth century. The first name on the list was that of Francisca de Paula Cavallero, from Lucena to the south of Córdoba, who had first been tried in June 1817 by the Seville Inquisition, under the presidency of the senior inquisitor there, a Carmelite friar from San Fernando near Cádiz, named Gregorio de San José. Francisca was suspected of suffering spiritual 'delusions', this being a somewhat amorphous charge which led to her being transferred to Córdoba, where the relevant tribunal had jurisdiction over her home town. The prisoner was despatched to the cells of the Alcázar, from which so many had gone to death by burning in previous centuries. In these late stages of the Inquisition's existence, though, local inquisitors seem to have had little self-confidence, referring this comparatively minor case to the Suprema. The result was an exchange of bureaucratic documents, but no *auto* took place before the second abolition of the Inquisition in 1821. Nevertheless, the 1819 *relación* contains in addition the names of two priests from the parish church of Lucena, and others held complicit in Francisca's supposed offences, including her sister María Dominga, a Dominican priest in the town, and the guardian of the convent of the order of San Pedro de Alcántara in nearby Puente Don Gonzalo. Also accused as followers of the supposed *ilusionada* were various other clergy and laymen and women of the town, including the local military commander, Brigadier Don Antonio Ortiz Repiso. The echoes of the sixteenth- and seventeenth-century *Alumbrado* trials are powerful, but others were also caught by the Inquisition's net, apparently for the last time, in the case of Córdoba. Most were accused of holding and uttering unorthodox views, which were referred to as *proposiciones* and, in the traditional manner, unspecified in the *relaciones de causas*. Some friars, however, were accused of the equally traditional offence of improper behaviour of a sexual nature towards penitents in the confessional.[18] It is likely, though, that the 'propositions' referred to in the Cordoban inquisitors' report were the openly atheistic ideas of the Enlightenment and French Revolution.

This suggestion may be tested by reference to the Court Inquisition in Madrid (*El Tribunal de la Corte*), which was naturally more central than that of Córdoba to national events in this disturbed period of Spanish history. Until the early seventeenth century, inquisitorial affairs in Madrid, which was a relatively unimportant town until it became

Spain's capital in 1561, were handled by the tribunal in Toledo. In 1620, though, a special tribunal was set up at the increasingly sedentary court. From 1650, the Madrid inquisitors had their own headquarters, complete with cells, in the present-day Calle Isabel la Católica, while public *autos de fe* were also held centrally, the smaller ones (*autillos*) in the Dominican church of Santo Domingo el Grande, and the major ceremonies in the Plaza Mayor. As was customary elsewhere, burnings took place in the outskirts of the then comparatively small town, outside either the Puerta de Fuencarral or the Puerta de Alcalá. It is clear that by 1800 there were very few prisoners in the cells of the Madrid Inquisition and, as in Córdoba, the main business was with spoken 'propositions', or heterodox views, and the censorship of books. This was apparently the general picture in the country, as in 1806 the largest number of prisoners recorded in any gaol of the Spanish Inquisition was fourteen in Palma, Majorca. Madrid, though, had only one, increasing to three in the latter part of the reign of King Joseph. The individuals in question were a chaplain to a gypsy confraternity, a surgeon, and the unfortunate Pedro Selva, who apparently just 'talked too much'! Things changed, however, both locally and nationally, when Ferdinand was restored to the throne in 1814. Immediately, there was an assault on freemasons, whose influence in Spain had grown greatly in the late eighteenth century, and particularly after the French invasion of 1808.

The Madrid tribunal had begun trials of supposed freemasons, at the rate of about five a year, in the 1750s and 1760s. This effort had declined in the latter years of Charles III's reign, but increased again in the 1790s and, once restored in 1814, the court Inquisition had launched up to ten trials a year. Between then and the second abolition of the

Inquisition, there were twenty-three such trials, involving fourteen Spaniards, six Frenchmen, a Fleming, an Italian and a Swiss: among them were three priests and one religious. In nearly all cases the verdict is unknown, but in the others the defendants were simply cautioned, and the Inquisition cells would remain empty until they were 'opened' by the Liberals in 1820. There had been a Masonic lodge in Madrid since 1724, when one was founded by an Englishman, the Duke of Wharton, but interest grew rapidly after 1808, when a new lodge was established by the French general Joachim Murat, and at least six more were soon added. Such was the expansion of freemasonry in the capital at this time that Blázquez Miguel estimates the total number of lodges in existence there by 1814 at over seventy. The restored Ferdinand VII immediately set out to ban such activity, however, and as well as issuing royal legislation he naturally turned to the Inquisition for enforcement. It quickly emerged, though, that even the Holy Office itself had been infiltrated by libertarian and secular French masonry. Sensationally, Vicente Perdiguero, a commissioner of the Toledo tribunal, confessed that he had become a mason, against the blanket prohibition of such an action by Roman Catholics which had been first issued by Clement XII in 1738 and renewed by Pius VII as recently as 1814. In 1815, the parish priest of the main church in Almagro was denounced as a mason, the lodge there being strong during the French occupation. Although the accused, Tomás Hornero, fled to Madrid, he was arrested there and cautioned like the rest of those accused of this offence. Even more sensationally, the then bishop of Havana, in Cuba, was denounced as a mason and the Madrid inquisitors dealt with the case, though they came to no definite conclusion. In the country as a whole, 103 individuals are known to have been tried by the Inquisition for this offence, about half of them foreigners, a caution being the usual outcome.[19]

Atheism and freemasonry were not the only ideas to be imported to Spain from France in this revolutionary period. A lesser-known but nonetheless well-documented facet of the work of the Madrid Inquisition was an investigation of the ideas on 'animal magnetism' advanced by the German doctor Franz Mesmer, whose influence in France had begun before the Revolution and remained strong during the Napoleonic regime, including the court of Spain both before and after the Restoration. A collection of trial documents from 1815 to 1818 which survives in the British Library outlines some cases which were investigated but, as in the case of freemasonry, the result was no more than a caution. The file also contains a printed work by licentiate Ignacio Graells, a doctor from Carabanchel, which was then just outside Madrid, entitled *News of magnetism and of its portentous effects on the animal economy* and published in Madrid in 1818. Graells takes a sceptical approach, which was clearly sympathetic to the inquisitors, who suspected in the ideas of Mesmer a heretical attempt to interfere with God's providential plans for Nature. The Spanish doctor states that most of the medical profession had rejected Mesmer's belief in the power of magnetism over humans and animals, but adds that it still had considerable power in both Prussia and France, as well as Spain. According to this account, the theory had only recently arrived in Spain and was taking the court, in particular, by storm, despite the fact that a French royal commission, set up in 1784 by Louis XVI, had totally condemned it. Graells explains that Mesmer was convinced that all human beings act as magnets, and that the use of the force they thus possessed could cure ailments such as rheumatic and other bodily pains, as well as epilepsy. The trials of 'Mesmerists' by the Madrid Inquisition started on 12 September 1815, ended on 17 February 1818, and involved a wide range of people, including men and women, clergy and laypeople, courtiers and state officials. The documents reveal that as the nineteenth century began the last inquisitors collected professional medical evidence and opinions in order to assess the apparent threat of Mesmer's techniques to the traditional Christian view of Nature and Providence. How things had changed since Torquemada and his colleagues started their assault on 'Judaising' Christians in the Spain of Ferdinand and Isabella.[20]

The last, traumatic years of the Spanish Inquisition are illustrated by the well-studied history of the tribunal in Valencia, which had been controversially refounded by Ferdinand the Catholic in 1484. In this eastern city, there had been signs of increasing intellectual freedom in the latter years of the reign of Charles III, and it is interesting to note that when an effort was finally made under his successor, in May 1792, to remove 'forbidden books' from libraries there, the initiative came not from the Inquisition but from Valencia's archbishop, Francisco Fabián y Fuero. The archbishop clearly intended to defy the policy of the then Inquisitor General, Agustín Rubín de Ceballos, which was to allow such works to be read by selected individuals under licence, without bans or burnings. From this time onwards, the Inquisition increasingly became the whipping-boy for both conservatives and liberals, though the main cause of its downfall was probably the fiscal crisis which hit the government of Charles IV between 1795 and 1808. One consequence of this was the decision in 1797 to sell off entailed property belonging to a number of public institutions, including the Holy Office. Thus the Valencia tribunal, together with its equivalents in other cities, was already losing its wealth, and hence its status, some years before the French invasion of 1808. As in other cases, this tribunal also had difficulty in functioning after its restoration in 1814, and throughout the succeeding six years before its second abolition it continued to experience severe financial difficulties, not least at the hands of rapacious royal officials. What is striking is the way in which the Inquisition, both in Valencia and nationally, reversed its position during the War of Independence (Peninsular War) of 1808–14, abandoning efforts to accommodate itself to the reforming ideas of the Enlightenment and instead joining the traditionalist battle against 'liberalism'.[21] Thus the Inquisition's traditional role as censor of faith and morals moved into politics, but it is now time to introduce the strongest character to emerge among the officials of the Inquisition, probably, for two centuries at least – Juan Antonio Llorente.

Known to his enemies in his own day as the 'cursed' Spaniard, and characterised by García Cárcel and Moreno Martínez as the man who destroyed the Inquisition from within, Llorente was born in Calahorra, of minor noble (*hidalgo*) stock, on 30 March 1756. As an orphan he was poor but showed exceptional academic ability, thus becoming a bachelor of laws at Zaragoza University, being ordained as a priest, and practising as an advocate in canon law. Initially, he had high ambitions in the normal secular clergy, but his hopes of becoming a cathedral canon and diocesan fiscal in Calahorra were frustrated, and instead he entered the employ of the Inquisition at nearby Logroño, as a commissioner (*comisario*). It should be added that he had previously shown a more worldly interest by writing libretti for the Spanish genre of romantic light opera known as *zarzuela*. His main passion, though, as a young man, seems to have been the study and writing of legal history, and he carried out various paid commissions in this field. In 1788 he went to Madrid, where the then Inquisitor General, Rubín de Ceballos, appointed him to the influential post of secretary to the court Inquisition. At this point the provincial boy's life began to correspond more closely to his ambition. He quickly became involved in Charles IV's court, and in 1790 obtained his coveted canonry of Calahorra without, of course, having to return to his home town to reside in it. He was frustrated in his aim of becoming archdeacon of Tortosa, but at this stage he was, to all appearances, pursuing the traditional career of a courtesan cleric, which the fifteenth-century Pope Alexander VI Borja would have perfectly understood. His life, and the history of the Inquisition, would however be changed when in 1793 the Inquisitor General, now Abad y La Sierra, commissioned him to produce a project, no doubt in the spirit of the Enlightenment, for the reform of the Holy Office, particularly in the matter of the censorship of books. Although the plan was frustrated, it did enable Llorente to cement relations with Charles IV's favourite, Manuel Godoy.

Meanwhile, the Inquisition secretary continued to supplement his income by writing historical works on commission. In 1796, for example, he wrote a piece to justify the removal of the historic tax exemptions of the Basques, but he now sought promotion in the Inquisition itself. In 1795, he had failed to obtain the post of inquisitor of Granada, but instead wrote his first historical work on the Holy Office, which was completed, but not published, in 1798 under the title *Discourses on the order of procedure in the tribunals of the Inquisition*. In it he outlined the history of the Inquisition and the reasoning behind its development, but already he was doing this only with a view to the institution's reform. Llorente presented the manuscript to Godoy, but it did not receive the positive reaction which he expected. At the time, the fall of Jovellanos as a minister forced the reformers into retreat and the inquisitorial secretary of Madrid suffered with the rest, despite the patronage and protection of the Duchess of Montijo. In 1801, Llorente was banished from the court to San Antonio de la Cabrera, north of Madrid, only returning four years later. In 1806, Charles IV paid him the singular honour of eleveating him to a canonry of Toledo but in April and May of 1808 he accompanied the king and his son Ferdinand to the meeting with Napoleon in Bayonne, and quickly declared his allegiance to the new puppet king, Joseph Bonaparte. Llorente's pro-French sentiments were now revealed for all to see.

Thus, when the Inquisition was first abolished in 1809 King Joseph entrusted to him all the available archives, 'with the object of writing the history of the Inquisition of Spain, in conformity with what results originally from the preserved documents'. At this time, Llorente was also appointed as director general of National Property, apostolic commissioner general for the Bull of the Holy Crusade, and as a full member (*académico*) of the Royal Academy of History. It was in this institution that he read and published, in 1811, his *Historical memorandum on what has been the national opinion in Spain concerning the Tribunal of the Inquisition*. A year earlier, Llorente had also been elected to the Royal Spanish Academy (concerned with the Spanish language and literature) and presented to this body the first volume of his *Annals of the Inquisition of Spain*, the second volume being published in 1812. A year later, though, the author of these works fled with his royal master to France, taking with him a large quantity of the Inquisition's archives. At this stage his work was about to gain international fame, and much infamy within Spain itself.[22] Although he would eventually return to Spain, during the period of liberal government after 1821, dying in Madrid in 1823, Llorente's most famous work, the *Critical history of the Inquisition in Spain*, was first published in Paris, in French, in 1817–18. Its four volumes, which now exist in a modern Spanish edition, use to good effect the author's privileged access to archival material.

Llorente begins with a consideration of the treatment by the western Church of 'heresy' before the introduction of specialised tribunals by Gregory XIII in the 1230s. Thus, unlike many modern scholars of the Spanish Inquisition, he placed the institution in its proper international historical context, going on to survey the earlier papal Inquisition as well as its successor, founded in 1478 and finally to be abolished in 1834. The author supplied copies of original documents to support his text, and to justify his fierce criticism of the Inquisition's denial of freedom of religion and conscience. The modern historiography of the Inquisition was born.[23]

Epilogue

The death of the Spanish Inquisition, as an institution though not in memory, went through several steps and reversals between 1808 and 1834. In December 1808, with his brother Joseph transferred from Naples and placed upon the Spanish throne, Napoleon ordered the abolition of the Holy Office along with other institutions in Spain which he regarded as relics of 'feudalism' – seignorial jurisdiction, the historic Council of Castile which dated back to the Middle Ages, and two-thirds of the country's monasteries and convents.[1] While Spanish traditionalists and patriots of a conservative disposition resented and tried to resist these drastic changes, and supporters of French ideas (the *afrancesados*) aided the new regime, those loyal to the monarchy of Ferdinand VII formed a central committee

(*Junta central*) to act as a continuing Spanish government and co-ordinate resistance. This failed, however, in the face of increasingly vigorous French military intervention, and at the end of 1809 it summoned a new, single-chamber parliament (*Cortes*) which was to gather in Cádiz, at the southern tip of largely loyalist Andalusia, on 1 March of the following year. This assembly had the potential to replace the now-collapsed *Junta Central*, and indeed it held wide-ranging and bitterly-fought debates concerning the future of Spain itself and of its increasingly rebellious colonies. In the event, the Liberal ascendency in the Cortes failed lamentably in its attempt to retain control in America, but as far as Spain itself was concerned, the so-called 'Constitution of Cádiz', promulgated on 19 March 1812, outlined a radical programme for the dismemberment and re-organisation of large tracts of Spanish society. Among these was, inevitably, the Inquisition.[2]

The attack on this venerable, but now highly controversial, institution formed part of the policy of expropriation known in Spanish as *desamortización*. This had an ideological base, in that it was aimed at the destruction of the most powerful vested interests in Spain, but it also had the immediate and pragmatic purpose of liberating funds for the resistance which its proponents hoped would shortly lead, with British military assistance, to the removal of the French Bonapartist regime. In this enterprise, at least, Conservatives and Liberals might combine, but the question of the future of the Inquisition would none the less cause fierce conflict, and help to create deep divisions in Spanish society which would far outlast the expulsion of the French in 1814. Inevitably, the Cortes of Cádiz debated the matter and eventually, in January 1813, enacted its conclusions. Three position papers on the subject had previously been submitted to this assembly, one of them resulting from the deliberations of a committee headed by the noted Liberal politician Agustín Argüelles, and the others by two priests with Liberal sympathies, Antonio Ruiz de Padrón and Joaquín Lorenzo Villanueva. All three gave prominence to the case of Archbishop Bartolomé Carranza in the sixteenth century (see Chapter 4). Ruiz del Padrón, a secular priest and deputy for the Canary islands to the Cortes of Cádiz, had formerly been a Franciscan friar, and claimed that his hostility towards the Inquisition arose from conversations he had had in Philadelphia in 1784, with Benjamin Franklin and George Washington, among others. He composed the final paper (*dictamen*) which was presented to the Cortes, with a long speech by its author, before the vote on the Inquisition was taken. Ruiz del Padrón listed the 'wise and learned men whom the Tribunal [of the Holy Office] has sacrificed to its fury'. He particularly castigated the inquisitors for their treatment of Carranza, but his general point was that the Inquisition had for centuries been the enemy of Christian virtue as well as freedom.[3] Villanueva adopted a more scholarly and dispassionate approach in his memorandum to the Cortes. Like Juan Antonio Llorente, he had been personally involved with the Inquisition, acting, from his position at Salamanca University, as a theological adviser and assessor (*calificador*) to the tribunal. He represented Valencia at the Cortes (having been born in Játiva) and argued for the abolition of the Holy Office on grounds of its illiberal attitudes and behaviour and its obstruction of necessary Catholic reform in his own day, just as it had suppressed the reforms attempted by Carranza and others in the sixteenth century. Yet the perception of the Inquisition held by Liberals, both lay and clerical, certainly did not go unchallenged. In 1814, in distant Mexico City where events in Spain were being closely followed, a 'discalced' Carmelite friar, José de San Bartolomé, composed a treatise entitled

Act of mourning for the Inquisition in which he denounced the verdict of the Cortes of Cádiz on the Holy Office. The friar condemned the work on the subject by Ruiz del Padrón and Villanueva, rejecting their list of notable victims, and in particular the supposed injustice done to Carranza, and describing them as '*anti-inquisicionales*'.[4]

Events in Spain in 1814 appeared to vindicate the approach of Friar José rather than that of the opponents of the Inquisition. During 1813, as a result of British military action led by the Duke of Wellington together with Spanish rebellion, the French position declined to such an extent that, by the end of the year, Joseph Bonaparte's 'kingdom' effectively consisted only of Catalonia. In these circumstances, it was possible for Ferdinand VII to make a comeback and thus, on 24 March 1814, he crossed the frontier from Catalonia, having already returned from effective captivity in France, and began the process of reclaiming his throne. He was met by conflicting and often irreconcileable expectations among his subjects, and these affected both the Church in general and the Inquisition in particular. In this case, the concept of 'restoration' was applied and a new Inquisitor General, Castellón y Salas, was appointed. But the institution, despite the local initiatives, including those of the court Inquisition in Madrid which have already been noted, never recovered anything approaching its earlier vigour, and the 1820 Liberal 'revolution' led to another attempt to end for good the Spanish Crown's lengthy experiment in testing and attempting to enforce religious orthodoxy. As in the case of other policies adopted by the incoming Liberal administration, the second 'abolition' of the Inquisition was undertaken on the basis of the decision made by the Cortes of Cádiz in 1813. It proved to be temporary, though, because conservative forces, both civil and military (and indeed the king himself), did not accept the new political orientation of the country, and worked to undermine the new government. In any case, there was also conflict within the ranks of the reformers, which even the return of large numbers of French troops to Spain, beginning in April 1823, did not succeed in quelling. Finally, all the Liberal strongholds in the country, including Cádiz, fell to conservative forces, and the reform experiment was placed on hold. Not only was the Inquisition restored, together with the 'purity of blood' statutes which had traditionally controlled entry to so many Spanish institutions, but a new process of political 'purification' was introduced, with the aim of purging Liberal supporters from large areas of public life.[5] The definitive end of the Inquisition was, however, merely being postponed, and it showed little or no life between its second restoration in 1824 and the issue of what proved to be the final edict of abolition, on 15 July 1834.

One thing is striking to anyone who studies the personalities of leading inquisitors over the period from 1478 to the nineteenth century. This is that the 'great characters' are all to be found in the earlier centuries. The 'typical' inquisitor was a lawyer rather than a theologian, a bureaucrat rather than an ideologue, though this did not prevent the development of the 'invented' inquisition of art and fiction.[6] One final point remains to be made. Just as the inquisitors largely failed to enter the minds of their prisoners, so it is effectively impossible for the scholar to penetrate theirs. Clearly, some very able Spaniards, who regarded themselves as devout Catholic Christians, felt that they were serving both God and their king by exercising, with varying degrees of vigour, the draconian powers of life and death which were granted to them. The reasons why each of them, individually, did so remain locked in the heart of *El Señor Inquisidor*.

Notes

INTRODUCTION

1   Caro Baroja ([1968] 1997), p.9.
2   Edwards (2003).

CHAPTER ONE: TOMÁS DE TORQUEMADA

1   Cross and Livingstone (1997): 1633; Sabatini (2001): 66-67; Sánchez
     Rivilla (2000): 276.
2   Cross and Livingstone (1997): 1632; Torquemada (2002): 87-
     121.
3   Pulgar (1971): 57.
4   Sicroff (1985).
5   Martínez Díez (1998): 92-95.
6   Ibid.: 158-59.
7   Ibid.: 160-61.
8   Ibid.: 168-71.

9   Pérez (2002): 90.
10   Llorente (1980): vol. 1, 219.
11   García Cárcel and Moreno Martínez (2000): 35.
12   Sabatini (2001): 66.
13   Meseguer Fernández (1984): 310.
14   Rodríguez Berné (2000): 4-48.
15   Martínez Díez (1998): 158-59.
16   Kamen (1997): 50-56; Edwards (1996c).
17   Torquemada (2002): 87-239.
18   Azcona (1993): 497-500, 508-09; Kamen (1997): 44-46.
19   Eymerich (1973).
20   Llorente (1980): vol. 1, 145-52; Sabatini (2001): 93-116.
21   Llorente (1980): vol. 1, 173-85.
22   Beinart (1980); Beinart (1981); Coronas Tejada (1988); Gil (2000–03).
23   Beinart (1981): 99, 114, 147, 148, 164.
24   Edwards (1999): 73-88.
25   Llorente (1980): vol. 1, 201-06; Sabatini (2001): 256-70.
26   Edwards (1996a).

CHAPTER TWO: CONFLICT IN THE CHURCH

1   Alcalá and Sanz (1999): 65-67, 175; García Cárcel and Moreno Martínez (2000): 35-36; Sánchez Rivilla (2000): 243-45.
2   Azcona (1993): 604.
3   Martínez Díez (1998): 304-07.
4   Llorente (1980): vol. 1, 255-58; Gil (2000): vol. 1, 210-11.
5   Llorente (1980): vol. 1, 253-54.
6   Martínez Díez (1998): 312-13.
7   Azcona (1993): 947-48.
8   Alcalá and Sanz (1999): 69-70.
9   Martínez Díez (1998): 304-05; 308-13; 328-35.
10   Llorente (1980): vol. 1, 262-68; Gracia Boix (1982): 31-134; Gracia Boix (1983): 6-8; Edwards (1996e); Kamen (1997): 72-74; Martínez Díez (1998): 358-67; Gil (2000): vol. 1, 231-38; García Cárcel and Moreno Martínez (2000): 37-39; Edwards (2000a); Pérez (2002): 108-14.
11   [Delicado] (2000): 177-78.
12   Edwards (2002).
13   Gil (2000): vol. 1, 235-37.

CHAPTER THREE: THE INQUISITION IN CRISIS

1   Rummel (1999): 1-28; Sánchez Rivilla (2000): 280-82; García Oro (2002): 19-168.
2   Martínez Díez (1998): 368-75.
3   Meseguer Fernández (1984): 350-59.
4   García Cárcel and Moreno Martínez (2000): 39-41.
5   Rummel (1999): 30-32.
6   *Ibid.*: 78-94.
7   Gil (2000): vol. 1, 229-85.
8   García Cárcel and Moreno Martínez (2000): 48-49; Cross and Livingstone (1997): 728; Meseguer Fernández (1984): 443; Sánchez Rivilla (2000): 277.
9   García Cárcel and Moreno Martínez (2000): 49-50; Sánchez Rivilla (2000): 253.
10 Llorente (1980): vol. 1, 311-32; García Cárcel and Moreno Martínez (2000): 233-34; Sánchez-Blanco (2000): 695-721.
11 Edwards (2000b): 194-221.
12 Nieto (1997): 83-85.
13 Rummel (1999): 53-65; García Oro (2002): 333-59.
14 Thomas (2001): 13-15.
15 *Ibid.*: 15.
16 Bataillon (1991): 10; Thomas (2001): 17.
17 *Ibid.*: 17.

CHAPTER FOUR: HERESY-HUNTING

1   Bataillon (1991b).
2   Pérez (2002): 131-33.
3   Kinder (1992): 215.
4   Nieto (1997): 84-85.
5   Meseguer (1984): 448, 450.
6   Bataillon (1991a): 254, 257.
7   Homza (2000): 49.
8   Partial facsimile text in Avilés (1980): 17-50.
9   Allen, Allen and Garrod (1906–58): vol. 7, 43-44.
10 Homza (2000): 49-76.
11 Avilés (1984): 448-51.
12 Kinder (1992): 218-19.
13 Homza (2000): 6-13.
14 Selke (1968): 31-32, 71-84; Nieto (1997): 88-90.
15 Homza (2000): 16-45.

16   Homza (2000): 20-21; Avilés (1984): 470-72; Sánchez Rivilla (2000): 253.
17   Wagner (1983): 349-50.
18   Avilés Fernández (1984): 473-74; Sánchez Rivilla (2000): 273-75.
19   González Novalín (1984): 549-50; Sánchez Rivilla (2000): 278-80.
20   González Novalín (1984): 538.
21   *Ibid.*: 544-56.
22   Kinder (1992): 225-29; Thomas (2001): 211-17; Alonso Burgos (1983): 103-16.
23   Tellechea (2004): 25-46; Edwards and Truman (2005).
24   Escudero (2004): 47-68.

CHAPTER FIVE: 'A COVENANT WITH HELL':

1   Henningsen (1983): ix.
2   Caro Baroja (1993): 19-20; García Cárcel and Moreno Martínez (2000): 284.
3   Cited in Caro Baroja (1993): 26.
4   *Ibid.*: 27.
5   *Ibid.*: 29.
6   Caro Baroja (1995): 19-29; García Cárcel and Moreno Martínez (2000): 284-85; Kieckhefer (1989): 194-201; Cohn (1993): 202-17.
7   Edwards (1996d): 17-18.
8   Kamen (1997): 270.
9   *Ibid.*: 269-70.
10   Ciruelo (2003): 20.
11   *Ibid.*: 15-28.
12   Kamen (1997): 273.
13   Sánchez Rivilla (2000): 408; Henningsen (1983): xxvi.
14   Henningsen (1983): ix.
15   *Ibid.*: xxv-xxviii.
16   Henningsen (1983): 6-25; Maxwell-Stuart (2003): 32-57.
17   Henningsen (1983): 27-36, 51, 69-355; Sánchez Rivilla (2000): 269-71, 309, 408.

CHAPTER SIX: CENSORED

1   Kamen (2001): 7-8.
2   Sánchez Rivilla (2000): 249.

3   Lynch (1989): 107.
4   Lynch (1989): 107-08; Kamen (2001): 82.
5   Kamen (2001): 83-84; Macanaz (1714); Vallejo García-Hená (1996): 216-17; Martín Gaite (1999): 29-307.
6   Sánchez Rivilla (2000): 249.
7   Lynch (1989): 108.
8   Macanaz (1735).
9   *Ibid.* (1744).
10   *Ibid.*: fol. 51r.
11   Martín Gaite (1999): 323.
12   *Ibid.*: 321-441.
13   Gracia Boix (1982): 280-83; Gracia Boix (1983): 500-02.
14   *Ibid.*: 503-31.
15   Martínez Millán (2000): 551-656; Torres Arce (2000): 657-93.
16   Gacto Fernández (1999): 31-81.
17   Peters (1989): 122-54; Kamen (1997): 305-20; Moreno [Martínez] (2004).
18   Scio (1824).
19   Martínez Bujando (2000): 773-828; García Cárcel and Martínez Moreno (2000): 316-24.
20   Quoted in García Cárcel and Moreno Martínez (2000): 325.
21   *Ibid.*: 326.
22   *Ibid.*: 224-28.

CHAPTER SEVEN: THE DEATH OF THE HOLY OFFICE

1   Lynch (1989): 375.
2   *Ibid.*: 375-78.
3   García Cárcel and Moreno Martínez (2000): 90-91.
4   Cross and Livingstone (1997): 862.
5   Peters (1989): 169-70.
6   Cited in Truman (2005): 194.
7   *Ibid.*: 194-95.
8   Cuenca Toribio (1990): 27-39.
9   *Ibid.*: 31.
10   *Ibid.*: 31-33.
11   *Ibid.*: 33-36.
12   *Ibid.*: 101-15.
13   García-Cuevas Ventura (1996): 69-72, 207-14.
14   Gracia Boix (1982): 286-92; Esdaile (2000): 40; Sánchez Rivilla (2000): 295.
15   Gracia Boix (1982): 293; Sánchez Rivilla (2000): 256.

16   *Ibid.*: 242, 295.

17   *Ibid.*: 294.

18   *Ibid.*: 294-302.

19   Blázquez Miguel (1990): 14-18, 23, 30, 51-55, 152-58; García Cárcel and Moreno Martínez (2000): 312-16.

20   *Noticias del magnetismo* (1815-18): MS fols 1r-70v, printed tract pp. 1-56 (fols 74r-101r).

21   Haliczer (1990): 346-58; Alcalá (2000): 201-14.

22   García Cárcel and Moreno Martínez (2000): 95-101; Fernández Pardo (2001).

23   Llorente (1980).

EPILOGUE

1   Esdaile (2000): 26-7.

2   *Ibid.*: 24, 31-34.

3   Cited in Truman (2005): 196..

4   *Ibid.*: 196-198.

5   Esdaile (2000): 54-55, 60.

6   Peters (1989); Moreno (2004).

Bibliography

PRIMARY SOURCES

(a) Manuscript

Macanaz, Melchor Rafael de (1744): *Breve compendio con adiciones o notas al Tomo Tercero de la* 'Historia civil de España' [by Fray Nicolás Belando] desde el año de 1713 al de 1733 (British Library Additional MS 15616).

—— (1735 [printed Madrid: Antonio Espinosa, 1788]): *Defensa crítica de la Inquisición contra los principales enemigos que le han perseguido y persiguen injustamente [...]* [= *Historia crítica de don Melchor de Macanaz contra los tres tomos de la* Historia crítica del establecimiento de la Monarquía francesa (by Abbé Die Ros, Paris, 1734)] (British Library Egerton MS 397).

—— (1714): *Representación hecha al Rey a justificación del escrito [...] que produjo el cardenal Judice, Inquisidor General, por edicto de 30 de julio de 1714, publicado en 15 de agosto del mismo año* (British Library Add. MS 28476).

Noticias del magnetismo (1815–18): Original letters, depositions and other papers connected with an enquiry by the Inquisition of Madrid relative to the practice of animal magnetism [...] (British Library Add. MS 33532).

(b) Printed

Allen, P.S., H.M. Allen, H.W. Garrod, eds (1906–58): *Opus epistolarum Desiderii Erasmi Roterodami*, 12 vols (Oxford: Oxford University Press).

Ciruelo, Pedro (2003): *Reprovación de las supersticiones y hechizerías (1538)*, ed. José Luis Herrero Angelino (Salamanca: Diputación de Salamanca).

[Delicado, Francisco] ([1528?] 2000): *Retrato de la Lozana andaluza*, ed. Claude Allaigre, 3rd edn (Madrid: Cátedra).

Eymerich, Nicolau (1973): *Le manuel de l'Inquisiteur*, ed. and trans. Louis Sala-Molins (Paris: Mouton).

Gracia Boix, Rafael (1982): *Colección de documentos para la historia de la Inquisición de Córdoba* (Córdoba: Publicaciones del Monte de Piedad y Caja de Ahorros de Córdoba).

— (1983): *Autos de fe y causas de la Inquisición de Córdoba* (Córdoba: Diputación Provincial de Córdoba).

Martínez Díez, Gonzalo (1998): *Bulario de la Inquisición española, hasta la muerte de Fernando el Católico* (Madrid: Editorial Complutense).

Pulgar, Fernando del (1971): *Claros varones de Castilla*, ed. Robert Brian Tate (Oxford: Clarendon Press).

Scio, Felipe (1824): *La Biblia o el Antiguo y Nuevo Testamento traducido al español de la Vulgata latina por el Rev. P. Phelipe Scio de San Miguel* (London: n.p., 1824).

Torquemada, Juan de (2002): *Tratado contra los madianitas e ismaelitas* (Madrid: Aben Ezra Ediciones) [Study by Juan José Llamedo González, pp. 87-121].

SECONDARY SOURCES

Alcalá, Ángel (2000): 'El control inquisitorial de intelectuales en el Siglo de Oro. De Nebrija al "Índice" de Sotomayor de 1640', in Pérez Villanueva and Escandell Bonet (1984–2000), vol. 3, pp. 829-956.

— (2001): *Literatura y ciencia ante la Inquisición española* (Madrid: Ediciones del Laberinto).

Alcalá, Ángel and Jacobo Sanz (1999): *Vida y muerte del príncipe don Juan Historia y literatura* (Valladolid: Junta de Castilla y León).

Alonso Burgos, Jesús (1983): *El luteranismo en Castilla durante el siglo XVI – autos de fe de Valladolid de 21 de mayo y de 8 de octubre de 1559* (El Escorial: Swan Avantos y Hakeldama).

Avilés Fernández, Miguel (1980): *Erasmo y la Inquisición. El libelo de*

Valladolid y la Apologia de Erasmo contra los frailes españoles (Madrid: Fundación Universitaria Española).

— (1984): 'El Santo Oficio en la primera etapa carolina', in Pérez Villanueva and Escandell Bonet, vol. 1, pp. 443-74.

Bataillon, Marcel (1991): *Erasmo y España. Estudios sobre la historia espiritual*, trans. Antonio Alatorre (Mexico City. Madrid, Buenos Aires: Fondo de Cultura Económica).

Beinart, Haim (1980): *Trujillo. A Jewish community in Extremadura on the eve of the expulsion from Spain* (Jerusalem: The Magnes Press, The Hebrew University).

— (1981): *Conversos on trial. The Inquisition in Ciudad Real* (Jerusalem: The Magnes Press, The Hebrew University).

Blázquez Miguel, Juan (1990): *Madrid: judíos, herejes, brujas. El tribunal de la Corte (1650–1820)* (Toledo: Editorial Arcano).

Caro Baroja, Julio (1993): 'Witchcraft and Catholic theology', in Bengt Ankarloo and Gustav Henningsen, eds, *Early modern European witchcraft: centres and peripheries* (Oxford: Clarendon Press), pp. 19-43.

— ([1968] 1997): *El señor Inquisidor y otras vidas por oficio* (Madrid: Alianza Editorial), pp. 15-63.

Cohn, Norman (1993): *Europe's inner demons. The demonization of Christians in Medieval Christendom*, 2nd edn (London: Pimlico).

Coronas Tejada, Luis (1988): *Conversos and the Inquisition in Jaén* (Jerusalem: The Magnes Press, The Hebrew University).

— (1991): *La Inquisición de Jaén* (Jaén: Diputación Provincial de Jaén).

Cross, F.L. and E.A. Livingstone, eds (1997): *Oxford Dictionary of the Christian Church*, 3rd edn (Oxford: Oxford University Press).

Cuenca Toribio, José Manuel (1980): 'Un conflicto cordobés a propósito de la religiosidad popular', in Cuenca Toribio, *Estudios sobre la Iglesia andaluza moderna y contemporánea* (Córdoba: Instituto de Historia de Andalucía), pp. 99-115.

— (1990): 'El episcopado español ante la revolución Francesa', in Cuenca Toribio, *Estudios sobre el catolicismo español Contemporáneo* (Córdoba: Universidad de Córdoba), pp. 27-39.

Edwards, John (1992): 'Defenders of the Faith: Spanish inquisitors in the reign of Ferdinand and Isabella', *Medieval History*, vol. 2 no. 1, pp. 83-91.

— (1996a): 'Bishop Juan Arias Dávila of Segovia: "Judaizer" or reformer?' in Edwards, John (1996b), no. X.

— (1996b): *Religion and society in Spain, c.1492* (Aldershot: Variorum).

— (1996c): 'Religion, constitutionalism and the Inquisition in Teruel, 1484-85', in Edwards, John (1996b), no. XIII.

— (1996d): 'Religious faith and doubt in late medieval Spain: Soria, *circa* 1450–1500', in Edwards, John (1996b), no. III.

— (1996e): 'Trial of an inquisitor: the dismissal of Diego Rodríguez Lucero, inquisitor of Córdoba, in 1508', in Edwards, John (1996b), no. IX.

— (1999): 'Ritual murder in the Siglo de Oro: Lope de Vega's *El niño inocente de La Guardia*', in *Proceedings of the Tenth British Conference on Judeo-Spanish Studies, 29June–1 July 1997*, ed. Annette Benaim (London: Queen Mary and Westfield College), pp. 73-88.

— (2000a): 'The culture of the street: the Calle de la Feria in Córdoba, 1470–1520', in *Mediterranean urban culture, 1400–1700*, ed. Alexander Cowan (Exeter: Exeter University Press), pp. 69-82.

— (2000b): *The Spain of the Catholic Monarchs, 1474–15120* (Oxford: Blackwell).

— (2002): 'Conversion in Córdoba and Rome: Francisco Delicado's *La Lozana andaluza*', in *Medieval Spain. Culture, conflict and coexistence. Studies in honour of Angus MacKay*, ed. Roger Collins and Anthony Goodman (Basingstoke: Palgrave Macmillan), pp. 202-24.

— (2003): *[The Spanish] Inquisition*, 2nd edn (Stroud: Tempus Publishing).

Edwards, John and Ronald Truman, eds (2005): *Reforming Catholicism in the England of Mary Tudor: the achievement of Fray Bartolomé Carranza* (Aldershot: Ashgate).

Escudero, José Antonio (2004): 'Notas sobre el proceso de Carranza', in Suárez Fernández, ed., pp. 47-68.

Esdaile, Charles J. (2000): *Spain in the Liberal age. From constitution to civil war, 1808–1939* (Oxford: Blackwell).

Fernández Pardo, Francisco (2001): *Juan Antonio Llorente, español 'maldito'* (San Sebastián: n.p.).

Gacto Hernández, Enrique (1999): *Cantabria y la Inquisición en el siglo XVIII* (Santander: Fundación Marcelino Botín).

García Cárcel, Ricardo ([1992] 1998): *La Leyenda Negra. Historia y opinión* (Madrid: Alianza Editorial).

García Cárcel, Ricardo and Doris Moreno Martínez (2000): *Inquisición. Historia crítica* (Madrid: Ediciones Temas de Hoy).

García-Cuevas Ventura, José (1996): *El cabildo catedralicio cordobés desde la revolución a la restauración* (Córdoba: Universidad de Córdoba).

García Oro, José (2002): *Cisneros. El Cardenal de España* (Barcelona: Ariel).

Gil, Juan (2000–03): *Los conversos y la Inquisición sevillana* (Seville: Universidad de Sevilla and Fundación El Monte).

González Novalín, José Luis (1984): 'La época valdesiana. A. El Inquisidor General Don Fernando de Valdés', in Pérez Villanueva and Escandell Bonet, pp. 538-56.

Haliczer, Stephen (1990): *Inquisition and society in the kingdom of Valencia, 1478–1834* (Berkeley: University of California Press).

Henningsen, Gustav (1983): *The witches' advocate. Basque witchcraft and the Spanish Inquisition* (Reno, Nevada: University of Nevada Press).

Homza, Lu Ann (2000): *Religious authority in the Spanish Renaissance* (Baltimore: The Johns Hopkins University Press).

Kamen, Henry (1997): *The Spanish Inquisition. An historical revision*

(London: Weidenfeld and Nicolson).

— (2001): *Philip V of Spain. The king who reigned twice* (New Haven and London: Yale University Press).

Kieckhefer, Richard (1989): *Magic in the Middle Ages* (Cambridge: Cambridge University Press).

Kinder, Gordon (1992): 'Spain', in *The early Reformation in Europe*, ed. Andrew Pettegree (Cambridge: Cambridge University Press), pp. 215-37.

Lea, Henry Charles (1906–07): *A history of the Inquisition of Spain*, 4 vols (New York: The Macmillan Company).

Llorente, Juan Antonio ([1817] 1980): *Historia crítica de la Inquisición española*, 4 vols (Madrid: Hiperión).

Lynch, John (1989): *Bourbon Spain, 1700–1808* (Oxford: Blackwell).

Martín Gaite, Carmen ([1969] 1999): *El proceso de Macanaz. Historia de un Empapelamiento* (Madrid: Espasa Calpe).

Martínez de Bujanda, J. (2000): 'Indices de libros prohibidos del siglo XVI', in Pérez Villanueva and Escandell Bonet (1984–2000), vol. 3, pp. 773-828.

Martínez Millán, José (2000): 'La persecución inquisitorial contra los criptojudíos en el siglo XVIII. El tribunal de Llerena (1700–1730)', in Pérez Villanueva and Escandell Bonet (1984–2000), vol, 3, pp. 557-656.

Maxwell-Stuart, P.G. (2003): *Witch-hunters. Professional prickers, unwitchers and witch finders of the Renaissance* (Stroud: Tempus).

Meseguer Fernández, Juan (1984): 'El período fundacional (1478–1517) (i) 'Los hechos', in Pérez Villanueva and Escandell Bonet (1984–2000), vol. I, pp. 310-43.

Monter, William (1990): *Frontiers of heresy. The Spanish Inquisition from the Basque lands to Sicily* (Cambridge: Cambridge University Press).

Moreno [Martínez], Doris (2004): *La invención de la Inquisición* (Madrid: Marcial Pons Historia).

Netanyahu, B[enzion] ([1995] 2001): *The origins of the Inquisition in fifteenth- century Spain* (New York: New York Review Books [1995] 2001).

Nieto, José C. (1997): *El Renacimiento y la otra España. Visión cultural socioespiritual* (Geneva: Librairie Droz).

Pérez, Joseph (2002): *Crónica de la Inquisición española* (Barcelona: Ediciones Martínez Roca).

Pérez Villanueva, Joaquín and Bartolomé Escandell Bonet, eds (1984–2000): *Historia de la Inquisición en España y América*, 3 vols (Madrid: Biblioteca de Autores Cristianos).

Peters, Edward ([1988] 1989): *Inquisition* (Berkeley and Los Angeles: University of California Press).

Perry, Mary Elizabeth and Anne J. Cruz, eds (1991): *Cultural encounters.*

The impact of the Inquisition in Spain and the New World (Berkeley: University of California Press).

Rawlings, Helen (2002): *Church, religion and society in early modern Spain* (Basingstoke: Palgrave).

Rodríguez Berné, José Ramón (2000): *El Concejo de la Suprema Inquisición. Perfil jurídico de una institución* (Madrid: Editorial Complutense).

Rummel, Erika (1999): *Jiménez de Cisneros. On the threshold of the Spanish Golden Age* (Tempe, Arizona: Center for Medieval and Renaissance Studies).

Sabatini, Rafael ([1913] 2001): *Torquemada and the Spanish Inquisition* (Thirsk: House of Stratus).

Sánchez-Blanco, Rafael Benítez (2000): 'La Inquisición ante los moriscos', in Pérez Villanueva and Escandell Bonet, vol. 3, pp. 695-756.

Sánchez Rivilla, Teresa (2000): 'Inquisidores generales y consejeros de la Suprema: documentación biográfica' in Pérez Villanueva and Escandell Bonet (1984–2000), vol. 3, pp. 228-437.

Selke, Angela (1968): *El Santo Oficio de la Inquisición. Proceso de Fray Francisco Ortiz* (Madrid: Ediciones Guadarrama).

Sicroff, Albert A. (1985): *Los estatutos de limpieza de sangre. Controversias entre los siglos XV y XVII* (Madrid: Taurus).

Starr-Lebeau, Gretchen (2003): *In the shadow of the Virgin. Inquisitors, friars and conversos in Guadalupe, Spain* (Princeton: Princeton University Press).

Suárez Fernández, Luis, ed. (2004): *V centenario del nacimiento del arzobispo Carranza* (Madrid: Real Academia de la Historia).

Tellechea Idígoras, José Ignacio (2004): 'Fray Bartolomé Carranza de Miranda, Arzobispo de Toledo. El hombre y la obra', in Suárez Fernández, ed., pp. 25-46.

Thomas, Werner (2001): *La represión del protestantismo en España, 1517–1648* (Leuven/Louvain: Leuven University Press).

Torres Arce, M. (2000): 'Los judaizantes y el Santo Oficio de Logroño en el reinado de Felipe V', in Pérez Villanueva and Escandell Bonet (1984–2000), vol. 3, pp. 657-93.

Truman, Ronald (2005): 'Pedro Salazar de Mendoza and the first biography of Carranza', in *Reforming Catholicism in the England of Mary Tudor. The achievement of Friar Bartolomé Carranza*, ed. John Edwards and Ronald Truman (Aldershot: Ashgate), pp. 177-203.

Vallejo García-Hená, José (1996): 'Macanaz y su propuesta de reforma del Santo Oficio de 1714', *Revista de la Inquisición*, 5, pp. 187-291.

Wagner, Klaus (1983): 'El arzobispo Alonso Manrique, protector del "erasmismo" y de los reformistas en Sevilla', *Bibliothèque d'Humanisme et Renaissance*, 45, pp. 349-50.

Brief Lives of
Inquisitors General
(1483–1834)

ABAD Y LA SIERRA, MANUEL

Born in Estadilla (Huesca) on 24 December 1729, he studied philosophy and theology at Calatayud, then canon law at Huesca, later becoming Doctor of Canon Law at Irache. A minor canon (*racionero*) of Huesca Cathedral, he joined the Benedictine order at San Juan de la Peña. In 1773 he was elected prior of the monastery of Santa María de Meya (Lleida). In May 1783 he was nominated by Charles III as bishop of the newly-created diocese of Ibiza, taking possession of it six months later. His previous experience in the Benedictine archives led to his election to the Royal Academy of History, with which he collaborated in several projects. After holding various other posts, he was appointed Inquisitor General on the nomination of Charles IV on 21 April

1793, but resigned in 1794, dying in Zaragoza on 12 January 1806. Although brief, his tenure of office was significant in that, while he strongly defended the rights and interests of the institution, he was equally determined to reform it, even being accused of Jansenism, though nothing came of this. Nonetheless, the king's favourite, Manuel Godoy, appears to have required a more compliant figure as Inquisitor General, and hence to have precipitated his resignation. [See Chapter 7]

ARCE, RAMÓN JOSÉ DE

Born in Celaya de Carriedo (Santander) on 25 October 1755, he was a member of the graduate Colegio de San Ildefonso, in the University of Alcalá de Henares, thereafter becoming a teaching canon (*canónigo lectoral*) of Valencia Cathedral. He was nominated as archbishop of Burgos on 18 December 1797, moving to the equivalent post in Zaragoza on 20 July 1801. He was Inquisitor General between 1798 and 1814, and resigned the see of Zaragoza on 15 July 1816. Having adopted a pro-French attitude during this period, he eventually died in Paris, on 16 February 1844. [See Chapter 7]

BELTRÁN, FELIPE

A member of the Royal Council, he was named as bishop of Salamanca on 18 July 1763, later becoming the prelate of the Order of Charles III. He took up the office of Inquisitor General on 5 May 1776, dying in office on 30 November 1783. Not long before his death, he began work on a new 'Index of Forbidden Books', which was continued by his successor, Rubín de Ceballos (see below). [See Chapter 6]

CASTELLÓN Y SALAS, JERÓNIMO

The last Inquisitor General, he became bishop of Tarazona on 10 July 1815, and Inquisitor General on 18 July 1818. He died on 20 April 1835, soon after the final abolition of the Spanish Inquisition. [See Chapter 7]

CISNEROS, FRANCISCO XIMÉNEZ DE

Born in Torrelaguna in 1436, he studied in Roa, Cuéllar and Salamanca, graduating in 1456 and taking charge of the local government of Salamanca, Uceda and Torrelaguna. In 1460–65 he was in Rome, where he obtained from the Pope a 'letter of resignation' which entitled him to the next suitable vacancy in any Spanish diocese. He chose Toledo, and hence took over as archpriest of Uceda. The diocesan, Archbishop Alfonso Carrillo, objected and put him in prison. He became a chaplain and then a canon of Sigüenza, and deputy (*provisor y vicario general*) to the bishop, Pedro González de Mendoza. In 1484, at the unusually advanced age of forty-eight, he professed in Toledo as a Franciscan friar, taking the religious name of Francisco and becoming guardian of the order's convent there, San Juan de los Reyes. He became a confessor to Isabella the Catholic in 1492 and archbishop of Toledo in 1495. A vigorous reformer of Church institutions, he began in 1500 the building of the new university of Alcalá de Henares. In 1503 he ordered the production, in that university, of a new translation of the Bible. After the death of Queen Isabella, on 26 November 1504, he became governor of Castile during the absences of her widower Ferdinand, and later regent for the young Charles V. On 5 June 1507, Pope Julius II appointed him as Inquisitor General of Castile, having already named him, on 17 May of that year, cardinal of Santa Balbina. In 1509, at the age of seventy-three, he led a military expedition to capture the North African town of Oran. He died in Roa on 8 November 1517, while on the way to meet the new King Charles, and was buried in the chapel of his university of Alcalá. [See Chapters 2 and 3]

DEZA, DIEGO DE

Born in Toro in 1442, he became a royal page on 2 August 1461. In 1470 he joined the Dominican order, becoming Prime professor of theology in Salamanca on 14 May 1480. He was appointed as chaplain and tutor to Prince John in 1486, in 1497 acting as one of his executors. In 1494, he became bishop of Zamora, taking possession of the see two years later. In 1497 he was named as senior chaplain and confessor to Ferdinand and Isabella and in the following year became bishop of Jaén. In 1500 he was transferred to the bishopric of Palencia and also appointed as chancellor of Castile. Meanwhile, on 1 September 1499, he had become Inquisitor General, a post which he held, controversially at times, until his resignation in April 1506. He had become archbishop of Seville in 1504, in which post he died in 1523, having reluctantly accepted, but not taken up, Charles V's proposal to transfer him to the see of Toledo. [See Chapter 2]

ENGUERA, JUAN DE

Born in Valencia, he was a Dominican friar who eventually became Master of that order. He was a confessor to King Ferdinand the Catholic and to his second wife, Germaine of Foix, and, having been elected senior royal chaplain to replace Diego de Deza (see above), he became bishop of Vich in 1505. After Deza's retirement, the Inquisition in the Crown of Aragon was separated from that of Castile, and on 4 June 1507 Enguera was appointed to the post of Inquisitor General for Aragon, Catalonia and Valencia. In 1510, he became bishop of Lleida and two years later was nominated to the see of Tortosa, dying in that post in 1513. [See Chapter 3]

GIUDICE, FRANCESCO

Born in Naples on 7 December 1647, he was descended from the Neapolitan nobility, as a young man becoming bishop of Ostia and Vercelli. On 13 February 1690, he became cardinal of San Sabino, and in 1702 was apponted archbishop of Monreale (Sicily). From February 1705 he was also viceroy of Sicily. On 7 March 1512, he became Inquisitor General of Spain, though he was deprived of this office two years later. He was restored by Philip V on 10 February 1715. Having been chosen as governor of the heir to the throne, in January 1717 he was once again deprived of all his offices in Spain, returning to Rome in June of that year and dying there on 10 October 1725. [See Chapter 6]

LORENZANA Y BUTRÓN, FRANCISCO ANTONIO

Born in León on 22 September 1722, he had a Jesuit and Benedictine education in his native city and then studied theology and law in Valladolid and Ávila. He held teaching posts successively as a canon of Sigüenza and Toledo, and on 5 June 1765 he was named as bishop of Plasencia. He did not take possesion of this see, however, and instead became archbishop of Mexico. In 1772 he returned to Spain, spent some time at court, and became archbishop of Toledo. He was subsequently elected as a cardinal on 30 March 1789. By papal nomination, he was Inquisitor General of Spain between 10 July 1794 and 15 November 1797, when he was allowed to resign the post. Having lost credibility in the Spanish court because of his apparent loyalty to the Roman papacy, he left for Rome on 14 September 1800, working subsequently for Pope Pius VII and dying there on 18 April 1804. In 1956, his remains were moved to Mexico City. [See Chapter 7]

MANRIQUE DE LARA, ALONSO

Born in Toledo, a member of the noble house of Manrique and therefore one of the few genuinely aristocratic holders of the office of Inquisitor General, he began his university studies in Salamanca in 1488. Becoming chancellor of that university, he combined the office with a canonry in Salamanca and the archdeaconry of Toro (Zamora). In 1499 he became bishop of Badajoz, moving to the see of Córdoba in 1515, and from there to Seville, as archbishop, in 1524. On 19 September 1523, Adrian of Utrecht named him to succeed himself as Inquisitor General of Spain.

Alonso retained this office until his death in Seville on 28 September 1538. In his last years, though, he had become increasingly ineffective. [See Chapters 3 and 4]

MERCADER ESCOLANO, LUIS

Born in Murviedro (Valencia) in 1444, he studied at Valencia and Salamanca universities and became a Dominican friar. He was prominent in the order and also acted as an ambassador for Ferdinand and Isabella in Germany and Hungary. In 1504 he became a confessor and councillor to Ferdinand and on 20 May 1513 took possession of the see of Tortosa. On 15 July 1513, Pope Julius II appointed him as Inquisitor General for Aragon and Navarre, now separated for this purpose from Castile. He died, however, in 1516.

MIER Y CAMPILLO, FRANCISCO JAVIER

His tenure as Inquisitor General was brief. Appointed bishop of Almería on 19 November 1801, he was given charge of the Holy Office at the restoration of Ferdinand VII in 1814, being succeeded by Castellón y Salas in 1818. [See Chapter 7]

QUINTANO BONIFAZ, MANUEL

An administrator of the archdiocese of Toledo who had refused the sees of Córdoba and Segovia, he was confessor to Prince Philip of Bourbon and Ferdinand VI. On 11 August 1755 he was named as Inquisitor General by Pope Benedict XIV, and he took a particular interest in matters of censorship. He resigned in 1774, briefly becoming archbishop of Pharsaly, before dying on 18 December 1775. [See Chapter 6]

QUIROGA Y SANDOVAL, GASPAR DE

Born in Madrigal on 12 January 1512, he studied at the University of Oviedo, in 1538 becoming Vespers professor of laws at the University of Valladolid, then a canon of the collegiate church of Alcalá and a judge in the High Court (*Chancillería*) at Valladolid. On 12 June 1545, he was elected to a canonry at Toledo, supporting Archbishop Juan Martínez Silíceo's imposition of 'purity of blood' (*limpieza de sangre*) on the cathedral chapter there. In 1555 he was appointed by Pope Paul IV as Auditor of the Roman Rota, as well as being non-resident dean of León. On 6 November 1565 he became a member of the Suprema, holding with this other government posts. In 1571 he was named as bishop of Cuenca, succeeding Bartolomé Carranza as archbishop of Toledo six years later. In the meantime, on 28 May 1573, he became Inquisitor General, dying in Madrid in November 1594. [See Chapter 5]

RAMIREZ DE GUZMÁN, DIEGO

A senior chaplain to the Holy Roman Emperor Ferdinand I, in 1500 he became bishop of Cuenca and soon afterwards of Lugo. In 1506, he received the post of Inquisitor General by delegation from Diego de Deza (see above). After the death of Philip I later in that year (see List of Dates), his powers reverted to his predecessor. [See Chapter 2]

RUBÍN DE CEBALLOS, AGUSTÍN

Born in Dueñas (Palencia) on 24 June 1724, he studied civil and canon law, becoming a canon of Cuenca. He became bishop of Jaén in 1780 and in 1784 was appointed as Inquisitor General. He supervised the preparation of a new 'Index of Forbidden Books' in 1790, and died on 8 January 1793, being buried in Jaén Cathedral. [See Chapters 6 and 7]

SANDOVAL Y ROJAS, BERNARDINO DE

Born in Aranda de Duero (Burgos) on 20 April 1546, he was brought up at court and studied theology and other subjects at the universities of Alcalá de Henares and Salamanca. In June 1574 he became dean of Seville Cathedral, and was bishop of Ciudad Rodrigo in 1586–88, then being transferred to the bishopric of Pamplona. In 1596 he left Navarre to become bishop of Jaén. In April 1599 he was promoted to the archbishopric of Toledo, having been made a cardinal by Pope Clement VIII, and in 1608 he became Inquisitor General, dying in Madrid on 7 December 1618. [See Chapter 5]

TAVERA, JUAN (PARDO DE)

Born in Toro (Zamora) on 16 May 1472, he was the nephew of the Inquisitor General Diego de Deza Tavera. He studied at the University of Salamanca, becoming a professor there, and being appointed as a minor canon (*racionero*) of Zamora in 1499. In 1507 he became deputy (*provisor* and vicar general) to his uncle in the archdiocese of Seville, subsequently taking up several senior political appointments. On 7 December 1539 he took up the office of Inquisitor General, dying in Valladolid on 1 August 1545. [See Chapter 4]

TORQUEMADA, TOMÁS DE

Born in Torquemada (Palencia) in 1420, he was educated by the Dominicans in Palencia and in 1455 was elected as prior of the order's convent of Santa Cruz in Segovia. He became an inquisitor under the new foundation in 1480, and Inquisitor General in October 1483, his powers being extended at this time from Castile to Aragon and Catalonia. This latter appointment was confirmed by Pope Innocent VIII in 1485. Later, Torquemada retired to the Dominican College of Santo Tomás in Ávila, which he had founded, and in 1498, because of his failing health, a committee of inquisitors was appointed to assist him. He died in Santo Tomás on 16 September of that year.

UTRECHT, ADRIAN OF

Born in Utrecht (Netherlands) on 2 March 1459, he studied at Leuven/ Louvain, becoming both vice-chancellor of the university and dean of the cathedral. In 1516, he moved to Spain to prepare the way for the new King Charles, and was named bishop of Tortosa, a cardinal, and governor of Castile. His brief tenure as Inquisitor General began in 1518, but in January 1522 he was elected Pope as [H]adrian VI, dying in Rome on 14 September 1523.

VALDÉS Y SALAS, FERNANDO DE

Born in Salas (Asturias) in 1483, he studied at the University of Salamanca, becoming dean of Oviedo Cathedral in 1528. He held this post until 1547, though largely as a non-resident. In the meantime he became a member of the council of the Inquisition in 1524, and vicar of the university town of Alcalá de Henares. In the late 1520s, he advanced his ecclesiastical career, successively becoming canon of Toledo and bishop of Elna, in Catalonia, of Orense and of Oviedo (1532). He pursued a career in government, as president of the High Court in Valladolid and subsequently of the Castilian Royal Council. In 1543 he was appointed a councillor to Prince Philip, the future Philip II, and in the following year he became archbishop of Seville. In 1547 Pope Paul III named him as Inquisitor General of Spain. He died in Madrid on 29 December 1568.

Source: Sánchez Rivilla (2000): 234-35, 239-46, 249, 251-53, 255-56, 264-66, 268-71, 273-80, 282-84.

Chronology

INQUISITION	SPAIN AND THE WORLD
	1474 (13 December) Isabella accedes to the Castilian throne
1478 (1 November) Pope Sixtus IV establishes a new Inquisition in Castile, at the request of Ferdinand and Isabella.	
1483 (17 October) Tomás de Torquemada appointed Inquisitor General.	1483–87 Violent resistance to the introduction of the new Inquisition to Aragon, Catalonia and Valencia.

	1492 (2 January) Ferdinand and Isabella capture Granada.
	(31 March) Edicts in Castile and Aragon order Jews to convert or leave.
	(12 October) Columbus sights land in the Caribbean.
1498 (16 September) Torquemada dies.	
1499 (1 September) Diego de Deza appointed Inquisitor General.	
1499–1508 Inquisitor Diego Rodríguez Lucero spreads terror in Córdoba.	
	1504 (26 November) Isabella of Castile dies.
	1506 (25 September) Philip I dies.
1507 (4 June) Juan de Enguera becomes Inquisitor General of Aragon.	
(5 June) Francisco Ximénez de Cisneros becomes Inquisitor General of Castile.	
1508 (June) 'Catholic Congregation' at Burgos meets and dismisses Inquisitor Lucero of Córdoba.	
	1516 (23 January) Ferdinand of Spain dies, succeeded by his mother Joanna ('the Mad') and her son Charles.
1517 (8 November) Cardinal Cisneros dies.	

1518 (4 March) Cardinal Adrian of Utrecht becomes Inquisitor General of Castile, having held that post in Aragon since 14 November 1516.	
	1519–21 Revolt of the 'Germanías' in Valencia.
	1520–21 Revolt of the '*Comunidades*' in Castile.
1523 (19 September) Alonso Manrique de Lara becomes Inquisitor General.	
1527 (July–August) Conference of theologians in Valladolid, to examine the works of Erasmus.	
1538 (28 September) Alonso Manrique dies in Seville.	
1539 (7 November) Juan Pardo de Tavera appointed as Inquisitor General.	
	1545 (1 August) Tavera dies in Valladolid.
1547 (20 January 1547) Fernando de Valdés y Salas becomes Inquisitor General.	
	1555 (25 October) Charles V abdicates sovereignty of the Spanish Netherlands to his son Philip.
	1556 (16 January) Charles abdicates sovereignty of Spain and the Spanish overseas territories to Philip.
1558–59 Convicted Spanish 'Lutherans' are burned in *autos de fe* in Seville and Valladolid.	

1559 (17 August) Valdés orders publication of the Spanish Inquisition's first 'Index of Forbidden Books'.	
(August) The Inquisition trial of Friar Bartolomé Carranza begins in Spain, ending in Rome in April 1576.	
1568 (29 December) Valdés dies in Madrid.	
1573 (20 April) Gaspar de Quiroga y Sandoval becomes Inquisitor General.	
1584 (9 August) Publication of a new 'Index of Forbidden Books'.	
	1588 (May–September) Philip II unsuccessfully sends an 'invincible' Armada against England.
1594 (November) Quiroga dies in Madrid.	
1610–1614 Logroño inquisitors repress supposed 'witches' in Navarre and the Basque country, successfully opposed by inquisitor Alonso Salazar Frías.	
	1701 (February) Philip V enters Madrid as king.
	1702–13 War of the Spanish Succession.
1711 (2 June) Francesco Giudice is appointed Inquisitor General of Spain.	
	1713 (19 December) Melchor de Macanaz publishes a paper critical of the Inquisition's independence.

1714 (December) Giudice removed from office by Philip V.	
1715 (February) Giudice restored as Inquisitor General.	
	1715 (February) Macanaz goes into exile in France.
1716 (June) Inquisition process launched against Macanaz *in absentia*.	
1717 (February) Giudice dismissed definitively as Inquisitor General, leaving for Rome.	
1725 (10 October) Giudice dies in Rome.	
	1734 Macanaz publishes a defence of the Inquisition against French Enlightenment ideas.
	1748 Macanaz arrested and imprisoned on his return to Spain.
	1760 (5 December) Macanaz dies in Hellín (Murcia).
1784 Agustín Rubín de Ceballos becomes Inquisitor General.	
	1788 (14 December) Charles IV succeeds to the Spanish throne.
	1789 (14 July) Storming of the fortress of the Bastille in Paris.
1793 (8 November) Rubín dies.	
1798 Ramón José de Arce becomes Inquisitor General.	
	1801 (May) Spanish troops join Napoleon's forces in the 'War of the Oranges' against Portugal.

	1802 (27 March) Peace of Amiens between Spain, France and Britain.
	1802–04 'Neutral' Spain in effect supports France against Britain and Portugal.
	1804 (12 December) Spain makes military alliance with France.
	1805 (21 October) Spanish navy suffers heavy losses in the battle of Trafalgar.
	1808 (March) Ferdinand VII takes the Spanish throne from his father.
	1808 (1 May) Uprising in Madrid against French occupation.
	1808–14 War of Independence in Spain (the Peninsular War).
	1810–12 Cortes of Cádiz, in opposition to French occupation.
1813 (22 February) Cortes of Cádiz votes to abolish the Inquisition.	
1814 (May) On the restoration of the Inquisition by Ferdinand VII, Arce is removed from office for collaboration with the French and King Joseph Bonaparte, eventually dying in Paris on 16 February 1844.	
1815 (21 July) Francisco Javier Mier y Campillo is named as Inquisitor General.	
1817–18 Juan Antonio Llorente publishes, in Paris and in French, his *Critical history of the Inquisition in Spain*.	
1818 (7 July) Appointment of the last Inquisitor General of Spain, Jerónimo Castellón y Salas.	

1820–21 Abolition of Inquisition	
	1820–23 Liberal government (*Trienio liberal*) under Ferdinand VII.
1822–34 Inquisition formally restored.	
	1822 Restoration of conservative government in Spain.
1834 (15 July) Final abolition of the Spanish Inquisition by the regent María Cristina, acting on behalf of the infant Queen Isabella II.	
1835 (20 April) Death of Castellón y Salas.	

List of Illustrations

10   Bernard Picart's engraving of an *auto de fe* in the Plaza Mayor in
      Madrid in 1723. Biblioteca Nacional, Madrid.
11   Goya shows the humiliating procession of a convicted prisoner,
      probably to his death. Biblioteca Nacional, Madrid.
12   Goya shows a convicted penitent at an *auto de fe*, listening either
      to a sermon or possibly to the reading of his sentence. Biblioteca
      Nacional, Madrid.

Index

TEMPUS – REVEALING HISTORY

Quacks
Fakers and Charlatans in Medicine
ROY PORTER
'A delightful book'
The Daily Telegraph
£12.99
0 7524 2590 0

The Kings & Queens of England
MARK ORMROD
'Of the numerous books on the kings and queens of England, this is the best'
Alison Weir
£9.99
0 7524 2598 6

The Tudors
RICHARD REX
'Up-to-date, readable and reliable. The best introduction to England's most important dynasty'
David Starkey
£9.99
0 7524 3333 4

The Covent Garden Ladies
Pimp General Jack & the Extraordinary Story of Harris's List
HALLIE RUBENHOLD
'Has all the atmosphere and edge of a good novel… magnificent'
Frances Wilson
£20
0 7524 2850 0

 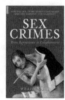  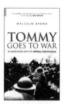

Okinawa 1945
GEORGE FEIFER
'A great book… Feifer's account of the three sides and their experiences far surpasses most books about war'
Stephen Ambrose
£17.99
0 7524 3324 5

Ace of Spies The True Story of Sidney Reilly
ANDREW COOK
'The most definitive biography of the spying ace yet written… both a compelling narrative and a myth-shattering *tour de force*'
Simon Sebag Montefiore
£12.99
0 7524 2959 0

Sex Crimes
From Renaissance to Enlightenment
W.M. NAPHY
'Wonderfully scandalous'
Diarmaid MacCulloch
£10.99
0 7524 2977 9

Tommy Goes To War
MALCOLM BROWN
'A remarkably vivid and frank account of the British soldier in the trenches'
Max Arthur
£12.99
0 7524 2980 4

If you are interested in purchasing other books published by Tempus, or in case you have difficulty finding any Tempus books in your local bookshop, you can also place orders directly through our website

www.tempus-publishing.com